THE INDIAN EYE

ON ENGLISH LIFE

OR

RAMBLES OF A PILGRIM REFORMER

BY

BEHRAMJI M. MALABARI.

THIRD EDITION.

———⁓⁓⁓———

𝕭ombay :

PRINTED AT THE APOLLO PRINTING WORKS

No. 6 DALAL STREET, FORT, BOMBAY

1895

TO

THE WOMEN OF ENGLAND

IN

GRATEFUL REMEMBRANCE OF

1890

CONTENTS

CHAPTER IV.

LIFE AS SEEN IN PUBLIC AFFAIRS.

CHAPTER V.

SEX.

CHAPTER VI.

LIFE AS SEEN IN THE STREETS AND SHOPS.

CHAPTER VII.

THE CONTINENT RECONNOITRED.

PREFACE TO FIRST AND SECOND EDITIONS.

THESE notes were jotted down during a brief holiday, mainly with the object of diverting thought. They are now offered to the British Public by a stranger in blood, in creed, and in language ; by a student too early withdrawn from the advantages of systematic study.

In contrasting the New Civilization with the Old, the writer cannot pretend always to maturity of experience or soundness of conclusion. All that he claims is a friendly conversation, in open council, with Englishmen on the one hand and Indians on the other. That granted, he hopes these rambles in the field of Humanity may not prove altogether to be the ramblings of a vacant mind.

BOMBAY,
Xmas, 1891.

THIRD EDITION.

OUR little journal may now be considered as up to date—if this be possible in such a case. The first two editions were put forward, in London, under a rather uninviting title against which neither entreaty nor protest could avail. And, as a bad name sticks faster than a good one, it is useless, at this stage, to try to turn the "Indian Eye" away from its appointed task. The owner of the eye has seen enough of English public life to acknowledge without demur the sovereignty of two of its principal factors—the Publicans and the Publishers.

This third edition goes out from India.

BOMBAY, 1895.

THE INDIAN EYE

ON

ENGLISH LIFE

OR

RAMBLES OF A PILGRIM REFORMER

CHAPTER I

FROM BOMBAY TO LONDON.

A Pilgrimage long deferred—Preliminaries—"Crocodile"—The Start—Organisation on Board—The Voyagers and their Fare—The Language difficulty—The Pastor—The Voyage—Aden—Suez—Port Said—Brindisi and Trieste—A Canter across the Continent—First Railway experience in Europe—On to Lucerne—Hard put to it.

A TRIP to London has been my dream for years, a hope long deferred. More, indeed, than wish or hope, it has been a faith with me, to be rewarded in the fulness of time. By the end of 1889 I find I have rambled over nearly the whole of the Indian Continent, comparing its past with the present, and catching a glimpse of the future, as afforded by the comparison. What could be more natural for a student of humanity, a pilgrim in search of the truths of life; than that he should now wish for a look at the other world, beyond the seas, whose fortunes are so closely knit with those

B

of his own country? There is so much to learn and to unlearn from contact with a different civilization, more robust and more real, in spite of its "falsehood of extremes." One could not expect to pick up the living facts of to-day so readily as by personal observation, or to apply them with equal force and precision to the shifting theories of yesterday. No study is so absorbing for man as a study of human progress; no method so successful for it as the comparative method. And where could one find a wider scope for the exercise of his observation than in the metropolis of the world? With London for its vantage ground, let the pilgrim look at the world's fair around. If he have eyes, he can see a panorama of happiness and misery spread out in wild profusion before him. If he have ears, he may hear the throbs of this great big heart of the universe, pulsating with the highest aspirations and the lowest passions of humanity. With all its unattractiveness, London is still a Mecca for the traveller in search of truth, a Medina of rest for the persecuted or the perplexed in spirit. Though centre of perpetual motion, it is still the Persepolis of human grandeur in repose. To the searcher after enlightenment it is a Buddha-Gaya; a Benares for the sinner in search of emancipation. Damp, dirty, noisy London, thou art verily a Jerusalem for the weary soldier of faith. There is no shrine on the face of this earth, where the pilgrim reformer could pitch his tent with a larger promise of grace from without, witnessing the Divine Man betrayed and crucified every day, only the better to conduce, as it is believed, to the glory of God and the happiness of Man.

Friends have asked me over to England repeatedly, even if only for a few months. Some of them have offered to relieve the guest of pecuniary anxiety, knowing how poor he is, and how freely he has had to give of his own to others more needy than himself. The invitations have been prompted more by public than by personal motives ; my visit has been contemplated on the same grounds. But it could not be decided on till the beginning of 1890. I am compelled about this time to slacken the speed of private correspondence and to suspend all literary effort. There is no immediate pressure of public affairs to keep me in India. Political interest seems to flag, and social movements are allowed to rest awhile, in sympathy with a quiet reaction that has been working for the reformers.

So, one day, in the height of enjoying a picnic at Karli, the subject of a visit to London is broached to the domestic circle. A brief discussion follows, ending in a liberal vote of supplies. An early day is fixed for the pilgrimage, so that there may be no changing of mind hereafter. All the same I dread the parting, and have hardly strength enough to sit at the same table. Is it not strange for a pilgrim, born for the service of others, that he should feel stepping out of the family orbit as one of his sorest trials, although as a matter of fact he has spent more of his life amongst strangers than amongst the dear *un*familiar faces at home ? In the present case parting is more than usually painful. With the home minister somewhat of an invalid, the junior members growing impatient with a new interest in life, which they lack the means of adequately gratifying ; with all parties having to give up a portion of their reserves in order to keep the wanderer in comfort; it feels anything but a holiday trip when the time comes for starting.

But there is no turning back now; no going forward hereafter if the present chance is missed. So, with the help of my valued friend Mr. T. J. Bennett, I secure a single-berth cabin on board the Austro-Hungarian Steamship *Imperator*, with permission to dine in my cabin and to have my man with me. It is a curious thing for a traveller to confess, but I seldom dine at the common table, at home or abroad. This habit of seclusion has grown upon me so much that I can hardly bear the idea of entering a common room; hence the need of a companion whenever I have a long distance to go.

This time I take up an old acquaintance whom (for purposes of an allegory on the banks of the Thames) we shall name " Crocodile." He is the eldest son of a gentleman at large, trained to nothing in particular, and accustomed from his infancy to a shabby-genteel existence. Neglected alike at home and at school, he has grown up a hulking baby, with his finer instincts half-developed and the growth of responsibility arrested somewhere midway. I have tried, in vain, to lick him into a useful member of society. But he tires very soon of a settled life of independence, and breaks away from it under various pretexts—weak memory, short temper, and bad luck especially. He is not born to be a servant, he thinks; and a master he cannot make, even on a small scale. He prefers to live upon his wits, and when at the point of starvation lapses into a sort of parasitism which he looks upon as his earthly paradise.

Poor Crocodile! What a puzzle, what a paradox he is! A willing worker, and yet useless to himself. Honest and faithful, without being acceptable to friends. Temperate, but with the temper of a demon; shrewd, without any business habits to speak of; a born gentleman, with the manners of a boor breaking out every now and then. His life is a failure, because he cannot see the purpose that underlies it. Hardened by its ups and downs, he looks upon life as a game of chance in which the victory is often for the swiftest. He runs swiftly enough, at times like a madman. But there is no method in his madness. With his fine presence, his tact, his pushing and pleasing ways, Crocodile ought to have made a capital ambassador, or a canvassing agent for a large enterprise. I put him in the way once or twice. But the situation was far too tempting; instead of confining himself to facts and figures he took flight into the regions of fiction. Latterly he has drifted towards a half-enlightened pessimism. The only way to keep him from sinking is to appeal to his manhood, and to the pride of family which seems to be the one strong element in his character. As a companion he has been very useful to me for small errands or purchases into which he throws all that remains to him of a heart. It is a good heart, too, this remnant, but soured by disappointments. Crocodile does not believe in friendship, though fond of making friends, perhaps with an eye to the main chance.

He opens business on board by getting the steward he and the doctor to allow him to occupy my cabin, representing his master to be so "religious," that would not have his meals from other than Parsi hands, and so weak in health as to be subject to fits. The steward believes our Crocodile, and admires his devotion. But the doctor is somewhat of a sceptic. He bustles up to my cabin about noon, and after referring to the cock-and-bull story told by Crocodile, pretends to feel my pulse. Before leaving, the doctor hopes I will not go off into any of my "fits" during the voyage, with such an attendant to look after me *and himself.* Crocodile has a bad quarter of an hour with me when I hear of his prank. But he pleads, with tears gathering in his eyes, that he meant it all for the best. He always means well, but can seldom show it by his acts. The only proof of his innocence he can afford is a copious flow of tears, hearing, speaking, eating or drinking. He cannot be charged honestly with eating or drinking like a whale; but he can weep like a Crocodile, unprovoked, when he has to clear his character. Hence his name, which I hope he may try to deserve.

About 11 A.M., on the first of April 1890, I say good-bye to friends once more. I read the last letters from contributors to the *Indian Spectator,* kindly undertaking to relieve me of all work. I bless my brother Dayaram for his words of comfort. Finally, I am about to drop into my deck-chair when I feel a friendly hand tap me on the shoulder from behind. It is Mr. Patrick Ryan, the Magistrate, heaving and panting. For a minute he cannot speak, though beaming all benevolence. On recovering his breath he explains that he heard of my sudden flight just before starting for Court, that he looked into the Court only to tell the clerks he would be delayed for an hour, and drove up to the harbour as fast as he could. " I dared not let you slip out without a shake of the hand," adds the honest old Irishman. "Who knows? we may never meet again." It is fated, indeed, to be our last parting on this side of the grave. A few months later, while still in England, I hear of Mr. Ryan's death at Poona, under very sad circumstances. Dear old Patrick Ryan! How kind and wise! Wise for every one but himself. Many a time have I consulted him on matters of extreme delicacy. Many a time have I recommended applicants to his unpaid service. He loved to help the needy, by purse and by pen. As a magistrate he was more humane, perhaps, than just, always siding with the helpless and the ignorant, as against the powerful police or unscrupulous limbs of the law. How often he turned away from the Police Inspector with a tactful compliment to his ingenuity, and turning to the accused with pretended severity, dismissed him or her with the remark, "Don't let me see you here again"! He was always for giving "a chance" to the accused, especially where the Police conducted the prosecution; and in not a few cases, I believe, he prevailed upon friendly lawyers to defend the defenceless. No wonder that he was one of the most popular men that ever sat on the bench. Personally he exhibited a rare power of friendship. He volunteered useful advice to me on complicated questions of law and procedure, put me straight on the Home Rule and other political problems, offered to grind for the *Indian Spectator*, and last time I went to the hills he offered to read the proofs for me, so that I could have a real holiday. Poor fellow, what was there between thee and me to lead to this extravagance of friendly regard? And I was denied the solace of watching over thee in thy last moments! Bombay will long remember this warm-hearted official Bohemian, with all his blunderings and improvidence. In his day he is said to have sowed his wild oats rather wildly; and a plentiful crop of them he had to reap. But that was long before my time. I knew only Patrick Ryan, the popular magistrate.

Two minutes after Mr. Ryan's departure the *Imperator* weighs anchor, and for the first time now I feel sure that I have left for the Land of Freedom, the land of my youthful dreams, which holds so much that is precious to me personally, and so much more that is of greater value to the land of my birth.

The *Imperator* is quite a little palace afloat, both as regards size and steadiness. From captain to cabin-boy it has over eighty hands at work day and night; and yet everything in every department goes on with the regularity of a clock. The principle of division of labour is so well maintained, that there is not the slightest friction observable amongst officers or men. Not only is there no grumbling as to overwork, or other kind of work than that contracted for; there is scarcely any ordering about found necessary. Every hand seems to know his own work; its why, when, and how. Every hand goes through the work cheerfully, humming or whistling a tune, or smiling at the on-lookers who stand gaping in admiration at some perilous feat he may be performing on the top-mast.

This *esprit de corps* is what strikes one most on board. How much we Indians differ from Europeans in the matter of organization! We hardly understand the word. I doubt if we have it in our vernaculars. At any rate, the spirit seems to have been almost lost to us. What a comprehensive word, this organization! It includes order, discipline, presence of mind—the best form of individual and collective responsibility. Think of a vessel like the *Imperator*, officered and manned by natives of India. What sulks, what shirkings, what disorder, each blaming the other for his own fault! In no respect are we so inferior to Europeans as in that of organized effort. Yet the root-idea of our system of caste is so akin to modern organization! Caste in India was once the most perfect type of organization. Others seem to have borrowed from us both the idea and the institution. How fallen we are from our original selves! Too much credit could not be given to the P. & O. and other Companies for the employment of Indian Lascars. They make capital sailors, and have more than once proved themselves worthy of their salt in times of danger. In fact, the Indian sailor ought to be found equally efficient with the European sailor, and much less expensive, as is known to be the case with the Indian soldier. I do not know of more than two natives who have made capable ship-officers. Most of our coast steamers are officered by natives who know little of navigation, and would be found unfit for work on strange seas. Why don't our educated men take to this branch of the public service? Perhaps they are not alone to blame for the neglect.

And why don't they take more kindly to travelling abroad? Now that there is a chance of the National Congress holding one of its sessions in London, and an International Congress of Orientalists is also coming on, I should like very much to see a hundred of our best men sent over as delegates, and the expense defrayed by public subscriptions. It would prove a valuable investment if the delegates undertook to use their eyes and ears more than their tongues. The ceaseless activity of the English, their public spirit, their commercial enterprise, their philanthropy—all these, if properly watched, would tell our representatives how a country becomes great, and remains so. A study, on the spot, of the political development of England, would interest them no less than its material progress. I honestly believe that even such a brief training, given to the more promising of our public workers, would be more profitable to India than the founding of another college, or the employing of a thousand additional hands as quill-drivers under the Collector Bahadur. Is the expense too much for patriotic Indians to bear? Not at all, unless our patriot wishes to serve his country by sacrificing *others*— "I am prepared for any sacrifice if some one else suffers for it."

As to the attitude of caste regarding foreign travel, one cannot deny that it is more or less hostile, and not without reason. Caste loves contentment—to let things alone. Foreign travel brings discontent, under the happiest of circumstances. The priestly law-givers of India were shrewd enough to see the risk; in their day perhaps the evil out-weighed the good. We are now living under totally different conditions. If the educated Hindu is sufficiently educated to conciliate the reasonable prejudices of his elders, he has little or nothing to lose from crossing the *Kálá páni* (Black Waters), and certainly a great deal to gain.

The *Imperator* presents a very cleanly exterior, though a curious glance towards the kitchen, or a turn of the nose towards the pantry, meets with doubtful reward. We enjoy our bath daily; sometimes twice a day. We enjoy our meals, too, the dishes being more to our taste than English dishes generally are. The cold drinks are fairly good, as also the fruit, such as we get. Of the hot drinks the coffee is excellent, the tea execrable. Dinner is a tiresome affair, even when taken in the cabin. The courses are too numerous, as a rule. From the way in which Europeans eat their dinner, one would think they were going to starve for a week after. As they eat, so they drink, making a provision against a fast which, however, never comes. Happy diners! I envy your appetite just as you envy my tramp on deck all the livelong day. The deck might be washed earlier than it usually is, so as to enable one to enjoy the morning breeze longer. The company on board is rather miscellaneous; but it never runs into crowds— small knots of men and women sitting apart from one another. The Lord be praised for his mercy in dividing us here into sex and race and special interests!

We have mostly Germans for our fellow-passengers. A fine people—rather awkward in movement, but very good-natured. They eat heartily, like the Parsis. When they are not eating, you may find them drinking or smoking. They are large-bodied, and have to keep the inner machine in gear. Besides, they want to make the best of their holiday, and have little to do beyond turning the pages of a fat volume after a fatter meal. Their ladies make very kindly practical friends.

How formidable stands the language difficulty in the way of uncultured travellers like myself! The very first day on board I have some trouble with the steward, who has put another passenger into my cabin. But we get over it by a liberal show of fingers. It is by no means unpleasant, this talking by signs and numbers. But the thing grows tiresome, especially when leading to practical jokes. For instance, one is tempted to sit down and swear, when, on having asked for a drink of cold water at 10 P.M. in the Red Sea, he is presented with a jug of boiling water and clean towels for a shave; or, with roast beef when he has asked for bread-toast. When asked for ink, Dominico appeals to Maximilian, and Maximilian to Antonio, and Antonio to Franz, and he to somebody else, till they all run up to the steward, conjugating ink—*hink, hank, hunk.*

One evening I salute a lady whom I have been asked to look up, and whose brother has spoken to her about my presence on board. With my usual knack at blundering I go up to the wrong lady—that is, to her maid who modestly explains, "Me comb mit him"—I come with her. Shade of Lindley Murray!— a quadruple murder in a sentence of four words! Here is a clever-looking lady's maid who has been in Anglo-India for some time, and who defies her form of speech with such utter defiance. "Me comb mit him!" Talk of "Babu English" after this. A Babu school-boy would blush at it. But why blame the poor German maid? There are thousands of English *ladies* and *gentlemen* who cannot speak German, or any Indian dialect, better. Is it not curious that the average Englishman, who scorns to pick up foreign languages while travelling, insists upon foreigners speaking to him in English? You observe this everywhere on the Continent, as also in India, where hotel-keepers, railway servants, cab-drivers, and others are obliged to accommodate the grumpy islander so far. In no other respect, perhaps, does the imperial instinct of the Anglo-Saxon seem to be more imperiously asserted.

Talking of "Babu English," I should like to know how many Englishmen speak Bengali half so well as Bengalis speak English. How many are the English scholars who handle the language more effectively than, for instance, Sambhu Chunder Mookerji or Rajendralal Mitra, Kristodas Pal or Keshub Chunder Sen?

The Babu schoolboy furnishes an everlasting topic to English joke-makers. His knack of mixing up synonyms is notorious, and is, in fact, shared largely by other natives of India. The most amusing instance in point is where a Bengali matriculate is alleged to have paraphrased "animal spirits" into "brutal souls." Perhaps it was Roget's *Thesaurus* that betrayed the poor boy; perhaps he was thinking of some rampant Anglo-Saxon when he thus stigmatized the animal spirits of the English schoolboy, to which he is a stranger. But it is wrong to father all such vagaries of speech on the much abused Babu. Parsis, Marathas, and Mahomedans are equally eccentric, if not more so at times. Who has not heard of the unconventional cockneyisms of the Parsi, the gutturals and cerebrals of the Marathas, the feeble hyberboles of the Mussulman? But these faults are venial when compared with the havoc that the average Englishman plays with our vernaculars.

For purposes of interpretation I am tempted to make friends with one of the voyagers, a missionary returning home with his motherly wife and a troop of children. He is very zealous for the good of souls. On the first Sunday after starting he inveigles his stray flock into the saloon, and sings and prays and exhorts to such good purpose that the said flock keep inside their cabins the Sunday following. I like him very much myself, both as a pastor and a man of the world. He is shrewd but kind-hearted; seems to have been somewhat ill-used in life; and what wonder, with the little colony that has sprung up around him while yet he is very far from being a patriarch. There he is, at dawn of day, working as dry nurse, giving a turn to the little ones, or running after a truant, boots and towel in hand, just as he got out of bed. After breakfast you see him sallying forth as a scholar, the wife following with a whole class, baby bringing up the rear in the arms of the eldest girl in her capacity of pupil-teacher. Before lunch our scholar has sometimes to assume the functions of a nurse, which he does with more dignity than grace, the wife smiling her thanks from her cozy corner, as he runs about on odd little errands. After lunch our pastor gets together his domestic flock, and stumbling up the steep ladder, improvises a chorus of sacred music, bribing a delinquent now and then with a piece of orange, or the promise of something better "another time." The concert goes on till 4, unless baby insists upon joining it in a falsetto. In that case there is a hasty retreat by the back steps and a sudden interruption of the concert.

Towards evening the family turns out again, this time *mater* leading the way with her work box, papa carrying the crib on his shoulder, with baby purring complacently inside. Poor dear pastor! Old before thy time. What a quantity of wife and children on Rs. 150 a month, and that in a strange land! Well hast thou earned a holiday in thy German home.

The voyage is disagreeably smooth, so much so that I have to pray one evening for a squall, when tired of walking the decks, or of reading the three-volume novels with which the library has been loaded, or of hearing the music played by amateurs on board, perplexing even to my friend the German pastor. This morning the Captain asks if I am "all right." I thank him, and reply that his ship makes me "too much all right." He laughs, and adds, "wait, wait till we near the Mediterranean." As we go along I feel praying again for a gale. There is some response to the prayer in the Mediterranean, but it is too feeble to be appreciated. No one, not even the ladies, pays heed to it. We now make up our minds to wait till crossing the English Channel. But there, too, the gale is child's play. We walk up and down the deck, from starting at Calais to landing at Dover. We see some of the ladies huddled together, towels and smelling bottles in hand, and bowls at their sides, deserted at this critical moment by their lords who are fortifying the inner man at the bar, against the coming gale, or seeking corners in a very suspicious way. But the gale, much dreaded by many, and much prayed for by a few, does not come, and about 2 P.M. on the 17th of April, 1890, we step out on British soil after a voyage as uneventful as if we had left Bombay for Ceylon next door.

I am not sufficiently drawn to Aden to get out on the forward march, or indeed on the return voyage. The port has been reached at inconvenient hours; but I have had a good view of it, and, what is more agreeable, a good look at the Arab boys and the Jewish pedlars. The boys rush at us scarcely a minute after we have anchored, skilfully paddling their little canoes. Here they come with shrill cries of " aho-aho—heb a die (have a dive) aho, lard (lord) heb a die—leddy, heb a die. Lard, throw a rupee, half rupee—aho—quater rupee—I die—aho-aho." They run about like squirrels, with the jackal cry of "aho-aho." Two anna pieces are thrown to this boy and that; and down they plunge like flying fish, coming up again in the twinkling of an eye, holding the tiny little coin between the fingers, aho-ing again from the beginning to the end of our halt. Sprightly little imps of Satan; nothing frightens them, nothing discourages. They climb up to the ship at odd corners, all but naked, and chattering. The sailors take them by the neck or foot, and throw them back into the sea. The Arab boys mind it not, they are up in a minute with their "heb-a-die." They sing and dance and sit on the water like dolphins.

They are lithe and generally well-built; very fond of dancing to the accompaniments of some weird music and the beating together of the hollows of their hands. They are not so innocent as their dress, or rather the want of it, would make one believe. Here we have one of the clever little urchins, offering sundry coins in exchange for a rupee. "Gib a rupee change, sar, here four anna, two anna, two anna, eight anna ; complat one rupee, sar ; gib whole rupee." The coins, when examined, turn out ill-sorted foreign pieces aggregating about thirteen annas ! Is this primitive savage of Aden any better than the civilized sharper on the London Exchange ?

The Jews, dressed half like Hindus, half like Mahomedans, walk silently about, offering their curious goods to the passengers, receiving all rebuffs patiently, and pocketing the proceeds equally without emotion. They flit about like ghosts, assailing a purchaser fifty times before they give him up. How tenacious they are ! Everywhere the same—hard-working, long-suffering, money-making. It is a wonderful people.

During my second trip I am induced to go ashore with Parsi friends under the escort of Mr. H. Cowasji Dinshaw and his cousin. It is better to risk the sun than the coal-dust that insinuates itself into every crevice of your face and neck, and takes nearly a week to wash out. Mr. Cowasji has a large establishment, numbering perhaps a hundred hands, all told. He is good enough to place a couple of carriages at our disposal, with an intelligent guide who takes us over the town, English and native. At every turn we see some trophy of the Englishman's practical genius—roads, drives, tunnels, tanks. These last are admirable works of engineering. We see trees planted on the roadside, changing the aspect of the bleak, barren country. So far the English may be said to have redeemed a veritable hell on earth. Next to them Aden owes its modern improvement to Parsis. They have built an Agiari, a public hall, and a Tower of Silence (never

C

visited by vultures). In the streets we meet a variety of faces representing almost all known types. The faces don't interest me much, except for the greed or hunger depicted on them.

The Suez Canal is a splendid piece of work; but the passage through it is dreadfully slow. It becomes too monotonous as we drag our way painfully along. The wild and weird-looking country beyond, on both sides, interests me more than the immense feat of engineering before me.

Whilst the steamer is crawling, you more than once realize the force of the expression—"Dull as ditch water." It is seldom, indeed, one finds that phrase so vividly illustrated as in the Suez Canal. The arid desert on both sides, with its heated sand heaped up on the banks, heightens the desolation of the scene. If you recall to mind the plague of flies that hover about your face, like Egyptian tax-gatherers, you complete the picture of desolation.

Port Said is an undesirable place to get out at—a mixture of European and Asiatic vices. The part of the town facing us looks tempting enough; the back part looks dirty and woebegone. The people generally wear a sinister look—seem to be sulky and tricksy. Turkish underlings in office bully the Egyptians at every turn. Here for the first time I see an Egyptian woman walking in her hideous veil. Her degradation appears to be reflected in the character of the people around. As it is daytime I get out for a stroll, but return to the ship as soon as the coaling operations are over. Another time I have to go out in the evening, to send off a wire. The telegraph office is just opposite. I go out in a boat by myself. The boat-man charges twice the fare stipulated. I hand him a sovereign, mistaking it for a franc. He coolly walks away with it. In the telegraph office I find out my mistake. The wire has been sent, and I have not enough silver to pay for it. I ask the European sig-naller to send his man with me on board, explaining my difficulty and offering to go after the boatman. He very kindly undertakes to recover the sovereign. He sends for the "boss" and speaks to him something that makes the man jump up. The boss goes after his boatman, who comes up to the scene, panting, and tells me he has been hunting after me ever since he discovered he had got a sovereign instead of a franc. The telegraph signaller knows better, and asks the fellow to take himself off. He then tells me some-thing about the place and the people. He says he has known me by name, and used to have a look at the *Indian Spectator* while on duty at Cairo, where he was anxious to get back from this God-forsaken town. On my way to the steamer I find three European ladies, evidently pilgrims returning from a shrine, anxiously waiting for somebody to get them a pas-sage on board. They arrived only this noon, and are determined not to pass a night at Port Said. A bad place that, and no mistake. On such a point I would take the word of one woman as against that of a hundred men.

During my second trip I am again obliged to go ashore at Port Said, in order to escape the storm of coal-dust and the babel of incoherent sounds. In the main street we see coffee, cigars, tobacco, liquors, sweets, and cheap curiosities hawked about or shown at the shops. After going the length of the street till it begins to emit very pronounced Asiatic smells, we re-trace our steps and enter a large café with a music-hall attached to it. The proprietor claps his hands as we enter—which is a signal for the orchestra to give us a lively welcome. We order a bottle of ginger ale, and sit watching the musicians and sipping the beverage by turn. The drink is good; the music is not bad. The orchestra is made up of half a dozen women, with one man and two boys. They play together on a number of instruments; and at the end of each air one of the young women steps down the platform, a tray in hand, and goes the round of the customers present. It is not much that the poor girl gets, generally a few coppers. A sad sight, reminding one he is not quite out of Asia.

In a corner of the room there is a gambling-hell, where a man stands with a box with dice inside and a table before him, on which he tempts his victims to place their silver. The play does not seem to be quite genuine—the " boss" seldom losing except to one or two decoys, as they appear to me. The faces of the players, as they stake and watch and lose, and stake again, are a pathetic study. I do not look at the play half so much as at the faces.

About 11 P.M. we wend our way back to the steamer, and are accosted by a number of donkey-boys offering to give us a cheap ride. The donkeys are named after prominent European politicians. Here is a beefy little beast which, as if by right, rejoices in the name of Lord Salisbury. There goes "The Grand Old Man," tall, gaunt, and full-mouthed. The ruffian who owns it

keeps persistently following us, with—"Try the Grand
Old Man, sir; a fine animal"! It is as unlike Mr. G. as
the other is unlike Lord S. The donkey boys are impartial, at any rate. A sorry old specimen of the asi-
nine tribe is named after the late Irish leader; and one
sorrier still represents the *brav général*. It is a very
incongruous sight; the florid English with which the
owners trot out their favourites makes it more ludicrous
still. I try to read in their faces if the fellows mean
the naming of their donkeys as a compliment to the
godfathers, or the reverse. But it is a dark night, and
the boys stand my scrutiny like true Arabs. Joke or
no joke, after all these savages are no worse than the
racing and betting gentlemen of Europe, who name
their animals after the most exalted personages of
either sex; and the ladies who acquiesce in such nomen-
clature. If the English ladies and gentlemen aforesaid
are not in good company, the Arab donkey-drivers are.

Brindisi offers a picturesque welcome to the eye
wearied of gazing on arid deserts and an endless expanse of water. The harbour is one of the prettiest I
have seen: it gives one a foretaste of European life and
climate. This impression is confirmed by the near
approach of Trieste, which looks pretty much like
Bombay, as the *Imperator* steams proudly into harbour.
Here one sees for the first time the contrast that
obtains between Europe and Asia, a contrast as visible
between the peoples as between the climates. One
has only to look at the women in Trieste, from those
carrying their baskets of bread, eggs, fruits, vegetables,
in their simple calico, and bare feet, to those dressed
up in the height of fashion, leaning luxuriously out of

balconies, or promenading on what appear to be the roofs of pleasure houses, as you drive past the tram-way lines. Everything speaks of freedom for them here—they have free movements and a free voice. Woman is a presence and a power in Europe. In Asia woman is a vague entity, a nebulous birth absorbed in the shadow of artificial sexuality.

On the occasion of my first trip I tarry but little on the Continent, and that little only to realize the con-trast that strikes me so forcibly, as also for ascertain-ing which part I should prefer for my headquarters if I ever got the time and the inclination to pass a summer in Europe. Within two hours of landing at Trieste we leave for Venice, and come in full sight of the Queen of the Adriatic before eventide. Leaving our luggage at the station, we go straight off into town, not by gondola but on foot, half a dozen of us, with a sharp young guide, who makes some of us pay for services done and to be done. Here we are, nearly six hours on the tramp, so that more than one of us have worn off the shoe-leather, what with mud and damp and hard walking; and one of us has actually to buy a new pair of boots before starting back for the station. It thrills one to see men and women enjoying themselves in gondolas in the limpid moonlight, singing under the archways—now a love-sick maid wooing back her swain; then a distracted lover breaking his heart in a hurricane of song over the flirt that has left him; the gondolas shooting forward and backward on the water; while multitudes prefer to take their pleasure on foot in the narrow streets and lanes, all abandoned to the excitement of the hour. The Venetians appear to me on the spot to be too free and light-hearted. But everything in nature is so deliciously tempting that I doubt if the heart of man could help going out in response to the call—Come and be happy.

Before returning to the station we take a light supper at what looks like a private restaurant. At about 11 P.M. we resume our journey. Crocodile gets into a second-class carriage with his friends, and next morning they tell me how he managed to remain there. He lay flat on the floor of the carriage, with his third-class ticket carefully concealed. When the inspector came in and shook him gently, he rubbed his eyes and sprawled in such a fearful attitude that the inspector turned away from him with a shriek of "Hoo, Arab"! The same scene appears to have been enacted at another stage of the journey, where the inspector shrank back from the prostrate form with the cry of "Hee, Afrique"! In this wise did Crocodile open his campaign on the Continent, and he has tried the same method everywhere, when away from me, sometimes with rather serious results. On the way we make shift with some *barfi* (sweetmeat), sent us by a friend at Surat. Though packed in a stout tin box, the *barfi* begins to melt in the Red Sea, and continues so doing till we reach Lucerne. On board it is a sight to see Crocodile melting at the eyes and watering at the mouth in sympathy with the melting sweetmeat. He breaks open the box, helps himself and me to a piece, and then makes a present of a few pieces to some of the hands on board. Up to Lucerne he manages to keep the tin box to himself, from which he doles out a little of the "dolce" to those who salute him, answer his inquiries, or oblige him in some other way. At the Trieste Railway Station he draws a crowd after him, all shouting for the sweetmeat, which they seem to like very much.

On our way up Crocodile sometimes enters my carriage to look after me, and remains there till the next station is reached. The guard on one of the Italian lines objects to this at one place, and asks for extra fare. I explain to him, as well as I can, how the matter stands. But although the man seems to follow me, he puts his hands to his ears, shrugs his shoulders, and demands extra fare. There is nothing for it in such a case but to leave the guard to Crocodile. They go on chattering like a pair of monkeys, neither of them the wiser or the richer at the end of the journey; for whilst the guard speaks Italian, Crocodile keeps firing at him in broken Persian. Here the guard and another official catch hold of me. They demand not only the extra fare on Crocodile's account, but 72 francs more for my having occupied the whole of a first class carriage. I protest that I have not reserved the carriage, and that it is not my fault if there are no passengers to fill it. We have high words, and in a fit of temper I call them robbers. The two men take off their caps mockingly and ask for the extra payment. We now get a German passenger to interpret. When he fails to bring the men to their senses I flatly refuse to pay. Crocodile is boiling over with indignation. He is "prepared to go up to the Queen of England" for justice. I am more modest, and offer to put the case before any English-speaking railway official; or, that failing, to wire to Lord Dufferin, the ambassador. That offer of an appeal to Cæsar, or rather to Cæsar's young man, takes effect. The guard now leaves the matter to the other man, and starts off. That man offers a compromise. If I pay the extra charge on Crocodile's account, he will let us off. There is some reason in this: the other charge for 72 francs was preposterous. But I ask him to give me an acknowledgment for the overcharge on Crocodile's fare. He says he never gives a receipt. I again decline to pay, till the man undertakes to have the extra item formally entered into one of the books at the station. I thus make sure that the five francs won't go to him, and he walks away fairly grinding his teeth. This is our first encounter with a railway sharper in Europe. I find travelling very expensive, more than three times what we have to pay in India; very inconvenient at times, and very annoying besides.

St. Gothard's Tunnel is a stupendous work of engineering—more so than I imagined. The views around are magnificent; it takes me some time to realize that the white substance that litters the roadside is snow. At first I take it to be cotton, and wonder why it is spread all along the passages. The whole roadway seems to be covered with a carpet of *pasham* (flakes of wool).

We are helped to a very good hotel by a porter at the Lucerne Station, whom we both mistake for the station-master. Lucerne and the neighbourhood are delightful about this time, and after a day's excursion I make up my mind to return there for a few weeks. The railway porter introduces us to a very quiet little family who live in a cozy little nest of a house, and speak English. They are willing to take me in, if my companion can shift for himself. For the present I do not wish to remain. We have another stroll next day through the town. I buy a pair of shoes, as my boots are beginning to give way. I like the new pair very much; they are so soft and light. Later on I find that they are lady's shoes; the railway porter has them re-heeled, and I am happy. The porter is very useful, as he speaks English. We could hardly get on without him, and he is very attentive. Why? Because we gave him the tin box with all the *barfi* that was in it. His family enjoyed it so much, he explains gratefully, and he wishes to keep the tin box as a memento.

At Basle I feel so done up, that it is found necessary to engage a berth in a sleeping-car. Unluckily, there is no berth in the carriage which I am asked to enter. When the position is explained, a husband generously offers to give up his seat, leaving his wife on the other seat, who is too tired to go out into an ordinary carriage. To this I could not, of course, listen, though Crocodile thinks that nineteen shillings of extra fare entitle one to every form of selfishness. After much shuffling of cards, however, it is arranged that an American gentleman and I should have a small compartment to ourselves. I shake hands with the gentleman who so promptly left his seat for me, and am rewarded by a smile from his lady, which makes me sleep soundly. Had I insisted on my right, I know I would have had a miserable night of it.

CHAPTER II.

IN AND ABOUT LONDON.

First Impressions of a London Crowd—The Weather—The People—The Air they Breathe—The Dress they Wear—The Houses they Live in—The Food they Eat—The Drink they Drink—unto Drunkenness—The Pipe they Smoke.

FROM Dover to London is an exceedingly pleasant drive, through a country as different as could be from our own. Travelling first-class, one is comparatively safe from fatigue; but he loses little, so far, even when travelling second or third, if he can stand a crowd. The British crowd, in a railway carriage or other public conveyance, is, as a rule, orderly and well-behaved; the presence of women makes it more so. This remark hardly applies to a crowd of holiday-makers abroad. What strikes an Asiatic most, on getting out at Victoria Station, is the noise and bustle around him. Every man and woman—one might say every animal, and even some of the inanimate objects—seem to be full of life. The streets and thoroughfares of London present a sight in this respect, which it is impossible for the stranger to realize save with his own eyes. I happen to have read a good deal about this, but what I actually see here exceeds my anticipation. To Crocodile it is all a new world. He stands apart, gaping at the scene

in bewildered admiration. The crowds of women in
the streets, walking rapidly past, pushing and elbowing
everyone who stands in the way, all intent on business
or pleasure, are a sight not likely to be soon forgotten.
For me it is a sight more striking than attractive.
After all, a woman's place is at home rather than in
the street. Of course, the climate and the conditions
of life generally impose this outing upon not a few
Englishwomen who are apparently unwilling to rough
it in a crowd. But it is none the less painful on that
account to see a delicate girl struggling to return home
in the midst of a traffic heavier than we see in India
during our annual fairs. This traffic is maintained
every day by railway trains, running under ground
and above ground, by omnibuses, trams, cabs, private
carriages, waggons, trucks, hand-barrows, tricycles,
etcetera, to say nothing of the immense pedestrian
crowds. In the large and more fashionable business
quarters, such as Bond Street, Piccadilly, Oxford and
Regent Streets, into which the various agencies mentioned above pour vast multitudes every five minutes,
and some of which are broad enough, besides the pavements, to hold a row of five carriages abreast, I stand
breathless of an evening, watching what goes on before
my eyes. Carriages and pedestrians alike seem to have
a hair-breadth escape of it now and again. But amid
this surging ocean of humanity, the police-constables
keep such order, the drivers are so skilful, and the
pedestrians so alert, that accidents are very rare indeed.
And yet the eye, if it can observe well, may detect a
good deal of suffering among the gay or busy crowd.
Here is some fashionable cad, nearly driving over a

fragile old woman. She rushes, trembling, to the constable's side. There goes a knot of boy-sweepers, running about between carriages, and even under them, in order to keep the ground clean. You could hardly expect greater agility from mice or squirrels. There is more safety, of course, on the pavements. But you are not quite safe here either, from dangers other than trampling. Few respectable women, I find, will venture out into some of these streets towards evening without a guide; so great is the rush therein of the unworthy ones of their sex, of their victims and tyrants. The back parts of not a few streets seem to have been given up to a Godless population, foreign and English. A large percentage of this, I should think, represents virtue first betrayed, and then crowded out, by vice.

To have an adequate idea of what a crowd in London means, one might repair to a railway station, Waterloo, London Bridge, Liverpool, or Victoria, especially on a bank holiday. The crush is indescribable. To say that it is tremendous, is to give but a feeble description of it. I wonder how people can stand the noise and bustle. If I were to be detained in such a crowd for a few hours, I am afraid I would either be stunned, or distracted beyond cure.

Of the principal cities of Europe that I have visited, London has by far the largest traffic to show. The heaviest goods traffic is to be seen, perhaps, about the London Bridge Station, and the heaviest passenger traffic about the Mansion House. Here you may see men of almost all nationalities rushing to the banks or driving bargains in the streets. There you see goods and commodities from all parts of the world, carried in enormous vans drawn by horses broad in hipbone and hoof. Even these large and sure-footed servitors find it dificult to keep pace with the traffic. On the wet asphalte pavement here and there you see the poor beasts slip down, perhaps never to get up again. Dead or alive, they are removed at once, to make room for others waiting impatiently behind.

Everybody in the streets seems to be out of breath. It is difficult to say how much of this hurry-scurry is a matter of necessity, and how much of choice or habit. The keen cold wind has doubtless something to do with this rapid locomotion, as also the keen pursuit of pleasure or business under the excitement of the moment. It is amusing to see men and women rushing frantically to the railway station or the omnibus stand, in the nick of time, hugging their packages under the arm and flourishing their umbrellas at the guard or the conductor. Here comes a matron, puffing and panting, just as the engine whistles departure. She runs from gate to gate, anxious to give chase if the gate-keeper will let her in. She is quite in a fluster, and as red in the face as her national roast beef. Now, why could she not have come in a minute earlier? But that is just what she cannot or will not do. In such a mad rush for life, people can hardly talk in words. They have to use brief, sometimes inarticulate, sounds instead. It is seldom that you hear a complete sentence. People in the streets have no time for dignity of language or of behaviour. If you don't move, they will push and elbow you out, without so much as looking at you. And when sometimes the offender apologizes by accident, for extra rudeness, it feels like insult added to injury. Yet, amidst all this furious bustle young people may find time enough to flirt—Jenny dropping her handkerchief, glove, parasol, or package, to be picked up by Harry. Jenny is a clever little general. She picks up the thing herself if she wants her raw recruit to come to the point. Some evening, perhaps, you may meet the Miss Push of Waterloo Station at a drawing-room show in her character of Miss Drawl, listening to your small talk in silence, broken by leisurely drawn out comments. Is not England a land of extremes?

I must not forget to add that all this hurry-scurry of the station subsides in a moment as soon as the gate opens to let passengers in, after getting their tickets punched. The crowd then tries to be solemnly decorous; and as you pick your way forward you feel as if attending your own funeral.

What strikes you most about Englishwomen is their look of health, strength, elasticity, all proclaiming a freedom of mind, to begin with. How they walk, and talk, and carry themselves generally! How they rush in and out, saying good-bye with the right hand turned towards themselves, *meaning* what our women in India always *say*, "vehela avjo," come back soon! How they kiss one another, and offer their children, even their cats and dogs, to be kissed by the friends departing! Does this last ceremony show heart-hunger, or is it affectation? Here they are, half a dozen of them rushing into my omnibus (the Lord have mercy on an unprotected orphan!) squeezing themselves into their seats. I am between two of the prettiest and quietest, feeling a strange discomfort. As the 'bus hobbles

along, I feel my fair neighbours knocking against me
every moment. *They* do not seem to mind it at all ; it
is a matter of course. Why, then, should I cry out
against the inevitable? Evil to him who evil thinks.
We are all too busy here, reading the paper, chatting
about the weather, minding our packages and our toes.
Further, I find both my neighbours resting their para-
sols between them and me on either side. A straw
shows how the breeze blows. The breeze that I have
just discovered is very refreshing to my soul. I have
also noted that respectable Englishwomen rather avoid
entering a carriage occupied by men. It is mainly
through such experience that I am learning to take a
charitable view of ladies sitting on the knees of gentlemen, or gentlemen on the knees of ladies, when three
of a family happen to be in one hansom, or more than
ten in a railway carriage. These sights, queer as they
are, do not offend me now. They would be an eyesore
amongst our own people. I myself could hardly bear
them at first ; but that is no reason why I should judge
others in such a matter, before I am well equipped
to form a judgment.

Less accountable to me, than the sight just mentioned, is the sight of ladies riding out with their
grooms. Why not with maids? Surely, this is not
impossible for England. Maid-servants could be
trained to ride and to manage horses, as well as men-
servants. I should like to see more girls employed as
riders, drivers, waiters, and personal attendants for
ladies. Is it not curious that male servants should
be more valued in Europe, indoors or out, than
females ? The latter do not outnumber the former so

much, after all, taking emigration and war itself into account. I suspect it is more fashionable to have the "lord of creation" in my lady's service, with his lordly airs and loud uniform.

I have said that the average Englishwoman strikes me most by her healthy looks and active habits. But, as usual, there is another side to this picture. One often meets with the anæmic and the consumptive, victims of overwork, starvation, or dissipation, in themselves or their parents. How pathetic is the sight of one of these girls, moving softly, like a ghost, with a frame so fragile as to be driven by the wind behind, with a transparent skin and glassy eyes, exhausted by the effort to creep on to the platform, and going directly to sleep in the carriage, with the delicate little mouth half open, as if to allow the breath of life to ebb out without a struggle! It fills me with grief to watch this fair slight being as if in the process of dissolution. And yet I sit there, fascinated by her presence, unmindful of time or distance.

Then, as to the modesty and candour of my fellow-passengers of the other sex; that picture also needs shading. You have sometimes the misfortune of having women beside you, with a trick of leaning on your arm or shoulder when they are quite capable of supporting themselves; of giggling, of laughing a dry hollow laugh, or of trying otherwise to draw you out of yourself. The conductor, entering into your feelings, or reading them in your face, may announce "Room up top, sir;" or, you may yourself get out before time. But why recall such experiences amid

D

so much that is beautiful and true? Let it be forgotten, like an evil dream.

The weather in England seems to be an odd mixture of all the weathers the world over. From extreme cold to extreme heat, with all the intermediate stages— snow, hail, frost, with the East wind eating into your marrow, the heavy, murky, fog-laden atmosphere, and an occasional glare of the sun that burns into the sockets of your eyes—you have to stay here a twelve-month to get a surfeit of each of these changes. With all the natural and unnatural varieties of weather at home, it is strange the English should be so eager for change of weather abroad. They appear to be blessed with more changes than one every week. There is a goodly assortment of damp, wet, sooty air for the sanguine pleasure-seeker, goodly enough to set Diogenes grinning in his tub. Then the delicate invalid may have his choice of cold or cramp, or of half-toasting and half-freezing, at the domestic hearth; whilst the butterfly of fashion may take a wide range between thunder and lightning, with a dash of perpetual drizzle. The worst of it all, for a sojourner from the sunny East, is that these changes take place without warning. There is no notice given, as to us in India, to take down or hang up the umbrella which is here a necessity of your nature, as you sally forth to take an airing or to return a friendly call. In less than ten minutes you may find the roads covered with pools of slime, produced by a shower. If you stand, you find your dress coat badly small-poxed in a minute, so great is the rush of carriages. If you run, you are not unlikely to come into closer contact with the slime aforesaid. Life then is little more than suspended animation. I have often wondered at such times why an eminently logical people, like the English, who have reduced everything, from weather to religion, to an exact science, and who have advanced sufficiently on the path of progress to be able to ask if life is worth living, should not take the matter into their own hands and put an end to all its uncertainties, oftener than they happen to do. If I were a Bishop, I don't think I would refuse funeral rites for experiments to which scientists of the advanced school might be driven, on a winter day in December, or a summer night in July. From what little I have seen of autumn, I can well imagine what an English winter is like—with all the forces of darkness gathering and the day of judgment as if drawing nigh. Is this English winter a visitation?—a punishment for national vice and sordidness of sorts?

These reflections were suggested to me by an experience of English weather during May 1891. As a rule, May is a good month. June is perfect, when London looks like a paradise. July is perhaps as good as May. These, I suppose, constitute the London season. What is trying for an Indian during the other months, even during some of these best months, is, as remarked above, the uncertainty of the weather. The only season that is certain is winter, and that is certainly a winter to be remembered to the end of one's days; though for myself I would rather have a spell of winter, for which I am well prepared, than the damp, wet, dribbling days of summer that abound all the year round. Sometimes you have an interval of sunshine ; but then it is opresssively close, more so during the night than the day. It is not often that you are fortunate enough to salute the bright orb of day in London. He is too fond of playing at hide and seek, and whenever he does come out, it is with a shy pale look, as if afraid or ashamed of the rôle assigned to him in the economy of nature. One day I see the sun about 12 A.M., exactly like our Indian moon. Next day, about the same hour, I find the city enveloped in fog, and myself overtaken by a dull throbbing head-ache. The rain is about to come down every minute, and yet it cometh not. The air is stifling—the fog, or mist, or whatever else the beast is, rising like steam out of the witches' cauldron. Although the gas is lit in the middle of the day, one cannot be too careful in picking his way up or down. All of a sudden, however, emerges the sun out of the sooty clouds—a small, lacklustre, emaciated orb without any of the halo that usually surrounds him in the gorgeous East. Evidently, he is ashamed to show his face to the world. But about 2 P.M., the same sickly little orb shines forth with a ferocity that would make his Indian cousin hide his diminished head, and that makes the wayfarer already long for the dim, moist, dirty morning.

Your troubles inside the house are about the same as those outside. You know not what you are to do with yourself five minutes hence. If you venture upon your morning plunge, you must at once retire to bed, half exhausted with the effort to make yourself presentable. If you take your stockings off your tor-tured feet, the chances are, you will catch cold and die of sneezing. Why, you could hardly trust yourself to a decent wash and a change of clothes during these uncertain days. What wonder, cleanliness is a virtue but rarely practised over here! The Doctor tells me he has to scrape the gatherings of years off some of his patients' limbs before he could see what the trouble is with them.

I am not sure that the moon is not visible in London oftener than the sun. The full moon in a clear sky is a sight worthy of the place of honour in all the picture galleries of England. What I myself dislike most in the English weather is the death-laden East or North wind, Son of Ahriman. May his face be blackened for ever!

The North or East wind sometimes grows into what they call a storm. To show what an ordinary London storm means I have only to detail my first experience of it. One afternoon I have to return the visit of a friend at the India Office. As it is not nearly four o'clock yet, I jump into a 'bus from Ludgate Hill, and am carried off to Waterloo. I take the ruturn 'bus then for Charing Cross; but the conductor points out another passing us half way, which, he says, will take me right into Whitehall Place. Whilst barely out to catch the other 'bus, I am overtaken, all of a sudden, by a heavy gale. Instead of making for the 'bus, I have, therefore, to run across under a bridge where many others have already sought shelter, as if by instinct. In attempting to protect myself from the gale I badly hurt my umbrella. My poor Gamp! She has her nose flattened and throws up one of her arms. Finding the rain does not cease, I hail a cab and ask to be set down at the India Office. The man puts me down at the wrong end, and I have to enter another public office next door. Here, in the open square, Sairy and I have to breast a fierce gust of wind. She throws up more of her arms, and I nearly lose my chimney pot and get a ducking in an attempt to regain my balance. In this plight I go up to the porter and ask if he could smuggle me into the right room. "You have to walk across to the Hindia Horfice, Sir," he titters, eyeing me from head to foot. Once more into the square, and then out at the end of Delahay Street. One more trial for my poor little Gamp. She moans and gasps for breath, and shuts herself up the wrong way. I am sprinkled all over with mud in my efforts to keep steady. On arriving at the porter's gate I try to doctor my companion with the aid of the porter. But the best surgical skill on the spot fails to set her fractured bones. The more we try to poke them back, the more we tear her flesh. It is a cruel operation, which we give up in despair. I am told it was a mistake to have carried an umbrella that afternoon, more so, to have held on to it when it wanted to go. In a storm people had better lose their umbrellas and hats rather than risk their limbs in saving these encumbrances.

On another occasion I see a stranger, smartly 'rigged out', running to catch the train that has just been signalled. As he runs down a sloping pavement, he feels driven by the wind from behind till he comes to a sharp corner, when, under the impulse he reels suddenly and falls, head foremost. Fast fly his chimney pot to the south, his umbrella to the west, his glasses and gloves to the east, his morning papers towards the north. This comes of pride—the pride of imitating the natural-born Londoner—and great is the fall of it. By main effort the stranger manages to save his head from too impetuous a contact with the wall adjoining. A servant girl looks at the scene, half dazed, as our knight of the rueful countenance picks himself and his effects up in a minute, and runs gayly along, as if nothing has happened. Oh London, here is a pilgrim from the East, scattered all over thy stony surface. What more couldst thou claim by way of sacrifice or homage?

It makes one laugh to hear the English talk of their "fine day," their "lovely, splendid, magnificent, glorious weather." Why, I never saw a whole day in London that could honestly be described as "fine," let alone the hyperboles. One may speak of a "fine" five minutes; a fine half-hour or hour. Nothing beyond that, so far as I could see. As a matter of fact, every five minutes of "fine weather" in London is worth recording in letters of gold.

Among other vagaries of the English weather it may be mentioned that you are sometimes overtaken by the shades of night at 5 P.M., not to catch a glimpse of the approach of dawn till 8 A.M. In some of the winter months you have hardly any such thing as the day. It is all night, from week's end to week's end. In summer you are rushed into the light of day about 2 or 3 A.M., seeing the face of night seldom before 9 P.M.

It is a settled point among scientists that with his naked eyes no man can gaze at the noonday sun. I am prepared to confound these learned theorists. On the 1st of August, 1890, about 1 P.M. in the afternoon, I gazed at the London sun from the top of an omnibus standing near Hyde Park Corner. I take my oath on it, that to the best of my knowledge and belief I did gaze at the sun, did stare at him boldly, did, in fact, outstare him and make him retire behind the gathering clouds. This is an historical fact, and I record it, therefore, with all the pomp and circumstance befitting it. I give date, place and hour; which is more than most of our modern scientists do in announcing their discoveries of mares' nests.

The climate of a country reflects itself pretty clearly in the temper, habits and general surroundings of the people. This is a scientific truth, the force of which is brought home to my rude intelligence most vividly in England. The people seem to be as changeable and restless as the weather. They are always on the move. Watch them where you like, at home or abroad, they seem to be full of the question—what next? No amount of walking, riding, sight-seeing satiates them —they will have something more, something, if possible, in another line. This is perhaps best seen during the holidays, when the Londoner strikes you most as an abandoned, unscrupulous holiday-maker. I know not if many parents will be deterred from enjoying their holidays by illness at home amongst their children; the majority of children are not so deterred by the illness of their parents. This may look unnatural, but is not so in reality. It is mainly the climate, and the peculiar mode of life the people have to live in obedience to climatic influences, that make them so keen about everything. They are as keen about business as about pleasure. The wear and tear of life in England must be terrible. But if it were less hurried than it is, I believe life would be shorter still. It is inevitable, under these circumstances, that life should be a mad scramble, and that keen enjoyment and keen suffering should exist side by side in most places. In every department of business people want to make most money in the least time, and retire at once, to live as ladies and gentlemen. That a life so artificial blunts human instincts, and lowers the standard of public morality, goes without saying; but it is equally certain that the mode of life is forced upon the people. It is bound to be a life of extremes, with the happiness of the family and of the community often sacrificed at the altar of individual interest. Nowhere could the law of the survival of the fittest be more inexorable in its working than in this vortex of high-pressure civilization. People live in a whirlwind of excitement, making and unmaking their idols almost every day. They seem to be consumed by a mania for novelty; everything new serves to keep up the fever of excitement. To-day they will set up a fetish—anything absurd, fantastic, grotesque—and worship it with breathless enthusiasm. It matters little what the fetish represents to the moral sense of the worshippers. So long as it is something unusual, they will bend the knee of fashion before it. To-morrow there must be a new sensation, to take the place of the old, pulled down with the same eagerness with which it was put up. In a word, the English seem to be as fickle as their weather. Flit about, poor butterflies of a brief season, and drink your fill of the poisoned nectar you so madly crave! I cannot blame you, though I will not join in your mad pursuit. Well it is for you that the weather is so capricious nine months out of twelve; otherwise, you might kill yourselves with sustained animation. And well is it, too, you make the best of your brief spell of sunshine; otherwise, you might die of *ennui*.

The air is no worse in London, I should think, than anywhere else, though appearances are certainly against the capital. If the towns suffer from smoke and gas, they make up by improved sanitary arrangements. Country air is decidedly purer, but it is apt to be tainted by noxious vapours floating around. London can hold its own, however, in the matter of sulphuretted hydrogen gas, escaping from street refuse of all kinds, and smelling very much like rotten eggs. But on the whole I am inclined to think that more people die in the metropolis from other causes than bad air. The incessant damp and cold, very injurious in themselves, do not allow of most of the houses being well ventilated. People have often to live with the windows shut, day and night, and breathe the same air again and again. In some of the poorer quarters, where ten to twenty have to occupy a room overnight, that is hardly fit to keep two in health and comfort and decency, the result can well be imagined. It is true that the sanitary arrangements for London itself are far from being perfect. I have seen dogs and cats and large birds lying dead on the pavements for two and three days, and I have seen some of the back slums reeking

with filth. I have known riversides smelling horribly
for weeks, with no one, in or out of office, anxious
to abate the nuisance. I have found large railway
stations in a wretchedly insanitary condition. All
these, however, are preventible evils, and they will be
prevented when there is less jobbery and more vigi-
lance on the part of some of the departments. At
any rate, such eyesores are rarely met with, and
then in poor districts. The air itself, on the whole,
both in the country and in towns, is pure enough.
Considering the climate and the habits of the people,
it is wrong to abuse God's air for want, or neglect,
of man's personal hygiene.

The Englishman's dress is perhaps as much under
the influence of climate as his temper; it is capricious, but not ill-suited to his wants, though one
would think it might be made more becoming in
some particulars. The Englishwoman's dress is
necessarily more complicated, but on the whole it sits
well on her, and is better suited to active outdoor
movements than is the Indian lady's, as a rule. The
tendency in this respect is markedly towards freedom. But it will be many years, I am afraid, before anything like real freedom is reached. The present cumbrous arrangement reminds one of the days
of female slavery, when everything was done by
their lords to keep women within sight. Englishwomen are advancing rapidly in every direction.
But they seem to be slow to improve in the matter of dress. Can this be from their own desire to
be easily caught when outstripping the limits of
womanly independence? Woman's instinct is said to

be sounder than her reason. For my part, I am not
ashamed of sympathizing with the movement for a
simpler, cheaper, more rational system of dress. It
would save many a milliner's bill, many an hour
wasted on the daily toilet, many a gap in domestic
harmony, and many a bonny English lass from
descending to the grave before her time.

It takes no close observation to see what important part is played by silk, satin, and clean linen
in the get-up of a daughter of Eve. At times you
hardly recognize the same person differently dressed. No wonder, women give so much of their time
to the toilet. So long as dressing is not overdone,
at the expense of more serious duties, I do not see
why they should be grudged a pleasure that spreads
gladness all round. Dressing is an art: it takes
something of genius to dress well. Simplicity is, of
course, the supreme test—just enough of art to aid
the work of nature. Most efforts to hide positive
defects are vain; to supply them artificially is ridiculous. And, after all, it needs a soul within to set
off personal attraction. A dressed-up carcase can
be shown by any butcher in the street. On the
whole, I think the English lady is more clever at
dressing than her Indian sister; firstly, because she
is always improving, and secondly, because she knows
better how to make a little go a long way. An Englishwoman thinks she owes it to Society to dress
well; her sister in India dresses well chiefly to please
her lord and master.

The weather in England imposes an amount of
clothing, and the manner in which it is to be used, to

which I could never reconcile myself. Oh! those horrible, abominable braces, and the ponderous, murderous overcoat! How I have revolted against their use, in spite of the doctor's vehement protests! A small, spare man, I have often been weighed down by coat and overcoat, and I do believe those so-called elastic braces have made me shorter by at least half an inch. Surely, it is not the dry cold of England that makes one shrink lengthwise from five feet two to barely one and a half?

For me the most pleasing dress is that used by the lady-nurse, of some dark material with snow-white linen tucked under the chin and running round the neck. One feels as if he would like to be ill, just a little, to bask in the sunshine of this bright and healing presence. Health and innocence follow thee, good sister!

The construction of London suggests serious thoughts to a stranger. What with railways under ground, running through the bowels of the earth; railways, tramways, omnibuses, and smaller vehicles working above ground, the city appears to have been perforated from end to end. Some of the latest improvements of science, when seen in a working condition, strike one dumb; the whole thing looks like a train laid for the destruction of the town. They could hardly have managed it better if they wanted London to be blown up into atoms. As it is, any passing shock of earthquake, or perhaps a flash of lightning or peal of thunder, might send the more incoherent parts flying about in the air. This is the impression left upon my mind: I dare say the Londoner knows better. Anyhow, it is hopeless to stem the tide of this modern civilization. If it shortens life, does it not make it more enjoyable? *Better fifty years of Europe than a cycle of Cathay.* This artificial civilization of the West, dominated by King Coal and Emperor Iron, and typified as Kaliyuga by the wise men of the East, has its price, which is paid every day in disease and death, in accident and crime. These go to propitiate the Moloch of high pressure material progress, and a daily record of them is to be found in newspapers reeking with realistic sensationalism.

The look presented by the average street in London is a dull monotony of ugliness, unrelieved by variety of construction or colour. At first sight one would think the people had no eye for the picturesque. But would not the best-assorted colours be out of place in a wilderness of fog and soot and mud? The exterior of houses in London is bound to be unattractive.

Jerry building is another eyesore to the lover of art and safety. But safety is inconsistent with the hurried life of sale and barter that obtains here; and for art you have the inside of houses, picture galleries, museums, parks, &c. The parks are the pride and glory of London. They are extensive, wonderfully well kept, and easy of access for the neighbouring population. Big and small, the parks and greens of London count by the hundred. And what a blessing they are to the millions, ill-fed and housed in miserable hovels!

If the outside of houses is generally uninteresting, it is quite the reverse with the inside in well-to-do quarters. Everything there bespeaks the latest appliance of art and science, to make life more enjoyable to-day than it was yesterday. That is the genius of the people. The drawing-room is generally well-adorned with cheap, but by no means inartistic, knick-knacks. Even the poor middle classes know how to live in some sort of what they call style. Let the Englishman alone to make a home for himself. A race that could conquer such a climate, and carve the utmost comforts of life out of it, deserves dominion over all the elements of nature and freaks of fortune.

In no respect, perhaps, does the average Englishman show himself so slow of imagination and wanting in taste as with respect to his daily food. He eats what his fathers ate before him. Bread-and-ham or cheese ; an egg by way of variety, with black tea or coffee; these seem to form his breakfast twenty-five days out of the month. His lunch may be a mere apology ; and for dinner he will have beef or pork, or fish with an odd potato or a slice of cabbage, all boiled separate. He may have roast beef now and then, or a little fish. He is a heavy eater, and enjoys the meat or cheese that appears to a stranger to be hardly fit to look at. He may have soup and German sausages, if he can afford them; pudding, custard, pie, and other side-dishes on a holiday. The better informed and better-to-do class seem to have borrowed French dishes, and imported French cooks. Indian dishes, rice and curry, for instance, with chutneys and condiments, are struggling into favour. But as a rule the Englishman's dinner is plain and monotonous to a degree. The cook knows nothing of proportion in seasoning his food; knowns little of variety, and has a rough, slovenly touch. The cookery is often worse than the materials, which may be seen any day hung up at the shops; carcases of large animals and small, beef, veal, pork, mutton, ducks, geese, rabbits, chickens, all dressed and ready for use. The sight is invariably unpleasant, and the smell is at times overpowering if one happens to be near the shops. It is an exhibition of barbarism, not unlikely to develop the brute instincts in man. I wish the people could be induced to go in more for vegetables and fruit, for grain, pulse, and other cereals. There would be less alcoholic drink necessary in that case, and a marked improvement both in their habits and appearance. A beginning seems to have been made in this direction by vegetarian hotels and restaurants. But what little I have seen of their culinary out-turn is far from satisfactory. Not until they learn how to draw the people by a variety of well-seasoned dishes will they compete successfully with "the roast beef of Old England." Why don't they employ Indian cooks for a time? Anglo-Indian ladies ought to set the example to their sisters.

The English are heavy eaters as a rule. I have never had a regular dinner with friends while in England, being unaccustomed both to their hours and their dishes. But I have had to put in appearance at lunch or breakfast, to catch a friend about to leave town. On one such occasion I see a company of poets, philosophers, and fanatics at table, presided over by a young lady, the daughter of the house. I sit there, wiping my forehead (they do the eating, I the perspiring) as I see slices of beef disappearing, with vegetables, mustard, etc. I am pressed to join, but pretend to make a horrified protest. The host then asks me slyly what I think of the food and their mode of eating? I reply instinctively, "It is horrible." The reply sets the gentlemen roaring, and my hostess blushing. But I could not help saying what I feel. How can a little stomach hold such an enormous lunch? Even women and children take large quantities. What vitality these people have, to be sure! The waste of vitality in their climate, and under their conditions of life, must be equally enormous; and it has, of course, to be replaced.

It is not only the quantity, but the manner of eating as well, that puzzles and sometimes frightens me. Men and women eat freely at shops, in the street, tram, 'bus, or railway carriage. There is an absence of delicacy and deliberation about the matter, at which the grave Oriental may well lift his eyebrows. Bismillah! How these Firanghis do eat! Oysters seem to be the ambrosia of adult invalids, as sponge cakes are supposed to be that of children in trouble. Nor is it a pleasant sight to see women devouring pork, bacon, beef, ham at restaurants, with the usual accompaniments. Many of them send for these things every day for dinner. I suppose it is easier, and cheaper perhaps, to do so. But how much better for themselves and their families if they knew how to cook a simple meal at home? The existence of so many hotels, restaurants, and tea-shops seems to be destructive of the home life of the people. It may

E

destroy the very idea of home, if it does not also dry up the spring of family affection.

Water is about the last thing the average Britisher thinks of for a beverage. Ale and beer and stout are the A B C of his alphabet of bibacity. He may wash a dinner down with tea, coffee, or other non-intoxicants. But have these as an aid to digestion and a fillip to the spirits? No. Never. He must have ·a something strong, you know. As a race, the British are hard drinkers, partly because they are heavy eaters; and they can stand much. The majority of respectable householders ought to know where to draw the line; but I doubt if all of them can do this. Mr. and Mrs. John Bull take a drop because it is so cold; then because they are so tired, or grieved, or disappointed. The habit grows on many till the victims are reduced to a state verging on lunacy. It is too much to expect self-control even in the majority of what are called moderate drinkers, unless they have some vital interest at stake, or are guided by high ideals of life. For idlers, or those that are feeble in character, the first glass is generally the first step to ruin. A good deal also depends upon the nature of the drink consumed in a country. The light sweet wines of the South, or a medicinal dose of something stronger, may not do harm to all constitutions alike, though it is very doubtful if they do real good in nine cases out of ten. This is my opinion, based on an experience of several years. There may be temperaments and occupations that need an occasional stimulus in the shape of wine or brandy mingled with semi-liquid food. But even in these cases alcohol is, I think, best avoided.

From drink to drunkenness is an easy transition, especially in a climate like that of Great Britain. What beastliness there is in the drunkenness of some of the backslums! It beggars description and defies all justification. People can hardly realize what a drunkard is, unless they have seen one in the streets of London or Glasgow—a sight saddening enough to make angels weep. What a desecration of the human form divine! The creature looks more like a seasoned cask of liquor, with the fumes escaping at the top. And he is a hundred times more noxious than the cask of liquor. The Continent appears to be almost free from this degree of drunkenness. It is said that Russia is much worse in this respect. Well, all I can say is that it is hardly possible to imagine a human being so soaked, so steeped, so absorbed in alcohol, as the drunkard I have referred to. If the Russian drunkard beats the British, the former must be allowed the distinction of being something other than human. India is quite sober, compared to England, in spite of her bhang, ganja, opium; in spite of her toddy, mowra, her Shirazi or Cashmiri wines, which are like milk beside the fire-waters of England. The drunkenness that debases, brutalizes, and maddens, seems to be peculiar to the British soil. Is it due to climate? I hardly think so. Paris, for instance, does not differ much in climate from London, and yet it presents a most favourable contrast. Is it occupation, food, personal habits? All these, probably, and other causes, including climate, perhaps, account for the phenomenal bibulousness of the Briton. Beer, ale, porter, stout, brandy, whisky, gin; these and other products of the distillery of Satan, sanctioned, and in a manner patronized by the State, spread their fumes over the land, poisoning men, women, and children. The evil prevails most, I should think, in mining and manufacturing districts, where the victims are more to be pitied than blamed. They have a hard life of it, their ignorance rivalling the squalor of their surroundings. A habitual drunkard amongst them, or in the backslums of London or Glasgow, is but little less than a brute. What talk, what dress, what general demeanour amongst men and women! Some of the worst crimes in these places, including violence and murder, are due more to this one cause than several others put together; as also the vice and suffering amongst a large number of those who disgrace the civilization of England, day and night. And who could say how many of the accidents that happen on land and sea, on railways, in mines and factories, or on steamers, might not be due to the brain muddled with beer, or the hand palsied by gin? Mysterious are the ways of an avenging God, as he sits chiding us in his thunder, or smiting us down with his lightning. More terrible warnings could hardly be given to the sinners themselves, or to those guilty of aiding and abetting, or acquiescing in, the degradation of their fellow-creatures. There are probably more liquor-shops in London, licensed by the State, than shops of any other description. And on Sundays, the Sabbath of the Christians, the day set apart for holy rest and orderly living, there are many more liquor-shops seen open than bread-shops and bible-shops put together. To one squalid eating-house open on Sunday there are perhaps a hundred liquor-shops, tempting the weak and the weary by their theatrical display of life and good cheer. Which of the two will the poor man prefer? And on week-days you will see more barrels of ale and beer in the streets than almost any other necessary of life, carted and conveyed from shop to shop. The men employed in the trade present a bloated and sickly appearance, and die off generally before forty.

Here I am tempted to cite an instance of hard drinking and its result. Even as an extreme case it is not without a lesson. A respectable mechanic in London marries the daughter of a gentleman of means. Shortly after the marriage he takes to speculation, the adverse effect of which he seeks to drown in the proverbial 'cup' of poison. The wife, who is a daily witness of this downward course, is drawn to it by sympathy. Things go from bad to worse till her own dowery has been squandered, besides the loss of the husband's income. It has become a sottish existence for both, in which there is not a grain of self-respect left, or respect for each other. One day, while the wife is in the kitchen, her clothes catch fire. No one notices this, certainly not the victim herself. When too late, the neighbours make a rush towards the kitchen, apprizing the husband who lies dead drunk in the parlour. Entering the kitchen they find the woman roasted alive, a ghastly lump of flesh and bone. She must have been incapable of crying out for help, even if she felt her danger. Of course, there is an inquest at the *public house*, which is usually the case. The gentlemen of the jury meet after an adjournment at the *bar*. And their verdict is in keeping with the *spirits* they have imbibed. The inquest is a solemn farce, the verdict is excellent fooling, and the tragedy itself a reminder of the hollowness of material progress.

It must be observed that drunkenness in England, as such, is confined more or less to the lower and the lower middle classes. But these are the very classes who need to be kept out of the way of temptation, and who have no means of rising, once that they have fallen. The middle class do not seem to be quite free from the vice. Hundreds of families have been ruined, hundreds of wives or husbands died broken-hearted, thousands of children have been thrown upon the streets by one or other of the parents of the respectable middle class taking to this fatal habit. A drunken man is bad enough; a drunken woman is infinitely worse. If she is a mother, she rages like a moral pestilence round the homestead. She spreads the vice around and through her. Her example is more catching than that of of her husband, though she generally takes her first lesson from him or from her father. Her children suck the vice at her breast; they are often born with an hereditary taint. And how many English-women nurse their babies on beer, ale, or gin—shame upon their motherhood! You see some of the results in the children, growing up with disease, ill-temper,

habits of wanton mischief; breaking windows, tearing up plants, their own clothes, and so on. Poor
women! I am told that many of them take to alcohol during their first confinement. If they only
knew what that means, they would turn away from it
with loathing. If they knew that it is more difficult
for them to be reclaimed than for men, more injurious
and more disgraceful, they might pause before im-
bibing the first cup of poison. But there are so few to
warn the young wife, and so many, perhaps, to lead
her on—generally well-meaning friends. I have seen
respectably dressed matrons reeling in the streets of
London. I have known of a number of cases, beginning with just a glass, and ending with the jail
or the lunatic asylum. It appears that the law ought
to be more flexible, allowing the victim a better
chance of cure. Drunkenness is a disease, and should
be treated as such, with the golden rule ever in
view—prevention better than cure. God forbid this
vice should ever approach our women in India, or
our men either. There is no custom so deleterious
as that of infant marriage. But if I were asked to
choose between drunkenness and that, I think I would
keep to my own national custom. For one thing,
infant marriages hardly ever lead to those cruel forms
of prostitution to which drunkenness in women sometimes leads. This is the most disastrous result of
drunkenness. Abate the latter evil, and you will see
the former abating itself sensibly. Drunkenness, to
my mind, is the chief cause of it in London and other
towns. Of course, want is a powerful factor. But the
victim in that case often wears the stamp of mar-

tyrdom in her face and demeanour. She grieves you by her mute appeal under the stress of necessity; the other outrages you by her wanton aggressiveness. What an amount of vice and crime in both sexes could be averted if the curse of drunkenness were to be overcome? Drunkenness is verily the curse of England. Will she, like Jerusalem, go on, heedless of the warning? What vast achievements would the Saxon race be capable of but for this drink crave! Or, is it the craving, probably created by the climate, that drives them to feats of valour?

Here the lunacy law seems to need revision, in order to prevent one man or woman ruining the whole family. A habitual drunkard is a lunatic, unfit to take care of himself and others. The difficulty is to make a law which unscrupulous parties cannot possibly abuse.

The upper middle and the higher classes, I am told, have improved in this respect. At any rate, ladies of real education and position are free from the evil. In its worst form drunkenness exists amongst the lowest orders, who are also the slowest to appreciate their own interests or those of their families. Happily, organized efforts have done a vast amount of good during recent years, both in the way of prevention and reclamation. The first, of course, is by far the best method. It is being tried by a noble band of workers, working under the banners of Total Abstinence and Temperance—men, women, and even children, very appropriately named the Band of Hope. They go forth amongst all classes of the people, preaching, setting an example, and inviting volunteers to sign a pledge. Preaching is good, personal example is far better. I am rejoiced to find that many in the highest ranks of society have undertaken to abstain from all alcoholic drinks, even though found beneficial to their health. This is an example that will tell most. Mild wine does not affect us all equally. It muddles some, while others feel cheered by a small quantity. Those who have enough self-control are none the worse for that quantity. But if not for their own sake, for the sake of others, I should like to see men and women in high places setting an example in self-sacrifice. Alcohol is not indispensable in any case. In most cases, especially of accident or sudden stoppage of the heart's action it is prescribed for temporary convenience; but the benefit is likely to be neutralized when the reaction sets in. That liquor sustains the nerves for any length of time, is as much of a fiction as it is a fact that it destroys them in the end. That, however, is a question for doctors. I speak from my own experience, having had a taste in my youth of almost all kinds of wines available to human ingenuity. If others have had different experience, may not the lasting welfare of society prevail upon the temporary convenience of individuals? The sacrifice would be but nominal, if moderate drinkers, as they call themselves, took more largely of real, genuine, fresh wine, drawn at first hand from the grape, the orange, the apple, the peach—delicious wine-producers of nature. There are also the fruit beverages and other non-alcoholic drinks that could be multiplied to any extent, at hardly one-twentieth of the cost of foreign imports. A change in diet and in personal habits, with a copious supply of water, would contribute largely to the success of experiments in this line, for the benefit of the people at large. It is not enough that these should be told about alcohol being poison. It is small comfort to the would-be suicide to tell him that he must die. The more effective, though perhaps the more difficult method, is to supply him with harmless and equally agreeable substitutes, to make life happy for him if you wish him to live on. Women will make the best missionaries in this vineyard of God, the best recruiting sergeants for the Temperance Army. With women as the life and soul of the splendid organizations that exist for the purpose, let us hope that the more revolting forms of drunkenness will gradually disappear from the land. Let us hope, too, that the Legislature will aid the masses in drawing nearer this consummation to be devoutly wished for.

As remarked above, India has very little to show, either of the drunkenness or the Drink Bill of England. The worst of our indigenous liquors are better than the best of the poisons imported from Europe and thrust down the throats of our working classes. As to our drugs, bhang and opium, their effect is not half so demoralizing as that of European drinks. Of bhang I speak from the experience of my school-days ; of opium from careful inquiries. The former, taken with its proper accompaniments, exhilarates without lifting you off your legs. When taken more than is good for you, it makes you see

double through a pair of rainy or thundery eyes.
I beg to protest against being mistaken for a victim of either of these effects even in my wild-oats-
sowing season. The reader will be pleased to distinguish between experience and observation. As
regards opium, the case will be best met by a
running comparison. Opium stupefies, alcohol excites; opium dulls the nerves slowly, alcohol quickly
destroys them; opium makes a coward, alcohol a
murderer. Even in small doses, taken over a long
period, opium makes a brute, alcohol a beast. Reader,
take thy choice, and then hide thy face from the light
of day.

Smoking is one of those small vices which seem
to be easily condoned by the social conscience of
England. To preach a crusade against it is like attempting to crush a pea under a fifty-pound hammer.
It is too venial an offence to be fought to the knife,
to be destroyed root and branch. And yet, judged
by its influence on the health and manners of the
masses, tobacco-smoking is scarcely a habit to be
encouraged. To begin with, it is very disagreeable.
See how the poor slave manages it. He takes the
thing out of his pouch, bites and half chews it, fills
his pipe with it, or rolls it up in a piece of paper.
He now fumbles for his box of matches, which he
carries about, perhaps more carefully than his watch
and chain. The victim then scratches two or three
of the matches, with an air of vacuous satisfaction;
lights his pipe, and goes at it puff, puff, puff. He
will light it anywhere, anyhow—in the street, 'bus,
or railway carriage; under shelter of a book, news-

paper, the side of his coat, against his trouser leg, even under his hat, so as to keep off the draught. He seems to smoke much oftener than he eats or drinks. I think he smokes oftener than he speaks. His tobacco is more pungent than pleasant; and the fumes he emits by perpetual puffing will give his neighbours a headache, if nothing worse. It often makes the non-smoker giddy, inducing a sensation of thirst which water only half quenches. On himself the effect is bound to be more unwholesome. Look at his hands, face, teeth, lips. Don't they proclaim violation of the laws of hygiene? Inordinate smoking doubtless tells upon health of mind and body alike. The victim may get shorter in stature as he does in temper, especially if he has begun too early. How many little fellows do we see in the streets of London, picking up the stumps of cigars and puffing away at them, as if for dear life? This form of smoking is worse than our Indian hubble-bubble—much worse than the poor man's *bidi* in India.

Among the upper middle and the higher classes, smoking does not seem to mean so much injury to the victim or so much nuisance to others. There is little harm, I take it, in two or three cigars a day, taken under medical advice. On the contrary, they may, in some cases, aid digestion, soothe the nerves, and sweeten taste as well as temper. But the habit is likely to be over-indulged, at the cost of health and good feeling.

How is this little vice to be controlled? The presence of women would be some check if they set down smoking as bad form. Do not Englishwomen deal with the question too diplomatically? There are some who rather encourage the habit. I have seen young ladies holding the umbrella or the hat under which their affianced might light the cigar. Will the fair hypocrites do this after marriage? I have also seen pretty little cigarettes between pretty little lips, and have been asked to share the privilege. The sight is very contagious. Is it, after all, so very unbecoming in these advocates of equal rights?

If I had a voice in the matter, I would advise the sex to refuse all osculatory rights and privileges to worshippers at the shrine of the fragrant weed. Perhaps a more shining and a more burning example might be afforded by some American judge granting damages to an aggrieved wife.

CHAPTER III.

LIFE AS SEEN AT HOME.

English Home Life—Life At School and College—Why Indian Youths fail amidst such Associations—The Home Life of England and India contrasted—Marriage—Over-Population—Polygamy—Mothers—Funerals—Child Insurance.

THE home life of England is practically a sealed book to us. I do not know why this should be so, if we wished it otherwise. At any rate, it may not be too much to attempt a rough estimate of it from a few glimpses obtained, both in India and in England. The life in a decent English home is a life of equality among all the members. This means openness and mutual confidence. Wife and husband are one at home, however different their creed, political or religious. They love, trust, serve each other as true partners, each contributing his or her share to the common stock of happiness. The children stand in the same position with the parents as the latter stand to each other. There are no secrets, and therefore no suspicion on the one hand, or reserve on the other. Mother and daughter live more like sisters ; father and son more like two brothers. The parent is as slow to assert his or her authority as the child is to abuse his or her freedom. The education of the heart begins very early, almost while the child is in arms. Then begins the physical education, followed after an interval by education of the mind. And how natural is the system of education! how pleasant the mode of imparting it! It never wearies or cramps the recipient.

All this is different in India. The mother must assume her true position before a country can expect to enjoy happiness at home or honour abroad.

The life at a public school or college is more or less of a continuation of the life begun at home. Progress is spontaneous, not forced. The body is as carefully trained as are the heart and mind. Habits of cleanliness, truthfulness, of observation, of decision and self-denial, grow apace side by side with the growth of the child in mind and body. The day is divided between the class-room, the dining-room, and the open grounds adjoining. The system is intended to make education a living force; to make of its recipient a whole man. Love of home and of country very likely predominates, but the mind is so trained that it will accept duty before pleasure any day, and make a home in any part of the world where duty lies. The same sense of equality, that obtains between parents and children at home, prevails between masters and pupils at school or college. The result, in either case, is a sense of independence rooted in a sense of discipline, all the sturdier because unenforced.

One often wonders why so many of our Indian youths return from England, soured and disgusted after a few years spent there at college. The reason is not far to seek, if one is in a position to find it. The Indian student cannot mix with his English companions on equal terms. He is ill-prepared for it by his early training at home. For one thing, he is so backward in the sports and games that enter so largely into the formation of character and friendship at an English college. He may be patronized for a few weeks by some good-natured fellows, but he works like a drag upon them, so little can he enter into their habits and feelings. When dropped after a fair trial, the stranger keeps his own company, or, in seven cases out of ten, is taken in hand by the worst set at college or in the neighbourhood. He learns to smoke, drink, gamble, to bet, and to squander his substance in worse ways. The life " in apartments," that he has often to accept, does not offer any relief from this round of vulgar dissipation. He may contract debts and disease, and return home with or without his degree. He carries away wrong impressions of English life, thanks mainly to his earlier home influences over which he could not soar. I am afraid this will continue in not a few cases so long as the difference in the home life of the two nations continues. That is a large problem. The question for the present is, how to offer the comforts and convenience of home to an Indian student in England ; how to enable him to make the best of his brief sojourn in the land of his rulers. Even this question I prefer to leave to wiser heads, to more practical friends of our students. But there is one aspect of the question, rather a side issue, on which I should like to offer a few remarks in passing. I refer to the relations that should subsist between Englishmen and Indians, whether in England or in India. We are all agreed that these relations should be friendly. Englishmen vie with Indians in insisting upon this condition. I have very little doubt myself that the majority of Englishmen, official or unofficial, sympathize with native aspirations; but I am equally certain that some of these well-meaning friends overdo their part of friendliness (real friendship, such as we Asiatics feel, it would be too much to look for in such a case), and it seems that the patronizing Englishman does us as much harm as he who always disparages and decries our merits. Strange as it may sound, I hold that it is as bad for us to be given more consideration than our due, as it is to be given less consideration. We should be treated exactly as equals, if we deserve to be. You must not give us less than our due; and pray don't give us more either —in the shape of words or otherwise. We must rough it out with you at school, college, and in public life. Equal justice—and no more. I have preached this doctrine in and out of season for nigh upon fifteen years, incurring the displeasure of some of my own countrymen, and perhaps ridicule from English well-wishers. The Englishman cannot understand why I resent patronage from a superior race. The Indian suspects I am angling for popularity with the governing race at the expense of my "poor down-trodden country." Well, I don't mind what the Englishman may think of it; but I appeal to my own people, the educated portion thereof,

F

to say if they love to wear the badge of inferiority. These remarks apply with equal force as between Natives and Natives; as, for instance, between Mahomedans and Hindus. As a true friend of each, I have always advised them not to rely too much on special favours or concessions. Let us ask of our English rulers and fellow-subjects to treat us as their equals; and where we are wanting, to push us up to their level, rather than keep us where we are, on a crust of comfort, such as they throw to the lame dog whom they do *not* wish to kick over the stile.

So strongly do I feel against differential treatment, that I have always opposed the suggestion made in India, from time to time, for separate carriage accommodation on the railway lines, in order to avoid race disputes which are by no means infrequent. I have myself suffered a good deal from the exclusiveness of English passengers. But rather than give in for peace sake, I have managed to keep my place and fought for it. In these tussles I have sometimes got the worst of it, but then I have found I was in the wrong.

To English friends in India, and more so to those in England, who are extra-polite to us, simply because we happen to be strangers, who stoop and bend in order to pat us on the back, I appeal earnestly to treat us more like fellow-subjects. By all means be kind and hospitable to us, as you are to your own people; but, above all, be just and impartial. Treat us as you treat your own brethren. Spare us not if you find us tripping. In a word, do not patronize but befriend us. Give us the right hand of fellowship at school and college, in the highways and byways of public life. Anything more from you we would rather be without. Habitual excess of forbearance is perhaps worse, in the long run, than an excess of severity.

The same equal treatment we ask for in the case of the nation as in the case of individuals. We want the public services to be open to Natives and Europeans alike; to be entered by one common portal, that of competition. We do not want England to send us her superfluous wealth; she has need of that at home. But we do want her to manage our resources in India as carefully as she manages her own. And the best way to do this, we think, is to associate with yourselves, in the conduct of public affairs, those of us who are competent for it, not by means of patronage—that is, on official sufferance—but by election mainly at the hands of qualified voters. In short, within the measure of our capacity and the circumstances of the country, there should be an approximation in the methods of government between India and England, with equality as the basis both of public administration and personal intercourse.

This, and much more, might be impressed upon the average English politician, if only he could be got at. But the difficulty is to interest him in the affairs of far-off India. His ignorance does not appear to be wilful. India is so large a problem that the majority of Englishmen give it up in despair. Those who are drawn to it by personal ties, or by

a more generous attachment, are distracted by the
proverbial multitude of counsel. I believe there
ought to be a central informing agency in London,
untainted by party bias and by pecuniary interest.
Anglo-Indians could be of great service in this connection. Some of them doubtless are; I wish there
were more. India has little to do with party politics. Conservatives, Liberals, and Radicals, are practically the same to her. Most of them are actuated
by honest, if not strictly honourable intentions towards us. But it would be idle to expect the
English, as a people, to concern themselves with
our affairs, when they have so many of their own to
occupy them. Their want of interest is excusable;
they make no secret of it. There is hardly any
excuse, however, for the ignorance of responsible
men who have the governing of India. Theirs is
sometimes a compound ignorance, as the Arabian
would call it, an ignorance that knows not it is
ignorant. My Lord Rattledrone is a good hand at
letting in the light of knowledge Indian on the foggy
horizon of his peers. Sir Evan Gossamer may get
up a flash now and then to dazzle the Lower House.
But when they and I come to close quarters, why
do these rulers of India so often think discretion
the better part of valour? Where is the need for
running away from Indian questions? Take heart
of grace, gentlemen, and face your duty. It is no
use putting off the evil day. The day will grow
more and more evil that way. India is getting on
but for the unnatural economic conditions imposed
on her by your ignorance. The drain on her re-

sources, perhaps inevitable in the beginning, has been so continuous, that she has hardly enough blood left in her now for healthy circulation. This process of depletion tells most on the peasantry, least able to bear up against it. The heavy expenditure incurred by the military departments, coupled with this drain of resources, cannot last for ever. The sooner you find a remedy, the better for us both. I do not care much what is to become of you in case of a disruption. You will probably find fresh fields and pastures new. But what about *us*, after this steady growth of a century? A French writer recently drew a picture of the coming struggle in India. The picture appears to have been ludicrously overdrawn. But the colours are not all equally false. The present generation of Natives are duly grateful for the blessings of peace and education they have received. To them it has been a matter of personal experience. Will it be the same to the coming generations? They may look upon the blessings rather as a matter of course, while they cannot but resent poverty and lack of employment all the more keenly because of the education they have received. How long are our responsible rulers to grope in the dark, with the light of knowledge and experience fully available? If England will learn to govern India more and more in accordance with natural conditions, she will not only be amply repaid for the task in itself, but will find a market for her goods, of almost every description, ten times larger than she is likely to find elsewhere. The experiment is as glorious as it is profitable to both.

I do not expect a political millennium to be reached to-morrow, any more than I expect a disruption to overtake us at once. But having discovered a mistake, we cannot set about correcting it too soon.

As to ruling India by the sword, my dear Colonel Swashbuckler, you ought to know better. How many swords do you keep in India? Sixty thousand?—eighty thousand?—a hundred thousand? And what is the population of India?—two hundred millions. Now, I defy you to cut off two thousand heads with one sword, even in imagination. You will use the armies of the Native States? How much will these swell the number of your swords? And you are shrewd enough to know that blood is thicker than water. Take my advice, dear Colonel; put your sword into a barrel of vinegar. It will improve vinegar and steel alike, and give you time to read up your school books of history again. How long can one nation rule another merely by the arm of flesh? Long may England continue to rule us, not by the sword, but by the rod. *   *   *   *

The home life of England is decidedly happier than one may be inclined to think, taking a surface view of the lower strata only. At any rate, they have a much wider extent of actual happiness than we have in India. On the other hand, actual misery, though limited in area, is certainly more keenly felt here. Marriage is not the be-all and end-all of existence; nor are children, male or female, the only means of salvation and the only object of earthly felicity. This ideal has its drawbacks, especially where the units of society become too much absorbed in self; but its advantages are obvious and manifold. There is more leisure in England for public work at home, or patriotic enterprise abroad; more freedom, more self-respect for individuals. Men and women may live free of the domestic fetters, and are none the worse for such life, if regulated on high principle.

Married life begins much later than with us, and amongst the better classes seldom without adequate provision for the future. The parties have a larger capacity for appreciating the duties as well as the privileges of married life. English children show a quicker growth of body and mind than children in India. Boys and girls are trained from infancy to a sense of self-reliance. They are generally fit to be so trained. In a word, the English enjoy a larger, freer, healthier life than we do. We have glanced incidentally at a few sharp contrasts between married life in England and that in India. One more contrast may close this section appropriately. In India, the little husband brings his wife, less than himself, to the paternal roof; and there, under its umbrageous shade, they grow into man and woman, father and mother. It is a parasitic growth, more or less, and perpetuates what we call the joint family system. In England, husband and wife set up a house for themselves immediately after marriage. The wife will not live with her husband's friends, though the husband may, in certain cases, live with his wife's parents. The mother-in-law of England is despised by her daughter-in-law. In India, the mother-in-law is dreaded as no earthly power is ever dreaded. The results of the two customs, pushed to extremes in both cases, are self-evident. In England, the separation caused by marriage is likely to blunt filial as well as parental instinct, whatever the Englishman may say to the contrary. In India, the living in-and-in weakens all independent growth. As in other concerns of life, so in this, the reformer will have to suggest a golden mean between the two extremes.

Marriage seems to be growing unpopular in England more perhaps in the higher and middle ranks than in the lower, and more so, of course, in towns than in the country. There are reasons for this growing unpopularity. The expenses of married life, of keeping a house, are heavy. Another reason is said to be the so-called independence of girls. Their idea of life is to pass for ladies, if they accept the marital yoke. Dresses, trinkets, servants, company at home, visits out; these are the main objects for which girls will marry. And they won't sell themselves under their own price. They do not care for cooking, and are too delicate to nurse their children. Young men, who have enough to do in the way of earning a decent income for themselves, cannot afford such expensive life companions, especially as they have within reach many of the privileges of marriage without its responsibilities. The result is often a bartering of affections on both sides, arrangements that could be broken off any day, and a dislike on both sides for settled home life. Our independent girls will do anything, from menial service to hawking flowers and newspapers in the streets; slaving at shops, hotels, restaurants, theatres; waiting upon men and women, engaging themselves as clerks, teachers, etc. In many of the small employments, referred to, they undersell the men. This widens the alienation of feeling. Even in cases of real attachment young people often hesitate to marry. If the girl marries and merges herself into the husband's existence, she ceases to be an earning machine, while as a spending machine she goes quicker than before. If she has to earn her living even after marriage, the husband is often left practically without home comforts. Few men, even of twenty-five or thirty, could be expected to go through the stormy waters of life under these conditions. It is a sad problem, and one turns away from it in despair. The vice, the shame, the suffering caused by this unnatural state of affairs amongst the lower orders can hardly be conceived by an outsider. It fills the streets of London with all that is repulsive in life, and much that is subversive of the welfare of society. That a certain number of men and women should be free to devote themselves to unselfish usefulness, is a state of things to be desired in every community. But here we are dealing with another class altogether, what may be called marrying men and women who won't marry. Young people dislike the cares of home life, forgetting that the house is intended as their little state. They are fond of gadding about, and look down on family life. They dread having children, when married. This anxiety not to add to the sum total of human life in London is due much less to prudential considerations than to other ignoble reasons. It is often for their own selfish purposes that this class of people desire not to have children ; and as children will sometimes insist upon coming, they think it safest not to marry. The results of such a course of life on the character of the people may be easily imagined. One can understand the dread of over-population, on the part of a civilized people, leading to poverty, disease, crime, pestilence and war. One may sympathize even with prejudice, so far. But what is one to say to mere self-indulgence serving as a bar to matrimony? Are they not fools who want all the roses of married life without its thorns?

This keen enjoyment of life in England, which a stranger may well be excused for envying, seems to be due mainly to its artificial character. Not to put too fine a point on it, the scramble after happiness indicates a low ideal, rather than a high one. Men run after money,—they are in dead earnest about it. When they have had enough of money, they run after pleasure. That seems to make an average of town life between twenty and fifty in almost all ranks. In the higher ranks, where wealth is pampered by leisure, and leisure enticed by wealth, one often meets with a look of settled cynicism, a sort of premature worldly-wisdom, not at all in keeping with nature. Can this be a mask? Not in all cases, I fear ; not, perhaps, in most cases. What makes one despair of the future of society is, that this spirit of negation is believed to be good form. It shows a superior mind to discard faith, to deny hope, to scoff at charity. There *may* be a God ; there *may* be an after-life. But we know little, and care less. It is the present that we live in, the self that we live for. That much is real, that much is certain. Why trouble about more?

If this be your English culture of the nineteenth century, let us remain ignorant in India. I had much rather that India remained superstitious enough to worship her stone-god. That means something of self-sacrifice; it lifts the worshipper out of himself. The worship of self is the worst form of idolatry.

Seduced by this example of high-born worldliness, what wonder if less favoured persons, and especially unprotected girls in the lower ranks of life, should startle you now and then with a show of shameless indifference? A large percentage of this class of girls live avowedly on the outskirts of shame. We must have money. Marriage is a risk, often a failure. So we shall have money without marriage. Of course, it is sometimes inconvenient. But what is life without money? Our employers do not pay us enough to live well. But we are free on Sundays, and on the early-closing Saturdays and Thursdays. We may have the company of men of our own class. Some of us are lucky enough to have gentlemen. There are the restaurants, chambers, apartments. There are men and men. Some ply us with drink, and leave us all of a sudden—the mean things. Others are liberal. There are some who are really kind, to whom we sometimes lose our hearts. But we cannot afford *that*. No, we can't live cheaper. It would kill one to depend upon unwilling people. We don't like this for itself; but where is the wrong? Everybody does it—it is give and take. It is better than beggary and the workhouse; much easier. One must have money whilst one is young. With £ 30 or £ 40 in the bank, there will be time enough to think of marriage. Of course, I have my own young man who knows nothing. He is trying to provide. I should like a home and a family. No, never after marriage, so help me heaven! How many of us do it? Well, all I can say is, it is few of our class who don't. Many of us begin it early, so as to end it before it is too late.

There thou art, London, with thy churches and chapels, and thy weekly charities trumpeted from the housetops. What dost thou think of this practical little woman?

Every such girl saved from the pavement is a gain to society. I am glad to see strenuous efforts made in this behalf by women themselves. That is the most effective agency. But side by side with such efforts I should like to see movements got up to induce employers of labour, especially skilled labour, to observe the same scale of wages between men and women, where the quality of the work done is the same. It is the small prejudices of the other sex that rankle women most.

Happily, it is with a few sections of the higher and the middle classes, and with one or two of the lower classes, especially in towns, that marriage seems to be losing its charms. Amongst the peasantry, the labouring class, the mechanics, and other wage-earning men, who have to spend much of their time out of doors in hard work, marriage is popular

enough. These men look back to a haven of rest
when they return from work. A wife and a home
alone can give this. They don't look upon marriage
as a bad investment; because, as they explain it
sometimes, the two find it easier to keep the mill
going. Home life amongst these people seems to be
happy and contented. There is a tendency towards
lowering the limit of age among some of them,
though no way approaching our Indian standard.
This tendency is observable even amongst the higher classes. Does it signify anything in particular?

We have glanced above at a very unattractive side
of married life in England. Of course, there is a
bright side to the picture, probably the brightest
that painter ever painted for humanity. The number
of happy marriages must doubtless be much larger in
this country than in India. By "happy marriages"
I mean those in which both parties are happy. Considering the essentials of wedded happiness, it stands
to reason that there should be more happy homes
here than in our country. Going by sex, I should
think there are more unhappy wives, both in England and in India, than unhappy husbands. But
wedded misery, though more keenly felt by wives
in England, is certainly less wide-spread than in
our country. In England wives know how to protest—if need be, to revolt. In India wives are
taught to be patient and enduring, nay, even to aid
and abet the offending husband in his lawlessness.
That is the supreme merit of the wife, according
to a spurious Shastra. But why pursue the comparison further?

It is being urged all around us that marriage means over-population. Stop marriage, say some; others say let marriage be, but stop its inevitable consequence in offspring. Science is asked to provide the human race with all the sweets of marriage without its health-giving bitters. Science can do much, but she will do it only in a fitful arbitrary manner. She is not to be relied upon when pitted against Nature. Now, it seems reasonable to say that no man or woman has a right to bring children into the world without adequate provision for them. It is equally certain, again, that over-population is becoming perhaps the most serious problem of the day. But it is by no means half so clear how the problem can be solved either by science or religion, or any other agency, without going to the root of it. Want of equality between the sexes seems to me to account largely for the evils of over-population. Let men and women be recognized as exact equals in the partnership of marriage, each loving and honouring the other, each consulting the interest, the capacity and the inclination of the other for a duty that is the most sacred in this sacred relationship of life. This is abstinence of the right kind, preached by the voice of Nature more eloquently than we are accustomed to hear it preached from pulpit and platform. And being natural, it is simple, safe, and healthy.

A good deal has been said of late in praise of polygamy. Mothers, who know not "what to do with our girls," may be excused for thinking with a sigh of this "goood old custom"; and the girls themselves,

seeing what a struggle they have before them, may
be sorely tempted at times to vote for the paradise
of Utah. The latest plea for plurality of wives comes
from that much abused colony. It seems to have
been urged, in all good faith, by one of the products of polygamy, no less than a daughter of Brig-
ham Young. The lady writes with generous warmth,
to say that all her father's wives, and all his children
by these different wives, sons and daughters alike,
have been healthier and happier than it is possible
to expect from the average monogamous alliance.

Now, this appears to be a hasty assumption. It
is possible that the many wives of one husband may
be freer from some of the ills to which the monogamous wife is exposed. But is she wise in buying
this small freedom at the cost of that larger freedom
she has secured after ages of hard continuous struggle, namely, the freedom from moral inferiority to
man? I think she will prefer to be man's equal on
any terms, sharing his joys and sorrows, rather than
revert to the yoke of comfortable slavery. Then, as
to the offspring of a polygamous marriage being
healthier in mind and body, it remains to be seen
what test we are to employ for an impartial comparison. Are we to judge of them as animals, as
being sound in wind and limb, apart from moral
and intellectual worth? The history of polygamous
nations does not seem to encourage a belief in superiority either of intellect or physique. At any rate,
if polygamy "pays" in an isolated tract, and under
exceptionally primitive conditions, it does not follow
that it will fit in with a complex and highly artifi-

cial civilization in the old world. Polygamy is losing its charms even for Islam, as the latter comes to the front in the battle of life. It is too late for a Christian people to think of it.

It can hardly be denied that many a monogamous husband practises polygamy in all but name. This is certainly more objectionable in a moral sense. From the social standpoint it is the open form that is indefensible—the doctrine of plurality of wives, encouraged by society and sanctioned by law.

Those who hold up the sex relations obtaining amongst animals seem to overlook the gulf that divides the latter from man, both as regards plurality and indiscriminate association. Think of man reverting to this primitive state without any of the inflexible safeguards of instinct under which alone can animals indulge themselves!

Equality ought to be at the root of marriage, whether it is regarded as a sacrament or a contract. Polygamy cuts at the very root of this noble conception.

Bad wives may make worse mothers. In England, wherever home duties are not looked down upon, the wives make excellent mothers. They may appear to be less careful than our mothers, but are not so really. Being grown-up women, with useful knowledge at the back, they know how to deal with children—to help the natural growth, to teach them self-reliance; in a word, to educate all their faculties conformably to Nature and their environments. They do not kill their children with kindness, as mothers sometimes do in India.

On the other hand, however, the life of the English mother appears in one important respect to be tinged with unpardonable selfishness. Too frequently her children are not nursed by her. Amongst the poor, children are reared more upon beer and ale than on nature's sweetest provision. Mothers in well-to-do families do not go to this extent. They employ nurses, or feed the little ones artificially. They seem to be ashamed of nursing their children, that is ashamed of being mothers. They are afraid of injuring their health or good looks, of making themselves unfit for balls and picnics or other social amusements. These are mothers who belie their motherly instincts. What do they become mothers for, if not to give the superfluity of their resources to the bone of their bone, the flesh of their flesh? In thus neglecting to utilize nature's bounty, they frequently bring ill-health upon themselves and the children. Except under medical advice, a mother serves herself as well as her offspring by obeying the law of nature. What she foolishly looks upon as her shame is, in reality, her glory.

It is no unusual sight in the streets of London to see mothers or nurses "give an airing" to infants in perambulators. This is "airing" with a vengeance; for the child sits exposed to the chill biting wind, whilst the mother or nurse stands chatting at a corner, making purchases, or gaping at the shop windows. You may sometimes see baby toppling out of the perambulator, whilst the mother or nurse is engaged at a distance; or you may see a sister of five or six in charge of baby, both in imminent danger

G

of being run over in the street, or both rolling together on the pavement. See how the poor thing
has its neck nearly broken by the jerks it gets in its
little carriage, as it sits, a picture of despair, with
arms and legs quite bare, catching its death both
ways. I touch the hand lying listless by its side;
it is ice-cold. I touch the forehead; it is burning
hot. It is evidently the child of well-to-do parents.
What is one to say to them, especially to the mother? These sights are impossible in India.

Such unmotherly mothers, however, must be the
exception, to be met with chiefly in the busy, selfish
towns. In the country, mothers and sisters often
make the very perfection of human relationship for
the Englishman, from childhood upwards. There
are thousands of happy sons and brothers in England, who seek no happier home than they have,
believing in none such, even as offered by holy wedlock. To me it is much more than amusing to hear
a brother addressing his younger sister as "mamma";
to see the little tyrant scolding and ordering him
about. One evening I call upon a friend rather un-
expectedly, on my way back from another. He is
not at home, but his sister receives me very kindly
and shows me her "Indian treasures." In less than
half an hour my friend turns up, and is greeted
with the playful remonstrance:—"You bad, wicked
boy, what have you been doing with yourself? Here
is an old friend waiting for you. Now go off at
once and get ready for tea. I am sure you do not
deserve it." " I *am* sorry," replies the laggard meek-
ly, kissing his pretty little caretaker, and extending

his hand to me, "but I did not know he was coming." If this is not home, I say to myself, watching the happy pair, there can be no such thing as home on earth.

How fond these people are of playing at papa and mamma! The husband greets the mother of his children as "mamma," returning home after the day's toil, to find the inner circle gathered expectant round the hearth, as the wife advances to relieve "papa" of his top-coat or the packet under his arm. This is very different from India: though, curious as it may seem, a Parsi wife sometimes addresses her husband as "mamma." For an Indian household the approach even of father or husband is often a signal for fluttering disappearance of the fair ones from the parlour. In the case of strangers the exit is, of course, more precipitate. Often have I scattered the ladies in a friend's drawing-room, like chaff before the wind, dropping the book or the work-box as they fly, sometimes leaving a pair of tiny slippers behind, as if to reproach the intruder for walking in unannounced. Ah me! when shall we have a real home in India? Poor, indeed, is the Indian in his mother; poorer still in his home.

We have seen that marriage is unpopular amongst certain classes of society in England. It is unpopular, mainly because it is expensive. The English might take a leaf out of the Rajput marriage code, recently promulgated, which forbids everything above a certain fixed outlay on marriage, funeral, and other ceremonies. Funeral expenses in England are generally far too high for the occasion. Amongst the better classes they cost from £ 50 upwards. People have to make special provision for their funerals, often by means of insurance. The poor follow the rich, and often outdo them in heartless extravagance. In many a case the survivors are left in destitution after paying for the paraphernalia of woe provided by the undertaker. In India we complain that they sometimes eat the dead man out of house and home. Here, in England, the cannibal of fashion carries this devouring process a little further. Besides eating up the insurance money, she sometimes runs the survivors into debt. I am assured, however, that the upper classes have been steadily discarding the fashion of late. Let us hope the lower classes will follow this example as readily as they have followed the other.

Child Insurance is a system of which the reader may have heard before. Parents insure the lives of their children, often only to neglect them in such a way as to cause their death, so that they may be able to secure money from the insurance office. With this money they get up a showy funeral, treat themselves and friends to drink, and otherwise have "a jolly time of it" over the grave hardly yet closed. Of course, this practice must be confined to a very small area, amongst the poorest and most ignorant, whom drink has already brought to the verge of brutality.

CHAPTER IV.

LIFE AS SEEN IN PUBLIC AFFAIRS.

The Poverty of London—Charity Organizations—Pangs of Hunger—Personal Appearance and Hygiene—Religion—What has Christianity done ?—The Future of Christianity—Going to Church—Heart·Longings—The Slaughter of Animals—Hunting and Shooting—A Wild Beasts Show—Vivisection—Labour Unions—Friendships—Militarism—The Navy—Other Careers—The Salvation Army—Racing and Betting—The Future of Royalty.

Poor as India is, I thank God she knows not much of the poverty to which parts of Great Britain have been accustomed—the East End of London, for instance, parts of Glasgow, and other congested centres of life. Men and women living in a chronic state of emaciation, till they can hardly be recognized as human ; picking up, as food, what even animals will turn away from ; sleeping, fifty, sixty, eighty of them together, of all ages and both sexes, in a hole that could not hold ten with decency ; swearing, fighting, trampling on one another ; filling the room with foul confusion and fouler air. This is not a picture of occasional misery ; in some places it represents the every-day life of the victims of misfortune.

In London itself there are hundreds of thousands who have a daily, almost hourly struggle of it, to keep body and soul together. So fierce is this struggle for existence that the victims can hardly find time to emerge from their work-holes for a whiff of fresh air. I am told of old Londoners who have never been out of their streets for years. Think of this in busy London, always on the move.

It is in winter, more than six months of the year, that you see the poverty of England at its worst. Thousands of men and women, disabled by accident, or thrown out of work, trudge aimlessly about, knowing not where to get a crust of bread, even a dry bone wherewith to allay the pangs of hunger that gnaw at their vitals; knowing not where to get an additional rag to keep the cold from eating into their marrow; knowing not where to lie down after the day's disheartening tramp, for fear of the policeman, or for fear of never being able to get up again. Hundreds of them may be found every month on the pavements, on the roadside, on house steps, starved, cramped, or frozen to death. Hundreds die every month for sheer want of means to keep alive. Thousands drag on a miserable existence, embittered by disease, from which death, too long delayed, is the only relief. The suffering in all cases is infinitely more keen than it would be in similar cases in India, though the extent of it is smaller.

And side by side with such heart-rending scenes of misery, one sees gorgeously dressed luxury flaunting it in the streets, dragged along by horses, better fed and better looked after than many a human family in the same neighbourhood. Here, again, one has a vivid picture of the extremes of wealth and poverty.

It is worth mentioning, however, that the contrast is becoming less rigid every decade. One observes a tendency towards a more natural distribution of wealth. It has been shown that the number of incomes over ten thousand a year is on a decrease, whilst incomes counting by the thousand and by hundreds are decidedly on the increase. This tendency is observable in India too, amongst corresponding classes. It is a good sign for the countries, for poor and rich alike, especially for the great monopolists in land.

For another contrast, let us turn to the little band of Englishwomen, who, discarding youth, wealth, position, walk about from street to street, wallet in hand, collecting such remnants of food as have been thrown away or kept in the refuse box, cleaning and cooking the morsels up into dainty dishes for the poor. Here we see the genius of Charity walking side by side with callousness. It is a noble contrast, this devotion of high-born Englishwomen to the wants of some of the lowest and perhaps most unworthy of their race.

These organizations, which are encircling Modern Babylon in a network of love and charity, forgiving sin, relieving disease, and raising the fallen, as it were from the dead, are amongst the brightest trophies of the Victorian era. Worked mainly through unpaid agencies, they undertake rescue work, ambulance and hospital accommodation, schools for destitute children, places of instruction and amusement

for girls and boys, homes for orphans, and for in-
curables. They embrace almost every stage of life
and every variety of trade, profession, business. They
are in themselves each a system of public beneficence, proclaiming the presence of the father, the
mother, the sister, at every turn, seeking to help
the helpless, to relieve the suffering, to bring the
strays and waifs of society back into the fold. Perhaps the most striking feature of these organizations
is their catholicity. There is no caste or sect here,
to stay the hand of charity; the workers in the field
of humanity work together as brothers and sisters,
giving readily unto all that are needy. Nor do we
see here much of the pride and self-righteousness of
the Eastern dispenser of charity; the pride with
which he scatters his superfluous wealth amongst
others; the self-righteousness with which he essays
to win forgiveness for past errors or make up for
past offences.

There is one danger, however, that may be detect-
ed in the working of some of these organizations, that
needs a passing remark. It is the tendency to cen-
tralize, to degenerate into a sort of state department.
This means delay, expense, possible injustice. And
although it may mean individual responsibility, may
it not also mean favouritism?

Perhaps the most beautiful amongst the charity organizations of London are what are termed flower-
services. They are as beautiful in deed as in name.
All kinds of floral offerings are brought to the church
by the congregation, in some cases prayed over and
blessed by the clergyman, and then distributed by

loving hands to invalids in the parish, the sick, the sorrowing, the poor. It is not a simple matter, this growing, collecting, or purchasing of flowers—the praying over and blessing and distributing of them. It taxes the powers of more than one capable organizer. Why don't they have fruit services likewise?

Among special organizations, not so pretty but of far greater importance, may be named the Hospital Saturday and Sunday. One Saturday and one Sunday in the year are set apart for money collections in aid of hospitals. Thousands of ladies, sweet volunteers, may be seen on either of these days, in churches and chapels, in the streets, at the shops, at railway stations, holding up the box to you with a coaxing look or a smile irresistible. How I love to be eased of my little gold and silver and copper! More than this, I love to see the sordid shopkeeper paying smile with smile, and a handful of silver with a mouthful of jokes. Joke away, old man. The fair enchantress knows how to take thy attentions. Latterly I have seen maidens enlisted in this labour of love—maidens tempting you with roses on their cheeks and in their hands. It is a pretty sight. But I should reserve the work for grown-up ladies.

In the city I sometimes see boys and girls thrusting their heads into kitchens under the houses and restaurants, or gazing hungrily at shop windows. They seem to feed themselves on the smells and sights of the food, smacking the lips every few minutes. What hunger theirs must be! Few that see these poor waifs, "living on nothing a day," can help feeling for them. Some of my friends say it is a dodge; that parents put up the little ones in order to excite sympathy; that the parents make a few coppers that way, and spend them on drink. This may be so in some cases. But many of the passers-by, I hope, will prefer to be imposed upon in one bad case rather than neglect two or three that are good. I never felt such a sensation of hunger as I have felt at times in England. During my travels in India I could live for days on a few biscuits with milk. In summer one hardly cares for solid food in our country. Quite different is my experience of an English summer. I have to go without regular meals for a few days. I find that I cannot do my work, that I feel feverish and miserable all over. It is not a matter, as in India, of the sinking of your stomach or its sticking to your back; it feels as if you had no stomach at all. You are driven as chaff before the wind. Practically, hunger in England is as keen as thirst in India. It is in London that I can realize the havoc of famine in my own country, the semi-starvation of 40,000,000 in India year after year. There must be thousands upon thousands in England, too, whose pangs of hunger I can well imagine, who suffer more keenly, though by no means so largely, as my own people.

Who can help helping these waifs and strays of society? Happy are they that share their happiness with others! Theirs is the only true happiness which comes of making others happy. It is happiness of the same kind that God allows to Himself. Therefore, it must be the best and the purest happiness In every thing let us strive to be as near to Him as we possibly can. It is but a little way we can go; terribly little. That little, however, is our all; it is enough for us all.

_

Who can give a definition of beauty, acceptable to all men and all races? One has but few opportunities of coming across the ideal of beauty he has set up for himself; and then, ten to one, he will not find it in busy London town. Photographs and pictures may not satisfy him. But he can see some very pretty faces, indeed, accompanying slight elastic figures. What strikes one about these faces is their extreme mobility. You may find the owners in almost all the tragic and comic moods conceivable, in the course of a single day. The other style of womanly beauty, that sometimes cheers your eye, is the Greek face and bust, with a stately figure. On the whole, however, there seems to be more of made-up beauty in London than perhaps in most parts of the world. Life is artificial to a degree. Time hangs heavy on those who have no earnest purpose to live for. There is plenty of money with which to buy a few patches and shreds of personal adornment every day. This is to be seen amongst the higher as well as the middle classes. But it must be remarked in passing that, whether natural or made up, an Englishwoman is decidedly attractive—her healthy looks, elastic step, and general freedom of movement, the outcome of a free mind, adding vastly to the attractiveness of her dress. The white and red of the skin may be as much a matter of blemish as of beauty, while a combination of regular features is very rare.

It is the fresh looks and the free healthy motion of the body that give Englishwomen their peculiar charm. These advantages are pushed to an extreme by professional beauties whose make up, sometimes hiding grave defects, costs an amount that might feed scores of the hungry and clothe as many of the naked. These are the languishers, as a set-off to the so-called mashers. They are so delicate in nerves that they will shriek and faint at sight of the very distress which their extravagance tends to create or to intensify. And when old age is on them, what a sight they present, these beauties of a bygone day! It is a sight, pathetic in the very falsehood of attire and demeanour.

But for every ten of this class, there are hundreds and thousands who prefer the simplicity of natural grace. These are the truly gracious, infinitely more interesting as a type of beauty. Perhaps the most noticeable thing about some of them is the character of their eyes. They are beautiful eyes, looking you full and straight in the face. Used to the languid, down cast look of the Eastern eye, one feels a strange sensation coming over him as he meets the look of an intelligent highborn Englishwoman. This is not at all a look of boldness, but of earnest sympathy and self-confidence. The English love to present you a clean, soft, shapely hand. But they cannot boast a good set of teeth, as we can. The men smoke and drink too much, and the women partake too much of injurious food, for that. They seem on the whole to be defective both in the shape of the ears and in the sense of hearing. The weather has, perhaps, something to do with this latter defect. As a rule, they have pretty noses, and well-turned ankles; but hist! whither are we wandering?

I defy the ordinary Briton thoroughly to appreciate the value of the teaching—cleanliness is next to godliness. How can he, poor creature? That teaching would take much longer to penetrate his conscience than does the climate of which he is a helpless victim. I speak feelingly, having had to go without a bath for days, making shift on a miserable wash-tub morning after morning.

There is little that is really attractive in the personal appearance of women of the lower middle and the lower classes, except where mixed blood has to account for a departure from the national type. Amongst the drink-besotted and criminal classes, one may meet with faces scarcely distinguishable from those of animals. Under-feeding accounts for a good deal of such physical deterioration. One also notices sometimes a beefy look, peculiar to Englishmen, apart from the well-known resemblance to the beast which supplies him with his pork. The faces of some of the costermonger girls belong to another order. They have somewhat of a lupine tendency, due to semi-starvation, which saddens one to look at. The most comely looks are to be found probably amongst barmaids, tobacco and other shop girls, girls employed at hotels and restaurants, for sufficient, though perhaps not always creditable, reasons. One or two really beautiful faces, which I happen to have seen in the streets of London, were

those of girls in an advanced stage of consumption
—a transparent skin, with eyes of meek resignation, lips quivering with expectations of a better life.
There is a beauty in suffering, such as can never
be found in health or prosperity.

No, reader, you need not scruple to ask me about
my own ideal of beauty in flesh. I am partial to the
Irish type. Further, I incline towards the French
and the Italian cast. Do not Englishwomen often
borrow their fashions from Italy or France? And
do not these latter partake of the Asiatic type? I
must be true to myself.

But, after all, beauty is not this or that gift of
the body, which is coarse and corruptible, environed
by animal functions, concealing, in the guise of attractiveness, what is really repulsive. Beauty is the
soul within, the pure ambient spirit encircling what
is divine in our nature. Thinking of this earthly
aspect of the attraction of sex, one may well sympathize with the great Pessimist of the East ex-
claiming—"Love and beauty, what are they? I steal
softly at night into the chamber of my queen, my
best beloved, my most beautiful. I see her stretch-
ed upon her bed, dishevelled, with the face dis-
torted, the teeth chattering." Ah! it is all appearance, *Máyá*, illusion!

*
* *

One of the strangest mysteries of reality that
press upon the notice of a student of human progress is the conversion of the early Briton to Christianity. The fact seems to me to be no less a reality
than it is a mystery. Was it possible, humanly

speaking, for that grim wanderer of the forest to be won to the fold of Christ? One would have thought him an almost impossible subject for grace to operate upon; with hardly the germ in him of that gracious evolution of which we now find traces around him and in him. Even at this length of time one may well pause to inquire, whether the rampant Briton of the nineteenth century has much in his nature to go out in response to the call of the Good Shepherd.

Taking advantage of a free Sunday, I have sought to read an answer to this question in the streets and churches of London, which may fairly be taken as a stronghold of all that is best and worst in the national character. The crowds are evidently on their behaviour. But it is hard to say if they move more in sympathy with their holiday attire, or the sacred surroundings amid which their souls might be expected to rest and to revel. The push and crash of the railway station are left behind for the hour; and yet, even in the house of God the preacher is not always secure from a yawn or a cough; sometimes from whispered conversation, whilst the service is proceeding. He may deplore this impatience; sometimes he mildly rebukes it. But he manages to wind up soon after, exhorting the audience to carry a little of the day's teaching into their daily life. This is what the congregation, the male portion particularly, seem to dislike. Why should the parson meddle with their business, with their everyday dealings with one another? What does *he* know about business? Is it not enough for the man that they contribute towards the maintenance of himself and his church, and patronize them both once a week with their presence? The men seem to be more eager to leave the house of God than to enter it. Once fairly out of its precincts, the average church-goer lapses into his habit of surly or reckless selfishness. His Christianity strikes one as being a religion mainly of flesh, bone, and muscle. It teaches him, more than anything else, how to live, to survive, to make the best of life. At home or abroad, he appears a good deal to be guided by this same muscular principle, to aggrandize, to conquer, and to rule. His life, at its best, is a high fever of humanity from which the divine has been eliminated, or in which, rather, the divine has not yet made a dwelling-place. It makes one wonder at such times if the life and teachings of Christ—Britain's most precious heritage—may not, after all, be thrown away upon a people whose spiritual appreciation is so defective. Are such a people likely to attain to anything like a perfect life, making for peace and righteousness? God knows his own time and his own ways. Who can say but that, perhaps, He has shown his grace first to those whose need of it was the sorest, who would take the longest to profit by the grace vouchsafed? That the grace is operating, and that it will operate all the more quickly with the quickening of the spirit in daily life, seems to admit of little doubt, if one is to judge from all the circumstances of the case before him. Appearances seem to be rather against the subject of our inquiry. But situated as life is, it will never afford a complete harmony between a people's religion and their material requirements. Natural surroundings are a factor to be reckoned with. With the majority of men, religion cannot be quite an abiding force. It is more a matter of convenience— a thing to be followed at leisure. It is a fashion, a persuasion with the average church-goer, in high life or low. And yet there are faces, one sees in the crowds, as they pour in and out of church, bearing the impress of an earnest abiding conviction. Not a few of these faces proclaim a life of glad self-surrender. Not a few of them, again, display refinement and culture, consecrated to the service of God in man. To this extent the religion of the English is a living force, wherever it exists. The area covered by it may be narrower than one expected; perhaps it exists in many more forms than going to church. At any rate, if one sees less earnestness in what is called society, he also sees less apathy than he was prepared for amongst leaders of society. Recent protests against dogma have served to quicken inquiry, and to kindle individual concern for the truths of life. In short, what was once a religion of society is becoming a religion of humanity, and women appear to help as well as to share more largely in the beneficent process. One striking feature in this improvement of the working spirit of Christianity, so to call it, is the tide of pure Catholicism that seems to have set in under different names and in different guises. Is the church of St. Peter going to regain its hold on England? That can hardly be. What is more likely is a reaction in favour of the doctrine of salvation by faith *and work*, with the divine humanity of Christ as a common platform for believers and workers alike. This appears to me to be the tendency of the age. A Church Universal is a dream, too vague even for the eye of faith. But if it is ever to be realized, to an appreciable extent, it will rest upon this common ground. Such a doctrine, preached as Christ preached it, and lived as it was lived by him in his own person, has no mean prospect in Asia, the birth place of all religious truths. Who can say if any of these beacon-lights of the future, which first shone in the favoured East, is to be perfected only there; or whether it is to be sent to its original abode, perfected and refined, perhaps with a change in name or form? It looks like a fair division of labour, that one branch of the human family should produce the raw material for the other branch to weave up into the fabric of life.

What is most perplexing to a stranger is the splitting up of the Church into so many sects, each setting down the other as false or inefficacious. Which is one to believe? Not that which depends too much on reason, nor that which demands too much faith. Let me have a happy blending of the two, making what the Society of Friends would call a Reasonable Faith.

⁎

It is sometimes asked—what has Christianity done for the nations of Europe? Has it softened the hatred of man for man? Has it not, rather, hardened the hatred and perpetuated it; raised war into a merit and a pastime; added vastly to the original selfishness of the race, making sin and vice and crime more easy at home and abroad? These evils, like others, perhaps, that may be suggested, doubtless mark the history and progress of Christian civilization. But why call a religion to account when it is the professors of the religion, not the believers, who are guilty of violating its spirit? The fact is, that the brute in man is still more or less rampant. It breaks out at different times and in different forms, and has to be controlled or subdued by different methods. The struggle has been co-existent with the progress of humanity. It is the struggle between good and evil, as the Zoroastrian would put it. The evil is the material side of our nature, which may or may not have pre-existed our spiritual nature. It is hopeless for man to reconcile the two. Such reconciliation, ready made to hand, would probably defeat the objects of Creation.

On the other hand, one need not be a Christian himself to be able to see that Christianity has tended powerfully to humanize one of the least human of the races of man. In its essence, it ought to exercise a threefold influence,—to humanize, to liberalize, to equalize. This, to me, is a very great achievement. Other religions have their special merits; but none of them claims to have rendered this threefold service to the race.

And nowhere, perhaps, is the force of this simple historical truth better realized than in our modern Babylon itself. It is along the darkest and narrowest tracts of life that Christianity seeks most to achieve her triumphs, correcting the infidelities of flesh and spirit, reclaiming vice from her lowest depths, arresting crime in mid-career. It brings sunshine into the prison, carries the blessings of health, peace and reason to the diseased and the demented. To me the most affecting sight in London is to see the highest in rank and culture stooping to the lowliest, offering to bear the burdens of life for those who find them insupportable. Is not this the highest form of religion, both according to its Eastern and its Western conceptions? This bearing of other people's burdens is by no means an uncommon experience in busy, selfish London, though one meets with it in rather unexpected quarters. Nor is it always accompanied by a spirit of self-righteousness or a hope of recompense.

Perhaps the most touching instance of bearing another's burden, that I ever witnessed, was at Mahableshwar in 1889. An old woman and a boy of about sixteen emerge from a jungle, with loads of fuel on their heads. The woman is apparently the lad's grandmother. She is trembling with age, bent in back, infirm of foot. The boy is strong-limbed, walks erect and with a steady step. But he seems to be out of breath, and stops short before an elevation. Thereupon the grandmother asks him to shift his burden on to the top of her own, stooping down in order to be within easy reach of the shifter. She then resumes her position as best she can, strokes the boy on his back, wipes his forehead with her hand, and totters cheerfully along, the boy following as a lamb follows its ewe. It is a sight I shall never forget. My first impulse is to go up to the woman and offer something to her as a tribute of reverent appreciation. But what right has a poor earthworm to detract from the merit of her self-sacrifice? Her reward will be higher and purer than I should expect for myself.

Such cases of burden-bearing it would be too much to expect in the haunts of busy life. But they are not confined to the land of Buddha, nor is the offering of such sacrifice always swayed by considerations of blood.

It is sometimes urged, not without a show of reason, that England should look after her own spiritual welfare before attending to the welfare of alien nations. Now, it is unhappily true, that after some fourteen centuries of active propaganda the Church has acquired but a precarious hold on the practical life of the English. England is still very far from a religious millennium. But that is more or less the case with all systems of religion. Anyhow, it would betray strange want of logic and liberality for the Church Universal to confine her efforts to an infinitesimal fraction of our race. Religion, like charity, may begin at home; but it must not end there. Because a large number of professing Christians in Europe are still grovelling in darkness, that is no reason why others, whom the light has not yet reached, should be deprived of it any longer. It is not unlikely that the influence of the life and teachings of Christ may be felt more readily elsewhere, with better materials to work upon. Asia is certainly a more congenial soil, with the seed of truth lying buried for ages, watered now and again by the spring of life, but withering, alas, in the process of growth.

Why may not the spring, that has wandered far and wide away from the source, be diverted homewards? In its journeyings back, after this generous pilgrimage, the spring may rid itself of the impurities it has had to gather from many a clime; and thus the harvest accruing from the original seed may be at least partially free of the husks and tares with which it has been overlaid. If Christianity is to have a chance in the land of its birth, it will have to be Christ's own Christianity. Faith is not a matter of words and arguments. Sophistry never conduced to the spiritual development of a people. What the people want is a direct appeal to the heart and the understanding. The golden rule of conduct—do unto others what thou wouldst have others do unto thee—if exemplified by Christian men and women in their actual lives, will do more good than any number of bibles distributed gratis, or any amount of empty brawling. As an evangel of love, freed from the jarring elements of sect and creed, Christianity has a field of its own. And for political reasons alone, if for reasons of no greater pith and marrow, this evangel should be carried home to a race prepared to receive it by heredity, by temper, by a long process of evolution.

Message of Love unconditional, emanating, not from this Church or that, this sect or the other, but from the bosom of our common Father, wing thy way abroad over all His Kingdom, for the benefit of His children at large!

* *

Though averse to crowds, I could not help going

into a church here and there. Service begins with one of the clergy *gliding* over the Exhortation, not reading it. Then come prayer and confession, in what strikes the unfamiliar ear as a sing-song, with sing-song responses. There seems to be a good deal of drawl in the reading, and a good deal of what may be called vocal gymnastics in uttering the A-men. But the texts, the hymn, the anthem, are all appropriate. They do not interest a stranger equally, because he cannot enter equally into their spirit. The sermon he can follow better. Here, too, there si no lack of mannerism. The preacher reads his sermon aloud, and yet he flourishes his hands and seems unconsciously to strive after effect. The interest somewhat flags till the preacher waxes eloquent. He is as practical as he is earnest. None but an Englishman could combine so much of commonsense with spiritual unction.

The music is very good, especially when the boy singers are present. I find it exhilarating, and think there may be others, like myself, in the church, who have come more for the music than for the service proper. This is wrong, but it is not always unnatural. Nor is it unnatural to see young women, here and there, looking too much at singers or preacher; though one cannot say it is not wrong. Poor hungry eyes! However, the audience are, on the whole, exceedingly well-behaved. What if the elderly neighbour on my left smells of cognac? Poor dried-up heart, let it moisten and well up when it can What if I recognize one or two faces behind me, that I saw yesterday gazing aimlessly at the shop windows? It is for them that the service is mainly intended. What if one of these poor girls naps during intervals, and puts the smelling salts to her nose? If there be sin in all this, let us reflect that such sin has its uses. For one thing, it calls forth our powers of resistance. Sinners as we all are, let us refrain from despising and trampling these poor souls. The worst of them have some good left in them. And at their worst they serve us as a warning. Who knows how much the best saints of history owe, in this respect, to perhaps the worst sinners of their time?

If I am not quite satisfied with the church, I know the church is not satisfied with me. May she be as charitable to me as I am to her! After all, for the few the best church is, not this or that church, not even the church under the canopy of heaven, so much as the church established in the sanctuary of the individual heart. For the many, the church has always been, and will always be, a palladium, a preserver from mischief. Yet in London—it is over the metropolis that my observations mainly extend—I see that her hold on the working classes is far from complete. Perhaps they think they have little to do with religion amid their social and material degradation. Perhaps they think religion has done nothing to lift them out of this degradation of ages. They judge hastily.

Better even than the music of the grand organ and the virgin voices of the choir, 'swelled by the mixed congregation, is the inarticulate eloquence of the bells. Oh these most musical of singers, the chimes!

They seem to call away the soul—"Come away, soul, come." Is it this that the chimes are singing?

My favourite resort for prayer and meditation is outside St. Paul's or the Abbey, with the bells chiming. It is seldom that I enter a church or temple, although attaching as much importance to prayer as to work, holding that the two should be used in sweet alternation,—prayer inspiring work, work confirming and responding to prayer. I find the interior more congenial at odd hours, but cannot bear the crowds and the formalities of a regular service.

*
* *

How sweet it is to live! To love is sweeter. Still more sweet is it to believe, so as the better to live and love. Oh, that I might believe always, always to live believing! What is it to live, without loving and believing? A veritable death. Let us live believing, if only for the sake of the dear ones who leave us behind, or whom we are likely to leave behind us. Such parting would be unbearable but for the hope of reunion. What this world calls death is but a change, one of the many links in the chain of evolution. There is life beyond that death, as sure as there is light behind darkness. But darkness and death are the portion of unbelievers. Many there are, who pride themselves on their unbelief. We believe nothing, they say, we believe in nothing. This is impossible for men. It is impossible, I hold, to live without believing, no matter what, in what. To believe is the sweetest experience of life below. To know may be sweeter, but it is also bitterer by far, at the same time. Knowledge is a sweet-bitter at its best; faith is sweet always. Doubt may do good as a tonic in small doses. Knowledge may serve as a stimulant, when it does not satiate and pall upon the taste, as it too often does. Faith is the only elixir of life, that satisfies without disappointing.

It is permissible to believe and yet to inquire; to try to catch a glimpse of the why, the how, the whence, and the whither of our being, although we believe it to be all ordered for the best. Each of us has certain heart-longings which he will strive again and again to satisfy, however hopeless the effort as shown by previous experience. I believe in the existence of a Creator, and in the beneficence of His design. I believe His law to be just, immutable, and universal. And yet I believe in the possibility of miracles, that is, of occurrences beyond my present limited vision, but neither impossible nor unconformable to the design and the law of His creation. I believe it is as well that man does not know all that is within and around him. But I cannot keep off certain vague yearnings to dip into the hidden. This curiosity seems to be a part of my nature. I sometimes feel as if it were more a necessity than a curiosity. It certainly is not the prompting of doubt, but rather of confidence in the justice of God's law and the faithfulness of his engagements with man. Is there anything wrong in this attitude of reverent inquiry? I have passed through many phases of thought, from intense religiousness verging on superstition, to occasional scepticism when clouds gathered and bore down upon my spiritual horizon. I have sought consolation in the childlike faith of

Aryans and Semitics alike, who claim a half-loving, half-fearing kinship "with Our Father in Heaven"; till roused by the thunder and lightning of Zoroaster's voice waging eternal war on corruption and self-righteousness. I have been subdued by the charity of Buddha, leading to nothingness as the goal of the something that is in me; till again roused by the larger charity of Christ, lifting me out of myself and bringing the regenerate life face to face with the Father once more. I have been fascinated by the vitality of Islam and the faith of its intrepid founder. I have dipped into shallower waters, too, running from one or more of these everlasting sources. Some of them have convinced me without satisfying; others have satisfied me without convincing. After all that has been absorbed or assimilated, there is still left a longing to be satisfied, a void to be filled. Often does my spirit venture into the region of the unknown, perhaps the unknowable, only to return from her search, bruised and bleeding.

Does the Western mind think much of the mystery of our being?—of birth and death? What was man created for? For the glory of his Creator, as some say; or for his amusement, as others would have it? Why such grievous inequalities in life?—the few getting more, the many less, than they need? Why are the few to be happy, the many to be unhappy? Is this divine justice? Or, am I suffering in the present for some past transgression of the law? Or, are happiness and misery the same to the subject of both? Is it all an illusion, *Máyá?* Is the sufferer more content with his lot than those who witness his suffering can make out? Are all conditions equal in the aggregate? That would be some explanation of this dread mystery.

Man is sin-bound; conceived in sin and surrounded by it all his days. Of his own unaided effort he cannot become one with the All-holy. The doctrine of atonement, therefore, comes in as a necessity of the case. It comes in, not only as a token of mercy, but also as an indication of man's kinship with his Maker. But does not this gift of vicarious atonement disturb the harmony of the original design and tend to a disregard of the consequence of sin, even though the grace may be intended only for those who do their utmost to work out their own destiny? In the masses it must slacken the sense of individual responsibility.

How is the doctrine of heredity to be justified? Why should children suffer for the sins of their parents? Firstly, because your children are but yourself reproduced; and secondly, you have to think of others besides yourself in choosing your course for good or for evil. The sinner has to suffer for three generations and four. Does this mean that there is a limit to the punishment of trespass, both in the moral and in the physical world? Or, does the limit refer to the period of expiation? Every trespass is followed almost immediately by its own punishment. This fact, taken together with the fact of the limitation above suggested, discredits the doctrine of eternal punishment.

Christianity hopes for the worst sinners. It is well that even these have a chance, after the necessary expiation. Is there any test of their sincerity, any limit to their power of transgression, any limit to the duration of repentance? Any distinction between degrees of sin as regards frequency? What is to distinguish the sinner who has sinned seven times from him who has sinned seven times seventy? Is there any distinction between sin of thought, of word, and of deed?

The body dies, but the soul lives on. Does not this theory of the immortality of the soul strengthen the theory of re-births? It seems to place the law of compensation into broad relief, and may account for the inequalities of human destiny. Whether animals have souls, and whether these souls are capable of rising, after release, to the level of human souls, or whether human souls have to rise and sink in spiritual importance, are questions of detail too vague even for speculation.

Does man ever get an inkling of the future state that awaits him? As he grows in spiritual experience, it does not seem to be quite impossible he may obtain some glimpses of the unknown into which he is about to enter. But it seems to be certain, on the other hand, that the veil is never lifted for the benefit of those left behind. Whenever it is lifted, it is lifted for his knowledge who is hereafter to be one of the enlightened. So far, it may be said that the Psalmist was wrong, when, in a panic of doubt and despair, he cried out:—"In death there is no remembrance of Thee; after death who shall thank Thee?"

Death is but a change, a release from physical environments. Though it is the most important change that overtakes man in this life, it is not in its nature quite unlike the changes that occur every seven or ten years. The soul, which is released at this change of changes, is not translated and settled again all at once. Has it to pass through further changes? Does this process of approximation continue through life after life, world after world, till at last the soul is fit to be at one with her original type?

But what avails this knocking at the door of doctrine in search of spiritual comfort? Can stone answer for the bread of life? The best life for the Christian is to be Christ-like. The highest life for all of us is the life of self-surrender. Let us pour out for others our gifts of mind and heart, so that on the day appointed we may be able to stand in the Presence of Grace, not as strangers or slaves, but in the assurance of conscious kinship with our Maker, and whisper to Him with filial confidence. "Father, Yes."

* * *

The sight of huge carcasses hanging at butchers' shops in London suggests curious thoughts to one unaccustomed to such a sight. If it is a sin to destroy life, why do we kill animals? Or, if it is no sin to take life, when such life-taking is useful for man, why do we object to the cannibals killing and eating one another?—thus illustrating the law of the survival of the fittest. Science has not yet come to that, but insists upon distinguishing "higher" from "lower" life. To some this may seem to be a distinction without a difference. Or, if a difference, only a difference in degree, not in kind. The brute nature still lingers in man, though sufficiently "advanced" to make the worse appear the better reason. Be that as it may, few of us meat-eaters can bear to see harmless animals put to the knife. And yet, it is for us that millions of them are slaughtered day after day. We do not mind the smaller ones cut up for our food. At any rate, we use them with less compunction. We try to explain away this further distinction by saying that the smaller animals are not likely to be missed so much as the larger. The larger may be more useful alive; but may it not be because they are so much the nearer to us that we are more careful of their lives? Be this how it may, the principle remains unshaken, namely, that all life is precious, and that small or large, low or high, we have no right to destroy or to harm it, except in self-defence.

Look at the eyes of the victim just before it is slaughtered, especially when it has seen its companions fall under the butcher's knife. How the eyes glisten, how the limbs quiver! Is it conscious of its approaching doom? Why not? It has feeling, as much as we have. It is endowed with hunger, thirst, passion, function, as we are, and can express these in its own way, as we do. Animals communicate with one another, as we do, perhaps compare notes; they muse and, perhaps, sing together in a fashion; declare war and make peace, like us. They are stronger in instinct than we are, if weaker in reason. For instance, they can espy danger better and from a longer distance than we can. But animals have nothing of our higher intelligence, you say; they are incapable of articulate sound; they are not conscious of guilt and shame. True, their intelligence is less developed than ours. But they are not altogether destitute of it. As to guilt and shame, may it not be that they seem generally to be unconscious of these, because they trespass so little against the laws of their nature? We know that animals are capable, to a certain extent, of expressing grief and remorse, though not perhaps repentance, just as they are capable of expressing joy and satisfaction. But even if they be unconscious of guilt or shame, it does not follow that they are without some rough dim idea of the fate that is about to overtake them, or insensible to the blow that has descended.

Will the day ever come when the slaughter of animals is to be given up as needless? Will the butcher ever cease to ply his trade, lower than that of the hangman who has to kill the guilty or those adjudged guilty in vindication of the so-called divine law of life for life? Those of the nations, who believe in the efficacy of animal sacrifice, will hardly ever be weaned from a practice as old as their oldest traditions. But will they never have the candour to admit, even to themselves, the possibility of animals having intelligence, however undeveloped? It would certainly be thrusting a terrible responsibility on these "poor relations" of ours, to invest them with souls. But what a consolation it would be to feel that the scheme of Creation is perfect even to this detail, making all the creatures of God ultimately equal in one another's sight, as they doubtless are in His sight! And what a blessing the mere thought of this might be to our race, keeping it away from the indulgence of some of the worst passions with which it is beset! At present, those of us who advocate laws for the prevention of cruelty to animals are perhaps amongst the first to kill and eat them wholesale. Well may the Buddhist say—this is straining at gnats and swallowing camels. But the doctrine of total forbearance, however pleasing in itself, is apt to be carried too far. It may be urged from the other side that if we are to deny ourselves all such food as involves life-taking, we must refrain even from eggs and milk, because both of these have the germs life in them. Likewise, it may be urged that neither the fruit or vegetable we eat, nor the water we drink, is wholly destitute of life. The answer to this will be that we are here dealing with *animal* life, that which is nearest to our own; and that even as regards animals, they are created for the use of man. That what is objected to is the abuse, not the use, of the creatures made for our own benefit. That it is the wanton cruelty, which so often accompanies the slaughter of animals, that is most to be deplored. Whether this answer satisfies the Buddhist or not, it is worth mentioning that in the East the butcher seldom uses his knife before asking forgiveness.

As to meat as an article of diet, one may be excused for asking if it does not stand to reason that habitual indulgence in flesh and blood may lead to

I

fleshly inclinations and thoughts? At any rate, it
may be safely assumed that man never feels so innocent as when living on an innocent diet. Whatever
the relative value of meat and what is popularly
called "vegetable" food, under different climates, and
on different constitutions, this much will have to
be admitted, that animal food is far from being
always innocuous, whilst its powers of sustaining
and strengthening are apt to be exaggerated.

To come back for a moment to our starting point;
what can excuse the sights and smells of a butcher's shop in London, gloated over by the people?
Is it nature or habit, this partiality for flesh and
blood? Who can say if, in some cases, the love
of blood does not lead to love of bloodshed?

Apart from this slaughter of animals, and the exposure of their dead bodies to the public gaze, there
are other forms of cruelty with which the East
is as familiar as the West; those, for instance, that
are witnessed in the street and in the field. These
latter may be due, in some measure, to every-day
familiarity with the former sights. There is little
excuse for hunting and shooting indiscriminately.
Even the sportsman, with all his privileges, might
distinguish between the noxious and the innocent.
It is, indeed, no paradox to speak of a sportsman
as tender-hearted. I have known many such men
who use their guns and spears freely whenever they
get the chance, but who would shrink from chasing
a mouse or trampling on a snail; men who are good
and tender in every relation of life. I know a friend
who sighs "poor fellow" as soon as he has brought

down a bird. He is quite sincere in his sympathy for the victim. Only he cannot see that the innocent little bird has as much right to live as himself. Tender as he is, how much more so he might have been but for the early training that has hardened his heart so far as to lead him to mistake destruction of harmless creatures for sport; to mistake cruelty for manliness?

It takes a very doubtful sort of courage to shoot an animal run to earth by hirelings, the beaters and the hounds; while, on the other hand, such cheap-and-easy sport engenders habits of cruelty. To our high-born Rajput or Moslem sportsman the game is *harám* (unlawful) to such an extent that he won't touch the meat prepared from a victim thus laid low. Probably there are sportsmen in England, who keep before them something of this ideal. But, judging from what one hears and reads, their number cannot be very large, even if their standard is half as high as that of our ideal Rajput. I once met a Bhil chieftain in a remote corner of Rewa Kantha, who used no safer weapons than a sword-stick in his encounters with wild beasts, although he had arms of precision in his camp. The chief used these only in *Nishanbazi* (practising at a mark), in bringing down a bird safely ensconced amid the foliage of a tree, or in shooting through a particular leaf or branch of the tree without disturbing any other part thereof. His son, a stripling of about twelve, seemed to be equally averse to foul play, and was known to sally forth on a holiday, sword in hand, seldom returning without the head of a foe worthy of his steel.

The Rajput sportsman is no less fastidious than this typical Bhil, that is the Rajput of the old school. In the summer of 1879 I breakfasted with one such in the north of Kathiawar. The meal consisted of large *Bajra* (barley) bread, fresh venison cooked with chillies, curds, cream, dry fish, and, for tea, a bottle of brandy! Discussing the merits of the venison, mine host regretted the decline of genuine sport in the province, owing to the bad example set by some of the English officials. He gave me an anecdote of how a British official had once asked the Raja of ——— for a real cheeta hunt, how he was put into a howda with the chief, how the sport was started in right earnest, how the cheeta and the elephant came to close quarters, how the Raja fired his gun and shouted for joy, how the youthful Briton sat paralyzed at sight of the angry animal showing his teeth and claws; and how, when the sport was over, the Sahib had to be helped out of the howda, smiling a sickly smile. I afterwards explained to my host that the young fellow was unused to a cheeta hunt. For, however conceited and frivolous an English youth may be, he is seldom a coward in the face of danger.

Women are in some respects, perhaps, the worse offenders. They are ready enough to cry out against cruelty to animals, and yet indulge in fashions involving barbarous cruelty, the plucking of birds and skinning of animals, after they have been destroyed for the purpose.

Animals may be soulless. Are they, therefore, to be denied the protection due to flesh and blood and bone? Look at that patient horse and his impatient driver. It occurs to me that on the day of reckoning the driver may have to stand abashed in the Presence of Grace, for wantonness and over-exaction of service from a fellow-creature, whilst the horse will show a clean card for duty done before the yoke is laid down for good.

Conscience and soul, how much of these do we discern in infants? Do we not meet with human beings in whom the highest attributes of our nature are reflected but by a negative quality?

There may be gradation in what we call conscience and soul, as there is in other things. They may be subject to development and deterioration, like the body and the mind. If so, it is hard to understand why animals may not be subject to the same process, in some manner unknown to us.

* *
*

During my stay in London I am induced, for the first time, to witness a Wild Beasts Show at the Crystal Palace. The beasts—lions, tigers, panthers, bears, and dogs—are led into the arena and made to go through a series of monotonous performances. The whole thing is painfully mechanical. To me it is a most depressing sight—no spirit left in the animals, no real pluck on the part of the showman, whatever the courage of those that caught and tamed the beasts. Think of lions and tigers, half-starved, emasculated, brow-beaten, in fact, idiotized; and you can understand how the poor creatures suffer themselves to be jumped about and worried by the dogs. These dogs alone, of all the animals, show life.

They are splendid fellows, and kept in a splendid condition, never having gone through the discipline imposed upon the others. I wonder what men and women can see in these shows, as dull as they are demoralizing. The itinerant *Madári* (showman) in India shows you more courage and intelligence for less fee, though he does not indulge in flashy advertisements. People in Europe often pay more for advertisements than for the things advertised.

* * *

Much worse than wanton sport and slaughter, and still more demoralizing, is the cruelty inflicted on animals in the name of science and humanity. Advocates of vivisection seem to make too much of their theory of a "painless death." Whatever the theory of it, in practice the death is often a protracted agony and torture, the tearing of limb from limb, nerve from nerve; the burning, cutting, sawing, boring holes into the organs of living animals, after partially stupefying or intoxicating the victims.

Vivisection (that is, cutting animals alive) may or may not have its uses. That is a question for European scientists. In the East we never seem to have had much faith in surgery, which we look upon in the light of science intoxicated. Guided by this natural aversion, our scientists would condemn vivisection really as science run mad. If experiments were found desirable in the old days, they were tried mainly with drugs, and even then their results were viewed with suspicion in the case of human subjects. It must, however, be confessed that the practice was not quite unknown in ancient India.

Here, in Europe, I doubt if a clear case has yet been made out for vivisection, as it is described by some of its eager practitioners. I speak only as a layman, without questioning the honesty of these advocates of scientific torture. The results, that one often sees published, appear to be miserably inadequate, taken at their best. And making every allowance for partisan zeal, at what frightful cost these results are generally obtained! A shock to the conscience, a blunting of our best instincts. Instead of cherishing and protecting the lives placed under our care, we destroy them by lingering torture. We do these poor victims to death inch by inch in order to keep up a superstition of doubtful utility. We do harm to others in the fond hope of doing good to ourselves thereby. Verily, if Religion has her fetish, Science is not without hers. And of the two, the latter is decidedly more debasing for its worshippers. Have we a right to take life?—to torture and kill the innocent? Lower or higher, it is life all the same. The vital principle, the richest of Divine gifts, is there. Who gave us this right? It is sometimes urged that the victim has no intelligence, and therefore does not suffer. This is a very poor excuse. And even then, what has *intelligence* to do with the question?—granting that animals are without it. It is a question of *sensibility*. Do not animals feel the torture inflicted on them? To deny this to the victims is more outrageous than to assert that their immolation on the altar of science conduces to the happiness of selfish man. Supposing they are insensible to pain whilst stupefied by chloroform or ether, they cannot but suffer on coming to, from the effects of the ghastly experiments performed on them.

To those who seek to justify vivisection by an appeal to the law of sacrifice, I am tempted to repeat the objections often stated before, almost in the same words—*Whose* sacrifice do you mean ? The sacrifice of *others !* That seems to be a travesty of the teaching of the Divine Master who, above all others, has ennobled and sanctified the word *sacrifice*. It may be noted here that vicarious suffering is another thing. But whatever the merits of vicarious suffering amongst men—you suffering for me, and I for you—it would be stretching the idea too far to *inflict pain* (quite different from *suffering*) upon unwilling parties. Such giving of pain to human beings, capable more or less of protecting themselves, is reckoned a sin as well as a crime. How much more so when it is inflicted on sentient creatures at the mercy of man—as innocent as they are helpless! Remember, these poor creatures do not suffer willingly, as you and I may in a good cause, but are *made to suffer.* Nor are they at all conscious of the merit, real or supposed, of their martyrdom. What have we, as responsible moral agents, to do with this "law of sacrifice," in which the victims are denied the exercise of their free will, and even the consolation of knowing that they suffer for "the larger good" ? I give the vivisectionists more credit than to believe they have never been struck with this view of the matter. Perhaps they are thinking of the law of *self-sacrifice.* And here we are all agreed, of whatever race, creed, or profession. Let us, each according to his opportunities, try to obey this law of self-sacrifice, which is the way to "the perfect life." But if we understand the law, we must instantly recognize the justice of putting up with our own physical ailments, often invited by ourselves, rather than violate our moral nature by a sacrifice of others who have as much right as ourselves to live and be happy. That the victims are at our mercy, entitles them the more to our protection.

India could well be consistent in her opposition to the practice. She would kill or torture none save the noxious. This would need some courage, and might serve a useful purpose. Very much the reverse seems to be the case with vivisection, as practised especially on the continent of Europe. Why, even their cock-fights, and dog-fights, and bull-fights show something of courage, as compared with the torturing of domestic animals lying at their mercy, muzzled, tied down, fixed to an iron bar.

May it not be this passion for 'science-worship that has partly to answer for the disregard of life which the European operator sometimes shows for his patient? The patient's life and comfort must wait till the claims of science have been fully consulted. What if a poor man or woman dies, so science gains thereby in the surgeon's eyes? From lower life to higher is but a step. One need not be a fanatic to be an honest opponent of vivisection, believing all innocent life to be worthy of protection by man, even though it be incapable of sharing the dignity and importance of his own life.

The practice of vivisection, to the extent sanctioned by law in England, may not in itself be open to serious objection. But the practitioners have hitherto shown no results to speak of, and are not likely to show better results in future, that might not be secured by fairer means. Considering this poverty of results, and the temptation to misuse the powers, which few vivisectionists can resist, the wisest course seems to me, as a layman, to have nothing to do with legalized torture of animals.

The horrors of the vivisection room are probably a good deal exaggerated by those who shrink from crossing its threshold. These have partly to draw upon their imagination. I am not at all surprised at vivisectionists complaining of a lady opponent who is alleged to have allowed her enthusiasm to run into such an excess as to print off diagrams of all the most formidable-looking surgical instruments she could get at, in order, as she thought, to bring to light the horrors of the secret chamber. But vivisection, at its best, is of doubtful and extremely limited value, whilst its tendency to blunt our finer instincts cannot be denied. The cry against it, therefore, even when proceeding from morbid emotion, is not unwholesome as a protest against the callous intellectualism of our age.

**
*

Fierce is the struggle for existence in the West. Life and health are being ground down under the wheels of modern civilization. Not a little of this cruel sacrifice seems to be due to the arrogance of Capital in its dealings with Labour, especially with

unskilled Labour.   Hitherto Capital has had it pretty
much its own way, in almost every sphere of activity. The day seems to be coming for Labour. Few
sights in London interest an outsider so much as
what are called working men's demonstrations and
strikes. Men, tired of ill-treatment, make a common
cause, and strike work. Happily, not a few of these
Unions are guided by principle and intelligence. The
men give due notice before they go out on strike,
and so far the inconvenience to the general public is
minimized, and business saved from complete disloca-
tion. Others, pressed by hunger, are ready to take
the place of those going on strike. Sometimes the
employers prefer to suspend business in the course of
negotiation with the strikers, or after the negotiations
have failed. If they could, they would perhaps like
to starve the men into acquiescence. Against this
danger the men seem to be prepared, though very
inadequately, thanks to the friends who advocate
their cause, and to the public who contribute to their
maintenance whilst out. Otherwise, the struggle
would be hopelessly unequal, certainly, more ruinous
to the aggrieved than to the other party. As it is,
I am not sure if some of these Labour demonstrations are not overdone. A new movement is apt
to run into excesses; and once it has seized the
popular fancy, it works like an infection. Miners,
gas-workers, dockers, railway, tram, and 'bus em-
ployés; tailors, carpenters, laundresses have, one after
another, struck work; some of them obtaining their
own terms when reasonable, others effecting a compromise; none, I believe, quite satisfied. In the

wake of this suspension of private works we have seen public servants follow, such as postmen, policemen, and even, in a modified sense, some of the military. Evidently, then, the Labour Union has become an institution; and if it keeps within bounds, it will have the sympathy of many thoughtful and disinterested men. The time is nearing for England, when Labour, in the field or the market, shall have to be distinguished from serfdom, and Capital from grasping monopoly. The question is one of great interest. God grant it may be solved in peace, to the honour of English Capital and the advantage of Labour!

I have witnessed some of the demonstrations in Hyde Park, for instance, where the workmen and their sympathizers, with the idle and the curious, pour in by thousands, to the tune of music, the flourishing of banners and so on, generally on Sundays. The processions are joined by hundreds of women, many of whom really help in organizing them, as also in preserving order. They are, as a rule, very quiet and orderly. The strength of some of these organizations may be realized when it is seen that at one time I had to wait in a hansom for over an hour and a half before it could be allowed to get out at a corner of Curzon Street. The general effect of the multitudes walking past, in holiday attire, more fantastic than picturesque, singing, cheering, shouting, but seldom breaking the public peace, is striking enough. But the thing strikes one more as a show, a fair, than a protest. Of course, there is some haranguing in the park; mostly, by crude young socialists who have a pronounced habit of getting red in the face and of dropping their h's. The crowds do not seem to pay much attention to these orators, whom they patronize for a few minutes by turn, just to save appearances. I have not heard a single leader in the park. In the absence of any serious discussion, the thing strikes one most as a huge turn-out where "Mary Hann" takes the field chiefly because her "'Arry" is out.

But how instructive the organization is for us in India! We are not likely to have much of it there, in the near future. For one thing, we lack the solidarity of interests. Our only organization worth naming is the National Congress. It is of the utmost importance that the Congress should go on working with a select body of educated men. When the movement extends lower down, or when other movements spring up on anything like the English scale, as between Labour and Capital, India will cease to be India. This latter event may be expected to arise only under the British Rule. India is poor, ignorant, and superstitious. But what can she not do with her numbers, if the numbers once acquire cohesion? It is difficult, however, to say whence the cohesion is to come—from politics or from religion. Politics cannot mould the social and domestic life of a people, as religion does. But religion in India is dead or decaying in the ranks where it is most potent for a wide-felt constructive influence.

To return to the strikes in England. Although one feels that sometimes the grievances of Labour

are unreasonable, they are on the whole worthy of
careful attention in the interests, not only of Labour
but of Capital likewise. Capital has no right to kill
Labour. What, for instance, can be so killing as
to insist upon drivers and conductors working sixteen
hours a day on the omnibus and the tramway lines?
These poor men are hardly asleep before they have
to awake. We have to think of them and of their
families also; that is, of the interests of society. So
far it is wrong of Government to stand aloof from
this struggle between Capital and Labour, on the
plea of freedom of contract. There can be no such
thing as real freedom of contract between parties
so grievously ill-matched. What free will is possible to a starving employé, as pitted against his
prosperous employer? The latter can wait in comfort, whilst the former has starvation staring him
daily in the face. It is absurd to postulate a free
contract between urgent want, on one hand, and easy
sufficiency, on the other. Freedom of contract is not
the same thing as freedom of trade. I doubt if
Capital will be able very long to resist the legitimate
claims of Labour. The spirit of the age is crying out
against such resistance. Not that the employers as
a body are cruel men. But vested interests are very
hard to move, and a false sense of *esprit de corps*
makes them oblivious to duties which individually
they feel sitting heavy on the conscience. On the
other side, representatives of Labour cannot be too
often reminded that the path of moderation is the
only safe path for them. They must, in certain cases,
be content with a shilling less for less work given.

Reform in such matters is very slow; it comes by lingering instalments. Of course, the State cannot interfere with the details of a contract, having satisfied itself that the contract has been a really free and equitable one.

* * *

An Englishman's friendship appears to be as fickle as his weather. It is warm and gushing for the moment, but lacks constancy. When in a fit of friendship, especially over his cup or at dinner, the Englishman may do anything for you. You have to take him at the high tide of breakfast, lunch, or dinner, when he is in love with himself, and cooing over the good cheer around. Though shy and reserved himself, he hates those who won't come to the point at once whilst asking for a friendly turn. The Englishman in London seems to have no time to dive after a drowning friend. In fact, he is angry at any friend of his happening to sink. Once you are down in the muddy waters of life, there is no rising for you, my friend : no hydraulic engine near can lift you out.

This is, of course, a picture of friendship in general. You may expect better from particular friends. But genuine friendship, such as we warm-blooded Asiatics cherish, laying down our lives and fortunes for one another, is seldom to be met with among a people so differently situated in climate, habits of life, and associations. Life is too hurried to enable them to cultivate true friendship. Every man has to live more or less to himself, absorbed for the moment in the pleasure or business he is pursuing. He lives in a state of perpetual tension—one pursuit chasing away another; this interest making room for that, day after day, hour after hour.

Even in serious matters it is almost hopeless to have a leisurely discussion with friends, especially during the season. At best you can do it by snatches, half-explained, half-understood. But this lack of thoroughness seems to be made up at public meetings, where they have it out to their hearts' content. They do it even more thoroughly in the House of Commons. If Parliament does not do all the thinking for the nation, it certainly does the talking.

Much of what has been said refers, of course, to town life, and to that brief fraction of the year, called the 'season'. It must be added, in justice to the London friend, that his life during this period is generally overcrowded. And for the rest of the year he is flitting about, in search of rest and change, often pleasure with business combined. What he wants is an escape from the worries of home life— be he father, son or brother. He must make the best of his holidays, so as to bring back, when he returns for the season, a store of energy and resource adequate for the purposes of public life. This he will do his utmost to economise. What wonder, my friend has no time for the sentimental extravagance of friendship? What wonder, I find him looking younger and fresher after an interval of three years, whilst I am myself conscious of having grown decidedly older during the period? It does not surprise me at all to meet with Englishmen of eighty, who are more vigorous and more

elastic, every way, than I am at forty. Apart from
Mr. Gladstone's phenomenal activity of mind and
body, I might instance the late Sir Harry Verney
talking to me familiarly of the times of Lord William
Bentinck with whom he was to have come out to
India as Private Secretary some sixty years ago. Sir
Harry was past eighty when he spoke to me of his
daily walks and rides and engagements. Another
instance is that of my good old friend, Mr. Samuel
Laing, whose interest in Indian questions is as keen
to-day as it was in the sixties, and who has done
some of his valuable work in the fields of religion
and philosophy after seventy. It were vain to look
for such cases in India where most of our strong-
est personalities disappear from the scenes of public
life before fifty. They age rapidly after forty, and
either die or become useless for purposes of active
citizenship. To be sure, we have men living on to
sixty and seventy; but few of these have done anything in their day to make history, and at an advanced age they claim to be no better than pensioners,
chewing the cud of their past uneventful careers.
Almost all the master-minds of modern India will
be found to have given way, before fifty, to the stress
of an unnatural social and political existence—caste,
infant marriage, joint family, poverty of resource,
lack of congenial occupation.

One or two instances may be mentioned here, to
make the meaning plain, of what I call distracted
friendship. Soon after arriving in London I invite
a prominent nobleman to join our Committee for
the improvement of the position of women in India.

K

He replies by asking me to go to dinner. I explain that I cannot dine after 6 P.M., that I have lost the art of dining out. After a fortnight he asks me to go to him for breakfast or lunch. Determined to hook a leading Liberal somehow, I accept a quiet day for lunch. On reaching the house I meet a strange gentleman who is to join us. We are hardly seated at table when I find a bright little lady walking merrily in and dropping into the chair opposite. The dishes are extremely tempting, but I sit freezing in my chair as mine host grows warm in his attentions. The lady of the house is more considerate, and keeps me engaged in small talk about India. The strangers now ply me with kindly offers. But my cup of misery is full; no wine for me, please, any more than meat. All that I have strength enough to accept is a glass of ice cream from the hostess—the best I have had in England. The lunch is soon over, and the host marches me off for a chat by ourselves. If feel rewarded for the martyrdom of an hour, as we sit in his study, arguing out some of the points of my programme. He sits there talking, smoking, and glancing at the letters just brought in. This, to an Oriental, is very bad form. But I know my English friend would deal with his own brother the same as he is dealing with me. He must make the best of his time in London. I resign myself to the inevitable. In this frame of mind I am trying to drive him into a corner on a crucial point, and hoping to secure his adhesion on the spot, when he jumps up suddenly with the words :—"Now I must fly. Come to the Hall.

Tuesday, very quiet. Will show you over." I am fairly stunned by the rapidity of this side move. He is quite sincere, I know. Only some other subject has occurred to him, which he thinks to be more urgent than mine. So I must lose just as I am within an inch of my prize. He gathers up his letters, and says good-bye in an off-hand manner. As I limp out of the house I make up my mind that this tough customer shall yet repay my trouble by joining the Committee. I keep pelting him with reminders every third week, till he surrenders at discretion. This success, however, is due more to my perseverance than to the constancy of his friendly regard.

Very much the same thing happens during my second visit to London. Here, our friend is a venerable prelate. Last year he fought our battle gallantly. But he seems already to have forgotten the movement as well as the man. He hurries up to me warmly, as I am ushered in ; and after listening for a couple of minutes, closes the interview with—"Let me hear from time to time." He shakes me again by the hand, adding, "God bless you!", and is off before I can recover from my surprise. O Cardinal, if you must needs cut a stranger, why cut him so kindly? That is the unkindest cut of them all, I have had in London.

Judging from what has been said above, one might conclude, as many a disappointed Indian has concluded, that the Englishman has "no shame of the eye." I cannot agree with this general conclusion. As just observed, life is so hurried in England, especially in town, that it cannot long retain the impressions of friendship. Friends come and go, apparently leaving no trace of their friendly contact behind. With so many daily interests crowding out one another, it is scarcely in human nature to expect more than friendship of the hour from the average Englishman. A friend once said. to me, he would gladly miss his dinner for the chance of seeing me. This is his uttermost limit of friendly regard. Be it said to his credit, however, that if the ordinary Englishman gives you no friendship of the right sort, he expects none from you. The friendship of the other sex appears to be more constant, and for obvious reasons.

* *
*

Militarism seems to be an absorbing passion with the English. You will always find a crowd round about the Horse Guards, gaping at the handsomely dressed guards mounted on their gallant steeds. It is not an idle London crowd; scores of honest country lads and lasses, who come to London on business, will stand there by the hour, with admiration streaming out of their wide-open mouths. Equally large crowds are attracted by military or police drills every morning. The average cockney is all eyes and all ears as soon as he finds a military band approaching. Multitudes of men and women follow the band to some distance, often to its quarters, dropping in and out as it suits their convenience, marching in a compact body, as if they formed part of the company. Belonging to the school of John Bright and other lovers of peace, I cannot affect a special leaning towards militarism. And yet, how my heart thumps and my whole body sways backward and forward at the sound of this military music! I can well understand the effect it has on London crowds—whether it be a band of the regulars or the volunteers, the trades unionists, the schoolboys, the police, the beggar brigade, or our friends the Salvationists.

Talk of the masses in India being gregarious. If anything, the English are more so. Let there be a house building, a hole digging, a horse tumbling, a shop window showing something new, something curious; and you will find men and women rushing breathless to the spot, at times jumping out of the 'bus. You often see old women running to the Punch and Judy show, perhaps for the thousandth time, drawn more by the crowd than by the exhibition of domestic amenities with which they are by no means unfamiliar.

A military career seems to be the ambition of many a well-born youth who can afford it. Even Anglo-Indian parents, who have the means, find their sons more inclined to that line than to others. Do the boys like it best? Is it the savage instinct for killing that stirs them, or is it their destiny? Who can say if England is not preparing for a very big war? The War Office may deny this; but it is no secret for the unhappy taxpayer that England, and all Europe, for that matter, is being crushed under the weight of military expenditure. It may be some consolation to the Indian taxpayer to count up the cost of the armaments of Europe, in these days of "piping peace."

Seeing that England is a naval power, one would expect the navy to be as much in request with the upper classes as is the army, if not more so. Such, however, is not the case. The navy has been falling somewhat into disuse. It is not so effective for purposes of destruction. And though England herself is a naval and a maritime power, she is not likely in future to have so many battles to fight on sea as on land. She is practical, and perhaps feels that the era of naval exploits is drawing to its close. Hence it is that the navy is ceasing to attract high-born English youths. Besides, the life of a sailor is probably less enjoyable in these days of luxurious ease. Well-paid idlers cannot find so much pleasure on the distant sea as on land, however remote from home. The conditions of service, also, may not be so attractive.

* * *

Next to the military, and perhaps still more attractive for the higher ranks, is a career in Parliament. That is as it should be. No occupation could be more profitable for the rising aristocracy of England than the sort of popular legislation that is more or less before the House of Commons in these days. It gives them a healthy interest in life, widens their sympathy and brings them more in touch with the people. A career in Parliament is as much needed in this case as it is needed in the case of Indians of rank and education—there in the Legislative Councils. In the interests of our Indian aristocracy one cannot but regret the miscarriage of the Duke of Connaught's scheme for a military college in India.

It is a wise and far-sighted proposal. The Duke is not likely to abandon it for want of immediate adoption. Things move more slowly in India than in England. But once the authorities take heart of grace, even for a restricted experiment, they are likely to be carried far enough in spite of themselves. Let us hope this question, with that of volunteering in India, may engage their serious attention.

The Indian career, as it is called, appears to be equally popular, both on its civil side and the military. It is, indeed, a prize in life for cadets of noble families, and for the eldest sons generally of the higher and the higher middle classes, who run after it in preference to a colonial career. Official life in India may be dull, but in spite of the depreciated rupee it is very handsomely endowed, and holds out still more handsome prospects of power and preferment. The career has now become historical, with brilliant examples to fire the imagination of a spirited youth, and to fashion him for wider usefulness abroad. The Indian service is as imperial as it is historical.

The Church is more or less in request with gentlemen's sons in England, and a most useful and a most hard-worked agency it is.

Next to the Church comes law to which the same ranks, more or less, seem to be drawn. This profession, more than any other, leads up to the avenues of legislation and journalism.

Then comes medicine, drawing the middle and a good many of the lower middle classes.

The next step seems to comprize business, trade,

manufacture, &c., including the shop which, more even than agriculture, forms the backbone of the nation, the distinguishing trait of the national character.

Arts, science, and literature may be included, for convenience sake, into one or other of the professions mentioned above.

It is hardly possible, and certainly not fair, for a stranger to estimate the influence on society of these various professions. Roughly speaking, the army must stand first as a menace to the moral welfare of the people, Next comes law in its power for mischief. The medical profession appears to be less mischievous, though avowedly more "irreligious" than either of those two.

All this while we have been thinking of the boys. What about the girls ?, asks my Indian reader. Well, the girls of England are only now beginning to carve out careers for themselves. Hitherto they have had but one career open to them—the matrimonial —to which they have clung with a devotion worthy, some of them tell me, of a better cause.

* *
*

Did General Booth take his cue from the spirit of rampant militarism obtaining in Christendom ? His organization, apart from its social side, strikes one as being an unconscious caricature of the crusades of old. It is no less interesting in this latter capacity than in the former.

When General Booth sent out his first contingent to India I viewed the movement with but partial favour. It appeared to be such an incongruous mixture of the church and the army—a combination which the Prince of Peace would shrink from. Its knee-drill, its shoulder-arms, its march past, came as a sharp and grating contrast to the sacred character of the work it had in view. But, as usual, I kept my prejudice to myself. God works in His own ways. They may be mysterious ; they may appear inconsistent. It is not for men to judge. Commissioner Tucker and his wife, moreover, had been known to me by fame. Their work in Northern India, while Mr. Tucker was a civilian in the service of the Crown, had won my sympathy. The Salvation Army uniform, the military slang, the tom-toming were not at all to one's liking ; and the risk was never absent from one's mind, of familiarity breeding contempt amongst the people, contrary to the fond expectations of those who wished to reclaim the masses by being with and of them, both in the spirit and the outer garb. But I also felt that the movement was not without its charms for those whom it intended to reach, and that after a boisterous youth it might perhaps settle down into a sober church militant, rousing the sluggish, rescuing the fallen, reforming the depraved, that came within its reach. Latterly I took personal interest in its prison brigade branch, and during its sallies on some of our strongholds of Parsi-ism at Bombay, I sought to exercise a moderating influence on the sons of Rustom and Zal.

During my stay in London I have had fresh and, perhaps, fuller opportunities of watching the movement. It is easy to see that the instincts of the people here are more in accord with its gunpowdery character. Whether an explosion purifies souls, depends upon the quality of the souls themselves. I see half a dozen Salvationists holding forth in the neighbourhood of a public-house. I see a few loafers drifting towards the spot, one scoffing, another jeering, but all drawing nearer. In a few minutes I see a change coming over the face of one of the most seasoned of these sinners. He throws away the tobacco he was chewing, and joins the chorus. One or two more follow, others skulking away, as if reluctantly. But the ranks are being swelled, especially by women. In less than half an hour the six Salvationists have an audience of about thirty. It is glorious work, surely, in spite of its eccentricities.

I make up my mind to witness the Salvation Army celebrating its twenty-fifth anniversary at the Crystal Palace. The crowds at the principal stations are enormous. Besides the soldiers of the Cross —a whole army of officers and men representing all England—there are contingents from abroad, Europe, America, India; supplemented by spectators and sympathizers like myself. The trains have to run every two or three minutes, at certain hours: and still we do not find accommodation for half an hour on our way to the Palace, not for two hours on our way back. Then, too, we have been packed like sardines all over the train.

At a distance, (I do not enter the Palace this evening) the movement seems to be well-calculated to strike the popular imagination in England; to lift the people from their grosser animal wants. It looks like a protest against the indifferentism of the period. Is not this inevitable? It is equally inevitable that in its early stages the movement should run into excesses of emotion. The extreme of emotion counteracts the extreme of apathy. As is natural, I find women to be the most frantically earnest. They are abandoned to the service of God. Salvation lasses are singing themselves into fits, into ecstasies, into paroxysms. Will they survive the night?, I wonder—poor fragile little things, all skin and bone.

By an accident I happen to be again in London on the day of the twenty-sixth anniversary of the Salvation Army. I make a point of studying it at closer quarters. I trudge over the Palace grounds, with Dr. B——, both of us in the most friendly spirit. Wading through ankle-deep mud below, and a steady downpour from above, we follow the march past. It is all managed in a rigorous military style, a few straggling camp followers bringing up the rear—pale, haggard, half-fainting. We are told of a wild beasts show at the Palace. I cannot resist asking which were the wild beasts—the lions and tigers trained like human beings, or some of the human beings I see there, looking like hunted animals. Indeed, there is too much emotion amongst the rank and file, especially the women, and too little of good sense.

After this " service " in the open grounds we are invited to a " solemn assembly " within. We are kept waiting for half an hour, and see a little bye-play that is by no means edifying. Captain Eager asks Lieutenant Grateful (a girl) "How is your

Sis?" "Thank you kindly," replies the fair Lieutenant, "she is better; you have done something for her; I know you have." Thereupon the Captain rejoins, "Wal, Maria, if I *has*, praise be to the Lord, and to the General." He flirts with the girl's hand for some minutes, using a copious supply of Salvation Army slang, and squeezing the hand till its poor owner looks blue in the face. Of course, there is nothing wrong in this vigorous expression of sympathy. The Salvationists pride themselves on being hearty friends. But an outsider might expect some limit even to the vehemence of fraternal affection.

Now begins the work proper of the "solemn assembly," with a prayer from one of the leading officers. While the prayer is praying, a hawker is hawking the programme of the evening to the audience, a penny each copy. Here is prayer and business for you in one breath. The business goes well enough. And how goes the prayer? Not wisely, I am afraid, but too well. Colonel Harrowby prays aloud, heaving and panting, and shaking the platform to its centre. He evidently thinks the audience is possessed, and is determined to exorcise the devil out of them by the power of his lungs. And what lung power the man possesses! Though sitting some twenty yards away from him, I feel knocked on the head by the ferocity of his tone and gesture. He is followed by others who take up his howl with such good-will that I am obliged to leave the "solemn assembly" in fear and trembling. None of the General's staff follow to challenge me to mortal combat. Perhaps they know me to be a lover of peace.

Seriously, now, is all this outburst and uproar called for by the necessities of the case? The Salvation Army is a movement of active dissent. As such it must be allowed a wide margin for roaring and ranting. But after every allowance made, I am bound to say that the sights and sounds I encounter this evening strike me dumb. There is a practice amongst some of the Orientals, of disembowelling the dead, in order to speed their souls on their way to heaven. The Salvationists seem to try the experiment on the living. Do they expect the saved to go to heaven by spitting their lungs out in prayer and exhortation?

They tell me that the movement is intended for the masses who can be best worked upon through the emotions. This is true; but it is no less true that emotion, carried too far, is dangerously akin to intoxication; that when a fit subsides, it leaves the victim all the weaker in moral responsibility. We are dealing with moral, that is responsible beings. Think of the reaction on them when the frenzy of excitement is over. In the streets, I am thankful to say, the Salvationists act more reasonably. I am often inclined to sympathize with them as against the Sabbatarians and the Philistines. Probably the excesses in the Crystal Palace, to which I have alluded, are reserved only for the annual field-day. But taken altogether, the movement seems to need uplifting. It needs, perhaps, a better class of men and women to guide it. General Booth may remain at its head, an autocrat on earth. He may well return public thanks, once a year, for the success of his cause. But I think the best thanks-offering that is available to him now is to make the movement his Master's. He doubtless means well; and it is because I respect his motives that I make bold so far to appeal to this boldest of our popular reformers, more readily than I could appeal to his now sainted wife.

Whilst the Salvationists are holding their high carnival inside the Palace, an unregenerate costermonger is holding forth to an amused audience outside. He is standing on what looks like a waggon, with a large doll in each hand, expatiating on their beauty to the "ladies and gentlemen" present :— "'Ere are them dolls, twin sisters, born of the same mother and father in holy wedlock—ha! 'tis a long story. Some day you may hear it. On'y half-a-crown each, ladies and gentlemen—you ain't likely to have another chance in your lifetime. Look at 'er height—Ah, what limbs! Ain't she a Princess of the Blood ? What arms, what ankles ! Why, 'pon my soul, the dress itself is worth a sovereign. Come, is there none in this assembly willing to throw in a crown for the two ? Here they go, go, go, go! The Queen of Hingland would be glad to 'ave them. Two shillings six ; going, half-a-crown, do ye hear ? "

There is no response. He pauses for a few minutes, fumbles about for nothing. "Now, ladies and gentlemen," he resumes, "having been to the Palace, you are perhaps lighter in your purses. Right. Help the Salvationists; your souls has a first claim. But

here's things for the little ones at 'ome. Come, I
consider, compromise, knock'em down at 1s. 9d.. 1s.
9d. for each, and that is the truth, upon my honour.
I have just said 1s. 9d., prime cost. That's the truth
for you. Do ye think I'd tell a lie? No—Never
(with a wave of the hand). Look at this face (wiping his phiz with a red rag). Look at them eyes,
ladies. If there's a lady that can judge of eyes, it
is my wife—(titters). Yes, I says it as oughten't
to. And what do you think she tells me this morning?—Says she, 'Ah! 'Arry, I never seen such eyes
before'"—(laughter and applause). At this stage of
the harangue a boy asks, "Come along, Puffin, when
did you marry, then?"—(shouts) "Ah, my boy," replies the hawker, lapsing into street-arabism, "where
would ye have been if I 'adn't married?"—(loud
laughter and applause). The women shriek and jump
about like mad over the joke that seems to have
gone home and demolished the marjoy of the evening. 'Arry sees his chance and makes a roaring
trade of it for some minutes—everybody going in
for dolls. He runs them on the cheap, to keep the
audience in good humour, anxious to get rid of the
supply. He has a joke here, a quip there, and polite
words for the ladies. I am myself so carried off by
the contagion that I offer to pay for a large doll if
Crocodile will carry it in his arms. Crocodile agrees;
and as we leave the place the crowds at our heels
lean eagerly forward to see the dark man nursing
his doll! Crocodile is beside himself with rage. He
rushes out of the crowd, and sells his doll for a
song.   *⁎*

Nothing comes so handy to the wealthy idler in England as racing and betting on races. This seems to be one of his favourite modes of wiling away an idle hour. It is somewhat of a revelation to a stranger to read an account of the Derby, the Oaks, or the St. Leger. And what enormous attentions the English pay to their horses. Here is a sample :—

Amongst the brood mares are Spud, by Hampton out of Thistle (dam of Common and Goldfinch), and another of equally fashionable blood in Pretty Dance by Doncaster out of Highland Fling (dam of Saraband, Superba, &c.), with her colt foal by Paradox. Amongst the yearlings chief curiosity, perhaps, will attach to the filly by St. Simon out of Morning Glory. Princess Victoria being a grand-daughter of Plausible (dam of the notorious Plaudit), who was by Springy Jack out of Pasquinade (an own sister to Touchstone and dam of The Libel, Slander, Caricature, &c.), whilst Little Lady, not to be confounded with the similarly named Orlando mare, the dam of Camballo, by Rosicrucian out of Dark Blue (dam of Preciosa, &c.), is a great-grand-daughter of Escalade, the only two-year-old that ever made The Flying Dutchman gallop when they met in the Mersey Stakes at Liverpool in 1848. Amongst the South Stud mares, four visited Hagioscope, three Galliard, two Exile II, one each Bend Or, Sheen, Hampton, Ayrshire, Bendigo, and Prism, and nine Silver (brother to Gold) this season, including Cartridge by Musket, whom Mr. Beddington bought in Auckland last winter. During his visit to Melbourne, Mr. B. offered Mr. Wallace, his owner, £ 3,000 a year for five years for the hire of Carbine, with the option of purchase at £ 20,000, less any money, paid for his lease in the interim, which offer "made his mouth water," as Mr. W. remarked, though compelled to decline it through fearing it might lose him his seat in the Legislature, owing to Carbine being such a popular idol.

Now, it seems to me that Homer and Firdousi were hardly so minute in their description of heroes and heroines of the epic age as is our modern chronicler in his description of horse-flesh. I am sure the chronicler could not write up his own pedigree with greater pride.

And what enormous prices they pay for the animals! £20,000 for one horse! Few Popes or Emperors could afford such a price for the most splendid work of art. After this, what is your tea at twenty pounds sterling for one pound avoirdupois, as sold by public auction? Upon my word, hundreds of Englishmen could buy their wives at cheaper rates; hundreds of husbands are bought in the matrimonial market for much less every year.

How sumptuously these animals are fed and brought up! Dear me, there must be millions of children in Europe, who would prefer to have been born horses by such and such sire out of such and such dam. No, I do not care to be sanctimonious. If I can't bless racing and betting, I won't curse it. But £20,000 for one horse, when there are perhaps 200,000 of human beings in London, writhing in the grip of deadly poverty! Come, that is too much for my unChristian conscience. Pray do not trouble to explain that much of the money goes to the poor in one shape or other. It is a false, unnatural, inhuman ideal. I cannot stand it. Away with you, and your horses and ponies, ye votaries of fashion!

As to betting; why, of course you cannot have an enjoyable race, or any sport or game, whithout a prize or a stake. I know that quite as much as you do. But without being pharisaic, I venture to ask why you are not content with nominal stakes? Why

L

hanker after money stakes at all? Do you know what we call honour stakes, and service stakes?—the losing side submitting to momentary service, such as undoing the shoe-buttons of the winner, fetching water to him or her, submitting to a kiss, bowing to the ground, standing on one leg, with clasped hands, &c., before the winner? or rubbing the nose against the floor, striking the cheek or forehead in repentance; catching hold of the ears and sitting down and standing up so many times, to make an open confession of defeat before the company? These are stakes worth playing for, in which all could engage without breaking the law. Oh ye cold-blooded, money-grubbing gamblers, can't you sin in good form, if sin you must?

₊

"How long are we to endure our royalty?", asks a very pretty politician of me soon after my arrival in London. "For ever," I reply, in easy good faith. My fair querist looks daggers. As we are not likely to meet again, I may as well explain myself to you. The world is groaning under the burden of so many unrealities, that any more added to it is a sin against one's soul.

Why are you in such a hurry for the advent of a republic? Has it done much for Europe? Even in the new world, with so many favourable conditions, how much real good has it been able to do for the people, with all its eagerness for the greatest happiness of the greatest number? Is not monopoly of various kinds still the bane of republican America? Let us put up with half-pleasant facts rather than court the pleasantest of fictions.

It is natural that the masses in our day should be in bad humour with vested interests in state and church, with the tyranny and monopoly of departments. With chronic indigence for his own lot, is it a wonder that John Bull should growl at perpetual privileges and pensions for others ? But say what he likes, John cannot live without his fetish. If he won't have a monarch in the name of monarch, he will have him under some other name. If he won't have a church in the name of church, he will have it under some other name. He cannot do without a symbol. It is for clever politicians, like you, to see that this symbol is made harmless. I, for my part, do not care much if the royalty of the future is to be a symbol for the people, to be kept in good condition, perhaps in a glass house, and worshipped once or twice a year. The people need something to look up to. It is well for them, well for us all, that they should.

It would be a sin to sympathize with the more odious and irritating pretensions of royalty. These must give way before the growth of the sentiment of brotherhood amongst men. And that they *are* giving way, not only in the West, but even in the "unchanging" East, is patent to the reader of history. The truth is beginning to dawn upon every minion of fortune, who prefers to be the slave of pleasure, that he is living in a fool's paradise, that sooner or later he will have a rude awakening and a heavy account to settle—that, in short, his own opportunities are but a measure of his duties towards others. But, to be just, there can be no imposition of duty

L 2

without a corresponding concession of privilege. The tendency of modern times in Europe seems to have been to stint this concession of grace while at the same time to exact the debt of duty. This is a utopian ideal, concealing more risks to the commonwealth than to the individuals envied.

And what are the royalties of Europe that we should envy them? They have to wear a sort of gilded livery; to live on the sufferance of others. During the day they go through a dizzy round of duties; through restlessness, long vigils, and perhaps constant dread, at night. They have few hours that they may call their own; many hours they are at the mercy of the footman and the fop. Have they not to eat and drink and sleep almost under prescription? I doubt if they can smile officially, without written orders; though they may weep to their hearts' content without the slightest mention of their misery in *The Court Circular*. Poor souls, I am sure I pity them with all my heart. And should they ever be in need of copper, they are welcome to this large quantity of brass placed before them in anticipation.

Seriously, dear Miss Peregrine (I take it you are not yet settled to a life of domestic politics), let us not destroy a superstructure of ages, before we have made sure of at least an equally lasting substitute. It may be easier, after all, to make England a republic, with all the advantages of constitutional monarchism, than to reduce it to a bald imitation of untried experiments.

CHAPTER V.

SEX.

The Mystery of Sex, and its Inequalities—Sex in the Affairs of Life—Woman as a Social Factor, in the West and in the East—The Englishwoman as a Moral Leaven—Crocodile a-visiting.

TERRIBLE as is the mystery of life and death, and of the inequalities of human destiny, it has always tended to keep out of view the other great mystery of our being, namely, the mystery of sex. But the latter is not so inscrutable as the former. And being a problem dealing more with the practical side of life, it appears throughout to have kept itself to the front, in spite of the comparatively limited attention it has received from the world's thinkers. Therefore it is, I believe, that whilst the problem of birth and death is as far from solution to-day as it was in the days of the prophets who communed directly with nature and with nature's God, the other problem seems to have gone on steadily unravelling itself under the stress of necessity.

Are there really two distinct sexes in nature? Nature seems to love unity in multiplicity. The unit varies and multiplies, only that the varieties and the multiples may return to the original unit. May it not be more correct, then, to say that there is *one dual sex* in nature? Man, that is man-and-woman, was made after the Maker's own image. "Man and woman created He them". Does that imply two created beings, or one? If the latter theory is accepted, it tends to shut out the assumption of a radical disparity between the sexes. If the former is the right theory, to which almost all the important systems of religion have been committed, then the balance of advantage, that is of inherent superiority, seems to be rather in favour of the woman. According to the Old Testament, for instance, God created woman from man. The only legitimate interpretation we can put upon this language of the infancy of our race is that, from man He created another being, more perfect than man. This interpretation would seem to fit in with the theory of Evolution. Woman is the latest created, therefore the best perfected, of the race with which the Creator has peopled this earth. If so, she is historically as well as by tradition the "better half" of man. Here, of course, we have to reckon with the story of the Fall. But even accepting the narrative of that event in its orthodox sense, one fails to see why the results of trangression are to be visited exclusively on one only of the two offenders, so far at least as physical suffering is concerned. That such may not be the real teaching of scriptures, we are encouraged to hope in view of the well-known fact that the trials of child-birth, which are held *in terrorem* over the woman's head, exist rather in some avenging imagination than in reality.

It is well-known that gestation, in itself, is no more painful than ordinary digestion, where the laws of nature are obeyed—as amongst primitive races; that the crisis itself is less painful than is generally apprehended, and that the pain of it is soon forgotten amid the pleasures of maternity.

It is not for an ignorant layman to pit the book of nature against the book of revelation; nor is there any need, I think, of forcing on such an antagonism. With an ever-widening sphere of knowledge vouchsafed to man, it may not be impossible some day to reconcile one with the other. In the meantime, we have already been told by scientists (with what degree of accuracy, remains to be shewn) that originally there was no distinction of sex in nature, that the hermaphrodite was the first distinct move towards separation, not completely established for ages. Be that as it may, one thing is certain, namely, that the idea of woman's inherent subordination to man in every concern of life has been set aside as gratuitous by some of the most advanced thinkers of the world; and by none so, in our times, as by the followers of Christ. It is now left to the scribe and the churl to dispute this truth, attested by the whole design and working of nature, that, in the aggregate, woman is exactly the equal of man. That if she is his inferior in some respects, she is also his superior in other respects. That man and woman is one, man the one half, woman the other; the two halves making one whole, each after its own fashion. That it takes man *and woman* to make an entire human being. It has

taken ages of a bloodless strife to have this simple truth of our being impressed upon the usurp-
er. It might have been impressed upon him earlier, had it dawned earlier upon the party wronged.
The position is better defined and better understood in our day than it ever was before. What
a stride this assured position of woman's equality
is, compared with that of moral degradation, bodily
slavery, and denial of soul, which characterised some
of the most glorious epochs of the history of our
race! To think that religion has been responsible,
to some extent, for this triple badge of slavery!
If the identity of sexes in nature is yet denied,
their ultimate equality is no longer doubted. Practically, there is no higher sex to dominate a lower
sex.

If this is so in nature, why should it be less so
in science, art, literature, in the professions, and in
politics? A uniform degree of equality in the practical concerns of life is not to be established at
once, amid a complex and highly artificial civili-
sation. It must result from a gradual process of
assimilation. That process has already begun, and
some of its greatest triumphs have been witnessed
during our own century. There are many obstacles
still in the way, but perhaps the worst of them
have been removed during recent years. The asser-
tion, that women are less able to bear the strain
of intellectual effort, is being challenged on almost
all sides. It is not to be denied that girls break
down more readily than boys under the strain of
particular studies. I have known some painful cases

in England and in India. But that may be owing to the fact that the course of studies was originally intended only for boys, as also to the other fact that girls are as yet new to it. Departures like this, after centuries of strict exclusion, cannot but lead to such results in the beginning. A few generations later, when our sweet girl graduates have settled down to the new line of study, and when this has been modified to suit them as well as the boys, they will be better able to hold their own. Already, they have begun to show a brighter record in some branches of study. I think too much has been made of the difference in weight between the two brains. Weight is not everything, as apart from quality. For a just estimate the two should be taken together. Under the same circumstances with men, women ought to stand the same amount of intellectual effort. The overworking of the brains may tell equally upon certain functions in both, though not perhaps on the same functions. If the effect of this overwork is, at present, more marked in woman than in man, it may be because the former has not yet had time to accustom herself to a full measure of intellectual exercise. Granted the same capacities and the same opportunities, the two individuals must stand eventually on the same level, though they may reach the level, here and there, by different routes. Then, as to women lacking originality which is the true test of greatness; there is much force in this way of looking at it. But what is originality? —and who fixed the standard of greatness? What opportunities have women been allowed of competing with their brothers or husbands, in this matter? There seems to be no reason why, with a wholesome change in ideals, such as would meet the aspirations of men and women alike, a woman should not make herself as great a force in the affairs of life as a man. Anyhow, if she is not recognized as great in herself, she is undoubtedly great as moulder of the world's destiny—including great men and little. Man alone is not much, by himself, in any sphere of life; certainly not all-sufficing, not even self-sufficing.

We have seen this in many spheres of life; and with the disabilities of the sex gradually dying out, and the laws of man approximating more and more to the laws of God, there is every reason to hope that sex in itself will cease to be a factor in determining the happiness or progress of mankind. Look at the law of inheritance as between the sexes, the laws of marriage and divorce. Look, again, at the position that woman has still to occupy, in some respects, in the Church and in the State. A woman can be a queen, assuming the divine function on earth; and yet she may not officiate at a church meeting. She may not offer up prayer or sacrifice formally. She is debarred from the exercise of functions appertaining to her specially as a ministering angel. And not only this: she is sometimes denounced from the pulpit as 'fiend', 'devil', 'daughter of Eve. Here we have a remnant of the old demarcation of sex, ordained by man on man's behalf. Reform in such matters comes very slowly; but come it must. Already we see that sex is being eliminated in science, art and literature. It will not be long before this elimination works more actively in the sphere of the learned professions. Then will come the turn of politics. It would be wrong to hurry on the process. But the time seems to have come for a moderate instalment of Women's Suffrage in England. Although the problem is beset with difficulties, none of these appears to be insuperable. Rightly understood, the demands of the Shrieking Sisterhood, as some of our monopolists of power are pleased to style them, will appeal to the sympathy of Liberals and Conservatives alike. Indeed, this question ought to be discussed independently of party politics. It ought to occupy a common platform. Where is the danger in a number of well-qualified women exercising the vote? It is but a small step in advance of the position already occupied by the sex. The talk about the shrieking sisterhood swamping the brotherhood of bores in Parliament shows how poorly the brotherhood aforesaid have grasped the situation. The time is too remote, even for the eye of faith, when women are to outnumber men in the active pursuits of life. Broadly speaking, that is a consummation neither desirable nor attainable. What seems to be wanted, in the present case, is that a certain portion of the national legislature shall be pledged formally to protect and advance the interests of the sex which is so jealously shut out from its deliberations. It is hard to see any danger to the commonwealth, lurking in this modest proposal. To say that women voters will be amenable to doubtful influences, is to set one's face against the teachings of history, so far at least as modern English life is concerned. The influence of women on the public affairs of this country has generally made for good. Women, such as those who are likely to be enfranchised to the extent indicated above, are more unselfish than men. Once in a position of trust, they will care more for the safety of the State, for the order and happiness of Society. Their presence ought to purify the political atmosphere. When settled down to actual work, they are likely to exercise more caution than they have had credit for. Naturally, women will always rule more from the nursery and the drawing room. But that is no reason why those, who wish otherwise, are to be cooped up in a political zenana, simply on account of their sex. Taken altogether, I believe the influence of women on the course of social legislation ought to be more useful and salutary than that of men. Justice and expediency both demand that this influence shall be directly exerted on the legislature of the country. Is it not singular, that whilst the English are governed by an essentially womanly woman, recognised as a most disinterested and capable ruler, they should pretend to be frightened at the very thought of qualified women safeguarding the interests of their sex in Parliament, and guiding its counsels in regard to questions of vital importance to themselves ?

Sad and pathetic is the story of woman's life. How great have been the moral and physical disabilities forged round her hapless existence in the past! Even in this enlightened age, when she is recognised as the mother, that is the maker of a nation, its law treats her distinctly as an inferior being. And society puts her seal of approval on this man-made law. Woman cannot err, as man often does, with impunity. She may be betrayed, branded, and burdened with shame. It is more or less the same story all the world over: man begets, woman bears; therefore, the one is born to rule, the other to obey. As if woman were intended to love, honour and obey man, regardless of his moral worth! How unequal are the laws ordained by Church and State alike? For instance, the laws governing marriage and inheritance. Some of these laws, and the customs arising out of them, strike one as a caricature of the relation that should subsist between two responsible beings. Happily, an incipient revolt has begun even amongst Eastern communities against this tyranny of law and custom. And in no part of the world has the progress of the revolt been more marked, during the last half century, than in England. This movement must grow with time. There is no external danger, that one can see, threatening its existence. The only danger is from within. Those who have at heart the interests of their long-suffering sisters will have to blame themselves in the main, if the movement is ever discredited or thrown back. The sexes are coming more and more into a line; already they stand pretty much on the same level, at least at home. The time has gone by to treat women as toys, as things to be played with and thrown away; or merely as breeders of the race. Men have begun to realise that what is good and pure in the mother's intelligence is really the making of a good and pure generation. That if it is woman's lot to suffer, it is also her privilege to save. This is just the time when tact and forbearance are essential for the winning side. Women cannot be too careful of undue aggressiveness. They sometimes ask—Where would man have been but for woman? And disdaining to wait for answer, they rush off to visions of an innate, immeasurable superiority, usurped by the tyrant in an unguarded moment. This superiority they expect to regain in as brief a space of time by using the divided skirt and flourishing the parasol. Now, all this is delicious talk. But it is neither good history nor good logic. Women will do well to understand that nothing is good for them that is not true. On the other hand, all thoughtful men have to remember that the sex are only now emancipating themselves. They must have time to realize the position after this process is over.

The guiding rule of life for the future is, sex equality before public morality. The trespass of the husband has too long been blinked. The wife of the future is not likely to stand it. She will have her rights better vindicated than hitherto; or, if weak in moral fibre, she may not scruple to pay him in his own coin. God forbid, in the interests of family life, that this should happen. She may learn to guide herself, as man does, by a utilitarian law of her own making, if the law of the land and the law of society continue their differential treatment much longer. As it is, infidelity amongst the married does not seem to inspire the same horror which it invariably does in the East; that is, infidelity on the wife's part. The husband is legally free amongst most of the Eastern races, and socially and quasi-legally in Europe, too. Infidelity on his part does not entitle the wife to divorce, unless coupled with cruelty.

It would be presumptuous to speak of the sex relations of a people of whose manners and customs one has acquired but a superficial knowledge. But it takes very little time to see that Englishwomen in the upper and more cultured ranks of society are pure as crystal. Could the same be said of men in corresponding ranks of life, especially those that are accursed with too much leisure as well as wealth? The great middle class seem to be equally pure, thanks mainly to the influence of religion, in both sexes, notably in the country where the English may be said to enjoy quite an ideal family life. It is the lower ranks that appear to be infected with poison, more so, as we have seen, unmarried girls in towns, who have to go into service of one kind or another. They fall an easy prey to monopolists of wealth and leisure, either through intemperance or love of finery. London girls of this class dislike poverty, and cannot bear want; they love to be ladies on any terms, and are prepared to pay for the whim. Here is an extreme of social progress. In India we are suffering, in this respect, from the extreme of stagnation. The nett result in both cases is about the same. Extremes meet.

It may be of use to note that women's education in England is still in a transitionary state. That poor girls are sometimes fed upon Euclid and Algebra, and then turned out, mostly to go into service. They soon begin to take airs, despise marriage and affect independence. Under these circumstances, the wonder is that the sin we are speaking of is not wider spread. But woman is pure by nature as well as by the conditions of life imposed upon her. She dreads exposure and loss of character more than man does, or cares to do. It is only when she is hard put to it, through one cause or another, that she succumbs to temptation. The first false step taken, often in ignorance, or in full hope of redemption, everything is over with her. She must die; that is the best thing she can do. Often she is denied this release, and lingers on for years on the charity of chance acquaintances or the workhouse. Sometimes she retaliates on the man, and on other men, through the vindictiveness of despair. In nine cases out of ten, however, she is a victim. Wealth and opportunity will always prey upon poverty and want. And where social institutions lend themselves to this system of sexual depredations, the misery of the victims is only intensified. But in spite of much that is discouraging, one observes a tendency toward improvement, both in the spirit of the law and the instincts of the people. The time seems to be coming when State and Church will combine to insist that a man's public life shall not be judged as distinctly apart from his private life.

What can men see in such an exercise of their manhood as involves the lowest form of tyranny over themselves and over others? Of course, there is the variety of attractions for the moment. But whilst the attraction is transitory and precarious, the shock of reaction on the moral system, if not on the physical, as well, is lasting. In his own selfish interest, man ought to see that the purchase of unlawful pleasure—cold, venal, irresponsive—a thing not given of the giver's free will, is a double loss instead of being a gain. How different is pure love reciprocated, the union of body and soul, secure for all from dread of conscience or shame of the world! For a well-balanced mind there is infinite variety in sameness. And even where such formal union is impossible, it is yet possible to cherish a disinterested, sexless love; to live on it, and through it, to a happier, freer, purer life.

Pleasures are proverbially fleeting. None is so fleeting, none leaves such bitterness of emptiness behind, as unlawful pleasure of the sense. We sometimes hear strange arguments used against this view of man's personal obligations. It is denied that such pleasure as can be bought is necessarily unlawful. It is urged that the law allows it, as it allows any other form of exchange and barter. That marriage itself is in most cases a matter of exchange and barter, and that where this particular form of it is not within the reach of a man, or when he has outlived its attractions, it is open to him to indulge his instincts in other ways, provided he acts strictly within the letter of the law. That puritans do harm to society, by setting up a false standard; so on and on.

Now, the answer to all this is simple. In the

M

first place, we have to deal with the interests of
society at large, those of women as well as men,
whilst those who argue as above seem to ignore
this dual interest. No honest woman will ever offer
her virtue for sale. Consequently, what you get
out of your 'exchange and barter' theory is less
than you bargained for. If you are content with
that, we do not grudge you the exercise of your
masculine instincts, nor envy the results that must
follow. If, on the other hand, you contrive to betray innocence, you are the meanest of mean monopolists, taking advantage of helplessness and want.
You destroy purity, instead of protecting it. You
dishonour yourself so far, as a man and a citizen. Of the consequences of your act on the victim
we say nothing, nor of its probable consequences
on society. That marriage itself is an exchange and
barter in many cases, is, unhappily, true. But even
when love is sold, in the first instance, on one side
or the other, it is often hallowed by association,
sanctified by ties of home, gladdened by the presence
of offspring. At any rate, the miseries of a mistake
in this case are visited mainly on the individuals
concerned, whilst in the other case the perpetration
of a wrong tends to destroy the fabric of society.
As to the absolute necessity of man indulging his
instincts, one wonders how far he is prepared to
give the benefit of this doctrine to the other half
of his being. Here, again, comes in the question
of equality between the sexes—all reforms in society must begin at this beginning. It can hardly be
denied that some men have stronger instincts than

others. But it is possible, even for the former, so to regulate their conduct, especially by means of intellectual and physical pre-occupation, as to be entirely above the necessity of social wrong-doing.

The pity is that most men learn this and similar lessons of life too late for their own use, when they have become saints in spite of themselves. It is not too late for anyone, however, to give the benefit of his dear-bought experience to others. I should think they need plainspeaking on this point in England. In India the social horizon is too nebulous to be penetrated by the rays of truth.

To an Eastern mind it is often a puzzle why the English make so much of balls, dances, and other exciting amusements. They cost so much in time, money and in health. If the climate requires a certain amount of warmth to be kept up in the body by active exercise, are there no other means? Or, if this particular method of exhilaration is necessary, may not members of the same sex engage in a dance? Or, further, if there is not sufficient attraction in that, why don't members of the same family dance together? These questions suggest nothing wrong; they are advanced by a stranger as they have been placed before him. He himself is inclined to think that the coming into contact, openly, of highbred men and women, engenders confidence as well as amity. But the thing is apt to be carried too far, especially amongst young people, married and unmarried. The by-play in deserted corners, and in that paradise of ballroom bliss, the conservatory, is an instance in point. May not some portion of the infelicity, of which we read almost every week, be due to this amiable excess of confidence ?

I believe there has been a great deal of improvement in the matter during recent years. This improvement ought to be maintained, if only for the sake of health. But late hours seem to be an inseparable condition of indoor amusements in England, just as these latter are an essential part of their life of hurry and bustle.

On the other hand, it is in the nature of things that the proud, Parda-ridden Oriental should misunderstand the scope and importance of the social amenities to which I have referred above, not in a doubting but in an inquiring spirit. It will be long before the Eastern mind can distinguish between courtesy and familiarity, as exchanged between the sexes in Europe. Oh that the nations of the East could be made to realise that it is the secret silent burning of the flesh that is sinful—and as cowardly as it is sinful ! That no zenana can save the sinner in such a case ! Where men and women are allowed to meet openly, on terms of equality, the glamour of sex is bound to disappear. Men and women then find it easeir to merge sex in friendship, or to eliminate it altogether from their friendly relations. What this glamour of sex is, and what fatal fascination it exercises on those who are doomed 'to burn from within', is best known to the heart and mind of the East. It permeates the whole texture of our existence and our national literature, corrupts the morals of our youth, and tends powerfully to keep up the artificial barriers that divide the children of God. It is sad to see some of our best Indian thinkers generalising, at times, from instances of the miscarriage of affections. Long courtships and flirtations are certainly not to be defended. But though flirtation is to be reprobated in all cases, there are many cases in which courtship is permissible as a prelude to wedded happiness. We are not likely to have much of courtship and the whole gamut of love-making in India, so long as we keep out the system of late marriages. Early marriages are best suited to our present requirements, though there is no excuse at all for infant marriages. But that is hardly a reason why we should look at the free and open air of English life, married or unmarried, through the lurid light of the zenana. As well may we ask the English to sit in judgment on the mysteries of our *Shraddha!* An Englishwoman can be as pure as any in India, without the prudery of the latter. Ever bent on enjoying her fill of freedom, she yet knows where to stop, and will slap your impertinence the moment you forget yourself.

It shows sad lack of charity to rush to a conclusion against a man and woman talking, sitting, or taking a walk together. A little reflection will show the harmlessness, even the usefulness, of the thing. If either of the parties happens to be married, so much the worse for him or her, in the eyes of the Indian critic. Needless to add that such a man cannot bear the exchange of partners at dinner or other public functions,—he will put his own construction on it. Even the natural display of affection between father and daughter, brother and sister, he will see with the jaundiced eye of the zenana, of which some of our Anglo-Indian friends are so enamoured. On this account I am always slow to cry up the zenana system, useful though it is in some respects for our present purposes. Certainly, I would be loth to admit to mixed gatherings gentlemen who did not bring their families with them.

Young Indians, visiting England, generally manage to see the darker side of life there, and away they run with their zeal for generalisation. This means injustice to themselves and to others. They are strangers to the purity of English home life. And having fallen amongst more or less impure associations, they are not likely to enter into, or even to admit, the existence of such pure home life. They return to India disappointed, having seen rather the abuse than the use of the institutions they came to study. They run down the institutions and the people, and in turn are run down by the latter.

Advocates of seclusion forget that it is the forbidden or the distant object of our quest, that excites most desire. There is nothing in the arm-in-arm walk, where the social code allows it ; but a good deal, often, in the same arm-in-arm walk, where it is looked down upon by society. The same kiss that confers nectar in the former case may impart poison in the latter. I do honestly believe that, in spite of the exhibition of flagrant vice and crime in England, on which the light of public opinion beats so fiercely, there is less of concupiscence in Englishmen than in Indians of the same age and position. If sexual offence is more violent in England, the climate and the habits of the people have a good deal to account for it. Such offence must certainly be more frequent in India, if you put the two standards of morality on a par; that is, if you bear in mind the very low ideal of woman prevailing in India. If it came to that, one might say there was something to choose between the cold-blooded 'respectability' of the Indian polygamist, with his well-stocked zenana of wifelings, and the occasional escapade of the English husband of one wife.

***

One of the trials of my life is to go out visiting friends. London is perhaps the worst place in which one has to pay homage to friendship. Apart from the uncertainty of the weather, a formal visit is a weariness to the flesh. The distances are so great that you have to spend hours on one or two visits. Evening calls are most tiresome. There is the inevitable tea, and such a variety of strangers, "just dropping in" to see how dear Lady Languish is. How I dread my Lady's At-home where not one in ten feels really at home! Then follow introductions—the bowings and smilings and how-very-pleased-to-see-you-ings, which the speaker is sure to forget next moment. I have managed to keep at a distance from breakfast, lunch and dinner, and thereby lost a good many advantages. But I do not regret the loss, considering how dearly one may have to pay for these advantages. As a rule, I have called oftener upon ladies than upon gentlemen; and, curious as it may seem, more often upon old maids. Women have hearts, and know instinctively how to set you

at ease. They are quick, and really less diplomatic
than men, when they get to know you. People may
talk of old maids being failures, and describe them
as sour. An old maid, who has a purpose in life, is
just the reverse. She is a great success in life.
Far from being sour, she is the very milk of human
kindness. As a rule, she is admirably well-informed;
an impartial and kindly critic; an earnest, open
friend. How many such have I met in London!—a
distinct type in themselves, standing far above the
idle tittle-tattle of society.

One loves to sit at their feet by the hour, listening to some fairy-tale of philanthropy. How young
in heart they are, entering into all your hopes and
aspirations! It is refreshing to see the girlish face,
the gentle free manner, the joyous sympathy peeping out of the bed of pain. Or, to enter the presence of a young-old dowager, holding her durbar,
like the Grand Moghul, with the same grace and
dignity, and with more intelligence. Or, to receive
wise, motherly counsel from another, quietly doing
you more service than you need, while offering to
do little. Or, to chat with the old maid, sitting at
her table, managing a vast charity organisation more
cheerfully and skilfully than your best paid Collector in India. Or, yet once more, to see another
old maid, getting through banking and other public
business in a spirit that might be envied by a
merchant prince. Gladly do I bow to woman's
genius in literature, science, art, business; in politics and religion. It is a fact worth mentioning
that amongst the English it is the good wife, mother,

sister, or daughter, that often makes the efficient public worker. She is earnest, unselfish, *womanly*. It is the frivolous and purposeless that lose sex. God bless the women of England!—wives, widows, and old maids in particular.

Talk not of crabbed old maids and crusty old bachelors. With all their faults, they have a distinct purpose to serve in the economy of home life. They are the buffers that often keep the engines of domestic interest from colliding. How many young wives and husbands have to refer their first quarrels to Aunt Mary or to Uncle Tom? And what would become of the spendthrifts and scapegraces of society but for the aunts and uncles whom they squeeze and spunge upon at every turn?

Of course, I pity those who happen to have very thin, and at the same time, very tall relations to look *up* to. Dear Aunt Janet, I am not unaware of your crosses and losses of old. Little wonder you have lost faith in this wicked world. But many of your young relatives have to go through the same ordeal. Try to sympathise with them, the more because they know not their fate. And oh Aunt Janet, do give up your habit of "putting two and two together" when the young people are trying to make something of this miserable life. That putting of two and two together sometimes leads to a moral murder. As for you, Uncle Gnash, all I can say is that it is not pleasant to have a tall, thin, self-absorbed beau bachelor for one's guardian.

The quietest people of quality, whom I have met in London, are some of the royal house of Egypt, now reigning in all the solemnity of silence in the British Museum. Of the numerous Majesties there assembled, it is Cleopatra, of course, who claims my homage first. Getting over all natural shyness, I offer my condolence to her in hushed tones. But there is not a word of thanks, not a look of recognition in return. What?—all thy sweet smiles and loving words still reserved for Antony? Poor Cleo! Perhaps it is as well. I envy him as little as I blame thee. Thou hast had enough to suffer. What a restless life! Even after life's fitful dream is over, they do not allow thy bones to rest. Here thou art, without veil or shroud, exposed to the vulgar gaze. Sad, indeed, is thy fate; sad enough to shake the avenging angel, though the recording angel has done his worst to thee.

Crocodile has been anxious to see "some England's Lord and Lady in his own palace." One afternoon I take him with me. On the way I miss my watch, and ask him to go up to a gentleman hurrying past, and ask what the time is. He runs and asks aloud—"I say, Mister, what is the o'clock?" The gentleman stares at him, but recognising his genus, gives the hour. Crocodile feels he has done something wrong, and stammers—"I beg your apology." The gentleman proceeds, smiling. On our way to the "Lord's palace" I explain to my companion why the gentleman smiled, and advise him to be more gentle in his politeness.

On reaching our destination I ring the bell. A rather flashily dressed maid opens the door. Crocodile, with better manners than myself, takes off his hat to her; and extending his paw, shakes her heartily by the hand, with the egregious salutation, "good by, Sir." The maid retires in hot confusion, opening the drawing room door for me. I deposit my companion in the cloak room, where he makes friends with the maid as well as the footman. They treat him to sumptuous tea. On our way back Crocodile speaks rapturously of how they showed him "the electric magic lanterns for cooking," (probably the gas stoves or some electric apparatus), the silver plates and dishes, the lift by which they went up and came down, the telephone at whose command a dish could be turned out in five minutes. The second Lord (the footman), he explains, is dressed in a suit worth thirty guineas. "His boots alone are worth two guineas," he flows on in a stream of eager eloquence.

CHAPTER VI.

LIFE AS SEEN IN THE STREETS AND SHOPS.

The London Policeman—The Postman—" Cabby "—The 'Bus—
The Tram—The Railway—" Apartments "—Expenses—"The
Daughters of India "—Business Morality—Tricks of Trade—
British Pluck—An independent Costermonger—Circulars and
Advertisements—"Living Pictures."—The Press in England
and in India—Exhibitions—The Houses of Parliament—
The Sights of London—The Parsi Burial Ground—Parks and
Markets—Roses and Kisses—Stray Sights—Street Arabs—
"Rum uns"—Street Cries—The London Rough—"Bloody"
—Farewell to London.

WHETHER the London policeman is a thing of
beauty, or not, it is for my fair readers to settle. But
every vagrant and street-arab will agree that Bobby
is by no means a joy for ever. The beggar runs
away at sight of him; so does the drunkard, when
he can, as also do the diseased and all others without honest means of livelihood. Obstructers and
breakers of the public peace, and those inclined to
commit what comes under the generic name of nuisance, hold him in horror. The policeman, yclept
constable by courtesy, is, as a rule, a burly fellow,
with a grip that he could tighten round a run-away
pig. He walks up and down his beat, always on the
look out for something to happen. In fact, he antici-
pates trouble. Is not that his business? He is paid
for preventing mischief more than for punishing the
mischief-maker. He is as quick as the cabman, as

cool as the 'bus-driver, as well versed in topography as both of them put together. He regulates the traffic, chaperons damsels in distress to the corner opposite; sometimes a bevy of them whom he gets to hang breathless on his arm (the artful dodger!) When there is a congestion in the thoroughfare, or a collision ahead, the policeman simply raises his finger, and the whole traffice in the locality comes to a standstill. From prince to peasant, driving or on foot, none dare to make light of the policeman's danger signal. In a minute he will move the finger this way or that, for the anxious pedestrians to rush out; and then he drops the finger or the hand, which means line clear for the general traffic. Verily, that man has the lion's strength; but he uses it not as a lion. As regulator-general of the street traffic he exercises his authority with such tact and temper that it is often a pleasure to obey him. Even the fat coachman, driving his gilded coach of luxury, takes his warnings kindly. He is tender and forbearing towards children, whom he leads gently out of a *mêlée*. How like a mother he walks the little trotters out! Courteous to women, and attentive to all; advising as to where you can have a cab or a 'bus for your destination, what you are to pay, how you can do the distance in ten minutes on foot, or take the train. Throughout my experience, I have come across no more than two policemen who were sulky; and one of them, I believe, had the spleen. The rest I have known to be pleasant and obliging; sometimes too much so. Once, in the thick of a Piccadilly crowd, I asked a policeman to put me in the way of going to New Burlington Street. Hardly had the words escaped me when he whisked me through the surging crowd, and landed me safe on the opposite pavement, my clerical coat, chimney pot and all. Before I could recover from my surprise and disgust, he muttered, "Here you are, sir; keep straight till you come to the turning." He had no time to enter into an explanation, because he was going to hold up his digital flag signal. That was a feat for Bobby, for, though only five feet two, if once I plant myself on a spot it would take more than one horse to drag me away from it.

Dear old Bobby; roughly tender in your attentions to all in need; seldom losing your temper, though distracted by a score of tongues at a time, or your presence of mind amid the confusion and clatter of a hundred feet! What a contrast you are to the stupid, peevish, insolent Patawala in India!

If I were a girl, I would prefer a London policeman for my knight to any Bond Steet merchant, whatever the ladies may say to that. As it is, I am prepared to exchange any three officiating priests in India for one London policeman.

Bobby on horseback is not much after my heart, however. Not that he cannot ride; but he makes such a droll figure as he stiffens himself up in his unequestrian uniform.

Bobby is not without his faults. For instance, he often points to the left of a street while speaking of it as the right. Sometimes he sends you off on a wild goose chase for "two minutes" when the distance to be covered is on the right side of twenty minutes. Perhaps he means two minutes by rail. He is not above small temptations, and can wink like a dummy in Dame Tussaud's collection. Well, well, why pick holes in poor flesh-and-blood when the sun himself is beginning to show spots? But it is ticklish to flirt with a spotted Bobby in London when the sun has hidden even his partial light.

**

There comes the postman's knock, exact almost to the minute. What a cheery knock it is, full of life and energy! How it startles one out of a reverie, with its *top top*, which I interpret as *get up*. On mail days I linger over my cup of tea till the welcome knock is heard, and willing feet run to bring me up the messages from across the sea. Sometimes it is a double knock, *top top*, *top top*, announcing a registered letter (which I like) or a large parcel (which I don't). Whether one likes it or not, however, he must open the door and accept his fate, after saluting the bearer thereof. The man is as like his knock as the knock is like him—quick, precise. He has his heart in the work, as he bustles up to you, with his modest " good mornin', sir." Off he goes, as fast as he came. He is not slow, that postman in London town. He can't afford to be slow. The weather drives him before it, and he is nothing loth to be so driven. What a contrast to our Indian tapalwala—slow, slovenly, unbusiness-like! I dare say the latter will learn some day to mend his pace and his habits. But he will never be like his London prototype. He loves rest as much as the other loves unrest. What wonder this restless mortal rules the world? Let him rule. It is his turn.

Let us not forget the telegraph boy, a veritable Mercury on the wing. Here he alights, top foremost, and gives a knock and a ring that may remind any sinner of the day of resurrection. He is a picture of rude health, singing or whistling, as he kicks about to keep the cold off his well-covered legs. Do you know, friend, what a sad message you are making merry over? Poor boy! he is not without his own troubles, which he bears like a philosopher.

**

Being new to the ways of London, I have spent nearly ten pounds in the course of my first week on cab hire. The hansom is an attractive vehicle, with sufficient protection from rain, with a looking-glass for dandies, and a match-box for smokers. It is light and neat, the horse is clean and well-cared for, with a bunch of flowers adorning his head stall. Cabby himself looks a picture of health, as he now and then touches his hat with "Keb, Sir"? Not knowing the distances, one is often tempted to jump in. More than once have I had to part with a shilling for not more than two minutes' drive,—for instance, from Grosvenor Hotel to Victoria Station. Cabby is a sharp fellow. He takes in the situation at a glance. No sooner is the touching of his cap and the cracking of his whip over than he puts me down at Victoria. "Come," I say reproachfully, "you haven't earned this," handing him a sixpenny piece. His right hand seems to be paralyzed. I put back the small coin and hand him a shilling. He takes it smiling, and replies, "A bargain's a bargain, yer honour. Next time it is from a point at Charing Cross into Spring Gardens. It is the same thing over again. On a third occasion I am within a stone's throw of Pall Mall East, and ask cabby to put me down at No. 1. "No need of keb, Sir," he answers, pointing to the place. I am taken aback at his generosity, and hoist up a shilling with a kind word. He looks at the coin very sheepishly, as if to say, "I have not earned it," but takes it at last with the apology, "Thank ye very kindly, sir, 'aven't 'ad one since mornin." I wish him good luck, and go my way. Seldom have I parted with a coin with so much satisfaction. During the first two or three days I asked for the fare, before getting in—How much? The answer was either half-a-crown or a crown. As I grow older in London, I grow wiser.

The London cab-driver is a very intelligent fellow, and exceedingly well-posted in the details of distance, situation, train time, etc. If pressed for time, he will take you off like a shot, dodging the crowds, as well as the policeman, and plunging deep into lanes and byelanes, till you are at your address before time. He cares for nobody so long as he is within his rights. He won't make room for a peer of the realm. But he dreads the hoisting of Bobby's finger flag. It has only to be lifted, to petrify cabby and horse alike. Instantly the animal comes to a standstill, and the reins fall loose in the driver's hand. Not till the finger is put down cabby resume his drive.

The best way of doing London is to tramp the

N

streets and lanes, if you can, in the company of a retired policeman, or a friendly clergyman. Nothing answers so well, if you want an insight into the life of the people. You will often find the street to be the best school for the study of those soul-problems that absorb a visitor. When tired, you may mount the top of an omnibus, and from your perch look down upon rank, fashion, beauty, all at your feet. It is delicious, on a clear day. One feels as if he would never tire of riding out. Oh the solitude of finding yourself in a strange crowd!

The omnibus traffic is quite a novelty to me. Look at the fussy little conductor, all smiles and bows, inviting passers-by to go with him to "Chring Cruss," "Stren," "Oxf Strit," "Pidly," "Toria," or "Roloke." He is too much in a hurry to speak out whole words—Charing Cross, Strand, Oxford Street, Piccadilly, Victoria, Royal Oak. But it matters little; people follow him right enough. Many of them who get in give him intermediate addresses, and he generally asks them out at those particular numbers. But he has an eye to his penny more than to the passenger's convenience. It is not infrequent to find people getting into the wrong 'bus, sometimes encouraged to do so, especially by what are called the pirates, or private 'buses. One day, after leaving Victoria Station, a conductor is asked by a lady if he is going to the Stores (Army & Navy), and directly he roars, "Yes, lady, come, come, come." There he stands, opening out his arms to the inquirer, fair, fat and forty, who glides rapidly forward in sympathy with his words and action. Out of breath, she is hoisted up gallantly and pushed into a seat. But she has hardly had time to recover her breath when conductor sings out, "Army Navy; here we are, lady." Out she goes with a bewildered smile on her lips, and eased of a penny in the twinkling of an eye. There is something like a smile on the fat conductor's face, too. But in the vast expanse of his smile I cannot see one speck of genuine sympathy. Ah me! men were deceivers ever.

How they bustle about of an afternoon, this tribe of gay deceivers! Here stands a Peri of the pavement, in search of prey. She is past her prime. But the conductor knows her weakness, and sings out—"Come on, young lady, penny all the way to Pi'dly Circus; penny all the way." The "young lady," neither young nor lady, nevertheless pleads guilty to the soft impeachment, as she struts up to the 'bus, to be helped in by her cavalier as daintily as if she were a Princess of the Blood. She has apparently no business at Piccadilly Circus; but these attentions are worth more than a penny to our professional enchantress who has lost her charms for the wayfarer, charm she never so well.

I have said that from the top of the 'bus you often look down upon the whole world at your feet. Well, yes; but you do this with amusement rather than contempt; sometimes with pity at the contrast between poverty and wealth. Amongst all who occupy this vantage ground with you, ladies and gentlemen alike, none perhaps looks so dignified as the coachman. He is generally a robust Briton, with a rubicund face, and a heavy rug wrapped round his waist. There he sits, with his jaunty little hat inclining to one side of the head, flourishing the whip often that he seldom uses. Man and beasts understand each other quite. What a presence of mind the driver has! What eyes! What a grip! Neck to neck, and foot to foot, he makes his horses run in one close line with others, 'buses, cabs, private carriages, costermongers' barrows; and yet he avoids collision just by a scratch. Half an inch this way or that, and the whole traffic must come to a deadlock. But coachy knows his business. Not only does he avoid collision, but spares the lives and limbs of many a pedestrian that crosses his path recklessly. He smiles at them struggling to get out, and even advises them how to do this best. There he sits, monarch of all he surveys, wrapped in his old rug and a free and easy dignity which will be ruffled by little short of the insolence of a cabman or a donkey boy. He is very jealous of his dignity, and keeps all small competitors at arm's length. When the baffled cabman sometimes threatens to teach him manners, the 'bus-driver cracks his whip and advises the luckless wight to "teach yer grandmother ——" a process which the old lady knew right enough long before either of them was born. Or, he cracks a joke that sets the passengers roaring. But he is seldom put out. I have never seen coachmen behaving rudely to a woman. The conductor, too, has his humours. Once I jumped into an Earl Percy, asking if his Lordship would take me to Chesterton Road. He replies quickly, "Yes, yer Majesty, right at the foot of the road." Another time, on a very hot day, I ask conductor to find me room up top, adding in a whisper, "it smells like a beefstall down here." Conductor laughs a deep gurgling laugh, and with the words "roit ye are, sir," helps me up the steps. 'Bus riding is very pleasant, except when you have to go over rough stone pavements. Then sometimes one feels a boring sensation in his brains, after which comes the feeling as if one's brains have been reduced to a pulp. If ever I have any brains left after death (not *before*, Dr. Vivisect.) you are at liberty to test the truth of this statement.

I prefer the 'bus to the tram. The latter is too tame for my nerves, though now and again I find a quick enough conductor. One evening I get into an East-end tram, and ask conductor to take me to the bitter end. He smiles a weary smile, and adds—"Right ye are, sir, it ain't sweet." But as a rule, conductor and driver are both dull, both having a very dull time of it. And the drive itself is a dull business,—jog, jog, jog, all the way. The horses, though working on rails, are none the better used for that—their reins pulled up any moment at the call of a heartless passenger. Is it not heartless of men and women to have the poor brutes pulled up whilst going at full speed, in order to save themselves a few minutes' walk up or down where another car is approaching? Talk of societies for prevention of cruelty to animals when such brutality is practised every hour in the streets. It is a torture to man and beasts alike, and could be easily avoided by fixing stations at a few mi-

nutes' distance. But if the horses are badly treated in this respect, they have a pleasant time of
it otherwise. They are well fed and looked after,
and worked by relays. No such good luck for the
driver and the conductor. Both of them, I find,
are worked daily for seventeen to nineteen hours,
have to be mostly on their legs the whole time,
especially the conductor, and to have their meals
as best they can whilst thus serving the public and
enriching their employers. It is distressing to see
a poor fellow take his cup of tea or milk from his
wife's hand, after a long fast, snatch a kiss from
baby who leans eagerly forward to be so caressed,
and in answer to the wife's wistful look, mutter
"12," the hour at which he is to be released that
night; then resume work at the tread-mill. This
has to be done all the year round, save when the
roads are blocked with snow. Think of the two
men's discomforts, exposed as they are to the chill
air, when the passengers inside, huddled together as
they are, feel it intensely. Think also of the misery
at home, the starving and stinting of home affection,
the neglecting of children, and so on. The horses
are much better treated than these men. Indeed,
some of the employers admit this, and explain that
the horses cost them more than the men, that the
latter are less difficult to get than the former. So
it has come to this—that human beings employed
on trams, 'buses, or railway trains, are to be worked harder and treated worse than animals, in return
for the daily bread they seek to earn for themselves
and their families. In India, things seem to be

somewhat better managed, except perhaps in connection with the tramway service.

Its railroads are amongst the most familiar sights in London, just as the whistle of the engine is the most frequent sound. The passenger traffic is enormous; so also, perhaps, the traffic in goods, carried on by night trains. As a rule, one sees trains running more frequently here than in India; the lines laid down at important junctions counting by dozens. The guards and other servants are quite a contrast to our railwaymen in their behaviour—"Yes, sir; no, ma'am, yes, lady." They have to deal with an intelligent, self-respecting public. The carriages are generally more comfortable than in India. This is not much to be wondered at, seeing that the fare is double, treble, at times quadruple, of what it is in our country. One has to pay a penny here, on an average, for the distance he is carried in India for a pice or a fraction thereof. Again, if there is more comfort for the passenger in transit, there seems to be less convenience for him, from the Indian point of view. As regards speed, I believe it seldom exceeds fifty-five miles the hour. Are the eighty miles of the Flying Scotchman a myth? In some parts, for instance, of the London, Chatham and Dover, the trains cannot be run faster than ten miles an hour. This line is perhaps the slowest and the tamest I have ever used. Carriages, rolling stock, stations, all bespeak an antediluvian age, whilst the brakes often begin to proclaim the approach of doom, that is the destination, from about half a mile of the arrival, making your bones rattle and your flesh crawl. The trains disdain to be punctual, taking their leisure between thirty minutes and fifty. No fear of collisions on this line, where trains wait patiently for one another outside every second or third station. The London, Chatham and Dover has done good work in its day. But, like an invalid veteran, it is slow to move with the times. It certainly needs modernizing.

Of all modes of railway travelling, the underground seems to me to be least desirable. I have had a thousand odd trips by railway while in England, but do not remember having tried the underground more than half a dozen times. I cannot bear the dark, damp, smoke-laden tunnels. Englishmen see no harm in it; and, in order to prove their sincerity, they travel underground by the million every day. I sometimes sit musing if these good people would not travel all the same if the way from London to Edinburgh or Dublin were one continuous underground tunnel. They would very likely enjoy the travelling, and might even assure me it conduced to health. Don't they tell me, when passing a brick-field, that the odours emanating from it are rather wholesome? They may be so; but I am not going to try these smells any more than the cheap and expeditious undergrounds.

Apart from risk to health, it surprises one to hear so little about other kinds of danger—robbery and violence, whilst the train is shooting through these nether regions of sulphur and smoke. Is the credit of this freedom from somewhat inevitable danger due to the people themselves, or to the police?

No, sir, for really enjoyable travelling, give me back my bullock cart, starting at 3 A.M., halting at 9 A.M., for rest to man and beast; resuming the journey for another five hours—the traveller chatting, laughing, singing with the driver, in all of which the bullocks sometimes seem to take an intelligent part. That is life sober, to the drunken existence of your railway traveller.

**
*

Unless he can live with a decent English family, it is best for the visitor to go to a hotel. Unluckily, I could do neither, owing to my habits both as regards quality of food and the hours of taking it. One cannot intrude upon friends, except for a very short time, and even then he may upset their arrangements, whilst himself feeling like a marjoy. Hotels are too expensive for quiet people, charging about a guinea a day. This is not to be wondered at, though one often hears Indian friends make a grievance of it. The rent of a hotel is enormous, as also the current expenditure on supplies, establishment, etc. The proprietor has to live, after enabling a multitude of servants to live; and he must live like a gentleman. Besides, unless you dine at the table d'hôte, he cannot but charge you for the whole quantity of food sent up to your room. He will send up a pot of milk, with another pot of tea or coffee; bread, butter, eggs, etc. He will send you a whole chicken, a whole fish, a whole vegetable, and a whole pudding, if he has to serve you to order. It is for you to take all or part. He must charge you for the whole quantity. I do not see how you can grumble. Besides, you are a foreigner, a bird of passage, here to-day, gone to-morrow. He and his tribe naturally make the most of your stay, just as your Khansamas do with English visitors in India. To be sure, the fleecing is done on a larger scale in England than in India. But an Englishman's wants are greater than those of an Indian hotel-keeper. The same remark applies to almost all other branches of trade and business.

For most visitors to England, who wish to have some sort of home comforts without the cares of home, perhaps the best thing is to go into private family lodgings, strewn all over the country, especially over the larger towns, and maintained by respectable families, and by others.

Of the infinite variety of sign-boards that adorn the streets of London and other towns, none is more ubiquitous than "Apartments." These are suites of rooms, let out by the week generally, with or without food. Most of the "apartments" speak of a shabby-genteel existence, being kept up by wives, widows, or daughters of broken-down traders, or others who "have seen better days." The landladies try to make both ends meet by taking in lodgers. My experience of "apartments" has been none of the pleasantest. And I believe many other Indian gentlemen, especially students, have had their worst disappointments here. Not a few of the housekeepers trade upon the lodger's ignorance, pile charge upon charge for things that have never been supplied, or supplied indifferently. Their object is to get as much as they can out of the strangers, and that in the shortest space of time. I have been told of "apartments" that have a skeleton in the cupboard, more hideous than needs to be revealed in this place.

Our second "apartments," for instance, were somewhat of this kind. The landlady was generally in her cups, with a lady lodger who had the knack of mistaking other people's rooms for her own, and of waking others up by delicate knocks at the door and asking after their health. There was a gentleman lodger, too, who dined elsewhere, leaving his room early in the morning and seldom returning till twelve at night. We were served with bad food, worse cooked, and charged at a rate which a first-class hotel might be glad to secure. And though we had a comfortable suite of rooms, with a bath, we were nothing loth when Dr. B——offered to release us from this fashionable bondage with starvation.

We had a still livelier time of it at Brighton. Dr. B——and a Panjaubi friend arranged with a lady for a room at three shillings a day, and simple fare for a simple charge. We stayed there two days and a night, Crocodile and I myself; and were presented with a bill running over three pounds odd. I paid off the bill, in spite of vehement protests from Crocodile, and was taken to task by the friends for encouraging fraud. On inquiry we found that this lady was widow of a defunct tradesman. She kept "apartments" during the season at Brighton, and spent the rest of the year in London or the country, as daugther of a gentleman at large.

Our first "apartments" were our best, let by a

quiet respectable family of florists. They keep a large house, and let out a portion. Mrs. M——, the landlady, is an excellent cook, having worked for the G——and the S——families. She made me as comfortable a home as I could expect, and I never grudged her extra items for extra dishes to coax a jaded appetite. Mrs. M. and I got on very well. But, somehow, she could not bear the sight of Crocodile. She called him a "hox," complaining that he ate "ever so much more" than I, and "never said so much as thank ye;" also that he went about half dressed. The two were so often at loggerheads that I had at last to leave "apartments" No. 1, to my lasting regret. I did not find another Mrs. M——in London. She had a large family, by a former husband as well as by the present, the eldest girl being under forty, the youngest boy about four. And yet she managed all the household affairs, did the marketing and the cooking herself, and gave me the best tea I have had in London, at six every morning—a luxury to me, before which other meals are hardly worth mentioning.

The family lived in peace and contentment; never a cross word did I hear from young or old. Mrs. M——'s second or third daughter, Annie, was a quiet, self-contained little lady, with a very fine devotional nature, fond of music, and a total abstainer. Living in the house, she hardly seemed to belong to it. She "minded" her father's flower-shop, but appeared to be more fit for a convent. Will Annie ever come out to India as a "Salvation lass"? She is too quiet for that. During our first drive to the bank and to the doctor's she unfolded to me a page or two of English domestic life, which has left a very sombre impression on my mind. Poor Annie! She felt for her sex, though disclaiming all sympathy with the shrieking sisterhood.

The girl of the house, however, was Maggie (to call her after her country's manner), a strapping Scotch lassie who had come to "Lunnun," she said, for the fun of it. Fancy the daughter of a respectable farmer taking service for the fun of it! I suppose the madcap did not like the dull monotony of a farm-house, and was fond of excitement. Mrs. M——had a very kindly feeling for her, and let her have her own way when not busy. Maggie made a capital maid-of-all-work. That girl never walked but jumped. Going up or down the steps she took half a dozen at a time. Crocodile stood in awe of her for the first few days, believing she was touched in the head. To me it was a sight to see her heaving up, like a steam-engine, with broom and mop and duster. At such times I greeted her as My Lady Margaritta Honoria Montgomery Tibs, walking up in her court dress. She would laugh at the conceit, supporting herself on the broomstick, till she shook the room from corner to corner. An honest, hearty, motherly girl was Maggie, in spite of her oddities. She never shrank from any work. The first evening she took hold of my boot, to pull it off, I objected. She laughed at the objection, explaining that she had to do it for all lodgers every day of her life. I told her, in our country we never suffered girls to do that, and I would not do so anywhere. This rather puzzled her. One day Maggie seemed to be fagged, and I asked her mistress to let her rest. Mrs. M——— spoke to her to this effect in my presence, when she jumped up with an hysterical explanation, " Poor girls have no business to be ill." That was the only bitter thought 1 heard expressed by this happy-go-lucky creature, full of life and animation.

Maggie had one weakness—love of finery and gadding about—like most girls of her class. She had two holidays in the week, and spent them with her friends or her " young man," a Scotch sailor who had given up the sea for her sake, and had followed her to London. Mrs. M———said she had presents from the poor fellow worth £ 20, in dresses and trinkets ; and yet, somehow, she tried to evade and avoid him. One day I spoke to her seriously, urging what a chance she was throwing away ; that it was cruel to her lover and unjust to herself to go on like that ; that it was far better to become the wife of an honest fellow, who loved her, than " a lady " about town and a servant-girl in apartments. She listened to me, weeping quietly, and then sobbed out the explanation that she could not make up her mind, because some of the girls had told her marriage " spoiled a girl in no time," and that her lover was rather dark. What notions for a girl in her position ! There may be hundreds in London, who are led away by such notions. I tried to laugh her out of the folly. A day or two after, we left Mrs. M———. When I looked in again to say good-bye, the landlady said Maggie had gone, in all likelihood, to make up with her young man. If this turns out so, it will be one of the matches of which I shall be very proud.

Speaking generally, one may find he has to spend a sovereign, on an average, in London, to a rupee that he should have to spend in Bombay. In a rough way the two coins may represent the wealth of the respective countries. If the proportion is too high, it may be so, partly on account of inexperience, partly because one is not a careful spender. This latter defect I suffer from wherever I live, but it is easily met by the manner of living—little meat, no wine or cigar, no theatre, no drawing-room, no dress, to speak of.

I have, however, seen Indian gentlemen in London, managing it much under the scale quoted. One Parsee lady, who is living here with her children, says she does not find much difference between London and Bombay; and that, on the whole, life is more enjoyable in London for about the same expenses that you incur at Bombay. Later on, while living with Dr. B——, I find it is not impossible to realize this modest little ideal. But it entails constant watchfulness, and a thorough mastery of the details of what they call prices current. It also means buying things wholesale, and saving cab fares by making light of time generally. For those who have settled down in London, the living need not be much more expensive than in India. But house-rent, and rates and taxes swallow up a goodly fraction of the out-goings.

A visitor may spend little on fares and other out-door sundries, if he is not pushed for time. But he cannot save time and silver likewise. Under Dr.

B——'s guidance I have tried various expedients. I have taken up Bradshaw, railway guides, maps, etc., with headache as a general result, and previous confusion of ideas worse confounded. My bump of topography is very defective, and often, after ridiculous blundering, I have got the 'bus to carry me off to the wrong place. I cannot bear underground travelling, nor a crowded train, which sends me into fever. As a compromise, therefore, I sometimes walk on straight so far as I can, with the constables in sight, and then hail a cab for short distances, if tired or out of time. Fares and postage stamps are amongst the heaviest items of my expenditure in England, as they are in India.

House-rent in the City is something inconceivable for us. A large warehouse fetches as much as £ 20,000 a year, that is Rs. 360,000. I doubt if it would fetch Rs. 1,000 a year at Bombay, or Rs. 100 a year at Surat. A small tea-shop in King William Street, with kitchen below, pays £ 800 a year for rent, that is Rs. 15,000. At Delhi or Agra you can buy a palace outright for less than that. As you pass the Exchange you read the words—" The Earth is the Lord's and the fulness thereof." No mistake about this sentiment, if, by the word *Lord* you mean the Englishman's God. Within an easy radius of its Exchange London may claim the overlordship of almost the whole of the commercial world. Verily, as Crocodile once remarked, rushing out of a shop in Piccadilly, " everything is *hot* in London."

My *Appeal from the Daughters of India* has cost a great deal more in trouble and money than its size and substance may seem to justify. I write it out at one sitting. It is quite an effort. I give a whole day to revising the draft before sending it to a printer for estimate. The rough estimate, nine shillings a page, takes my breath away. I have to go to three printers with Crocodile before I could have the job accepted at three shillings a page. A good deal of time is spent in receiving and revising proofs. Meanwhile, the friends who are to be consulted are about to leave town. In feverish anxiety I manage to send off proofs to these friends. But many of them are already off, like the unscrupulous holiday-makers that they are, promising to return proofs from the country. Days are lost in this way, and when the proofs come back there is a fresh difficulty to cope with. I find myself a victim of the proverbial multitude of counsels. Several of the friends have to be interviewed; two of them take five interviews between them, and as many letters each, before they could make up their minds to subscribe generally to the proposals embodied in the tract. By the time the revised proofs are ready, the printer finds it will be easier for him to set the matter over again. Nearly a month and a half passes since "copy" was first given to the printer, before I get the final proofs. The copies are ready in less than a week—folded, wrapped and addressed by a dozen pair of hands. Then arises a new difficulty—the tract exceeds the regulation weight. This is too much for my patience. In desperation I resolve to use a double stamp for each of the 5,000 copies. But the Postmistress kindly suggests a way out of

o

this heavy liability. Send all the copies to the baker, and have them kept in his oven—in the process of drying the weight may be reduced. Happy thought! Dr. B——clutches at it. I yield, but with an aching heart. Poor daughters of India! poor child-wives and child-widows! As if you hadn't passed sufficiently long through a fiery ordeal! Poor orphans, bear a little more for my sake. This may be the last act in the drama of your lifelong Suttee. Never mind the trouble and pain to me. You are all the dearer to me for the suffering you cause. I love you with a mother's love.

So the ruthless Doctor carries off the *Daughters of India* to the baker's, I stipulating piteously that none but the baker's wife shall bake them for the British public. Are our troubles at an end now? Not quite. The copies posted to the House of Commons are accepted. But the Clerk to the House of Lords declines to forward them unless we redirect each of the copies. That takes another night of torture.

*_**

If the English are a nation of shop-keepers, they are on the whole very honest for the character given them by Napoleon. Not that they have more scruples than others in making the razor that will sell— whether it shaves or no, it is for the buyer to find out. They are shrewd business men, eager to push their wares, to make money and to retire as fast as they can on a competency, to live as gentlemen at large. Small shop-keepers are about the same everywhere.

Dr. B—— buys me a pair of boots, on the express condition that they shall be quiet. But they begin to squeak within a quarter of an hour of the first wear. The worthy doctor thereupon goes up to the shopman and reads him a heart-rending sermon on the evils of selling goods under false pretences. The man listens patiently, and then stammers something like this apology:—"I am very sorry, sir, but if I am to stick to the truth always my master will kick me out. He pays me for *selling* the stock. How can I turn away a customer honestly? And, after all, what do *you* gain by my telling the truth? The next shop will sell you the boots as much with a lie. You gain nothing by my truth-telling, while I lose my custom, and very likely my place. The only party that gains is at the next shop; and he gains by telling the same lie for which you condemn me."

Is not there a ring of truthfulness in this false arguing? There is considerable force in it, at any rate. The man undertakes to stop the noise in his boots; and two days after returns them packed in a showy cask, swearing they are " all right." We find, however, he could do nothing to them, save packing them in the case. Having meant them for sale, perhaps he wishes us to keep them for show. The fact is, he cannot afford to tell the truth. It is as much as his place is worth. He is not so much to blame as his employer; and the latter may be less to blame than the public who want cheap things as well as good. Not a little of sharp practice at shops is due to this hankering for bargains.

I buy an umbrella for a guinea, which shows holes

innumerable within a week. I want an estimate
for a little printing which is to be done sharp,
and the estimate sent is three times higher than
the price for which I get the job done at a larger
press. Such sharp practice is very common in London, especially when you are not on your guard.
Look the shopman squarely in the face, and let
him understand that you understand him. Again,
keep well within the terms of your bargain. If
you want just a little more of this or that, you
will have just a little too much to pay all round.
The Englishman dislikes waiting upon an uncertain customer, and will make him pay "through the
nose." The best way to deal with an English rough
who is inclined to be vicious, whether at the shop
or in the street, is to knock him down before he
has the chance of serving you the same way. You
may give him your hand when he is down, and he
will like you all the more on getting up. On the
other hand, if you give him an advantage to start
with, you must be prepared for one of the hard-
est knocks you ever got.

In well-regulated business establishments you have
fixed rates to go upon, every article marked with
its price. This price may be very stiff, but, as I
have explained, everything is dearer here than in
the East—material, labour, living, etc. As to the
rest, nowhere in the world, perhaps, does business
morality stand so high as amongst the better class
of merchants, bankers, shipowners in England. Of
course, there are black sheep everywhere, and in
every business. A dishonest business man in Lon-

don is out and out the blackest sheep in devildom. But considering their enormous business relations with the world, it is a wonder we do not hear more about failures and frauds and embezzlements amongst the English.

Personally, I am not fond of your over-strict sabbatarians in business. They live as patterns of piety, as marvels of morality. But there is an air of unnaturalness about them, that repels one. Some of them go to church thrice on the Sabbath, and after the usual forty winks return to the well-ordered meal or the siesta. They will do nothing for the poor, will not allow others to do anything, it being Sunday. I wonder if they remember Christ's words to the pious "fool." My favourite business people are Quakers. Pity there are not more of them in business. Is the Society of Friends declining?

The more familiar tricks of trade, as practised everywhere at shops, are underweighing the articles sold, mixing them with others of an inferior quality, showing one quality at the window and giving another. Of the wholesale adulteration and spurious manufacture of wine, sugar, preserves, tea, cheese, butter, etc., London is supposed to enjoy a very fair monopoly. But there are sharp practices sacred to the London shop-keeper, which will bear the telling. One of these is to reduce the prices in order to catch the eye of the ignorant. What is the amount of reduction? A farthing, a halfpenny, or a whole penny where the figure stands high—1s. 11d., 3s. 4d., 2s. 11d., 1s. 2d., 5s. 11d., just an apology of a fraction to get rid of "our summer goods." A more ambitious plan is to offer a pony, a bicycle, a cow or some such bait, for so many tickets you may have collected at the end of a fixed period, indicating the extent of your dealings with a particular shop. On the day fixed, the pony or the cow is decked with flowers and ribbons, made to parade the streets, and then formally presented to the holder of the largest number of tickets. The recipient knows not that the cost of the present has been more than recouped by short weights, bad qualities, etc., ranging over a six months' custom. The present is a delusion and a snare. These are but a few samples of the sharp practice noticed by me.

Comparing the Indian shop-boy with the English, one finds very little to choose between them, except perhaps that while the former is more or less flurried in lying, the latter generally lies at his ease. In London you usually find a cool hand at the counter. The English shop-boy tells you a lie with lofty unconcern, passing one article off for another. He lies unflinchingly; tells a lie and sticks to it, unless you catch him tripping; and then he will whimper an apology, if no one is by. The Scotch boy can tell as round a lie as anybody, with this to his credit as shop-boy, that nothing will make him confess, even if you tear him limb from limb. The Irish shop-boy is easier to deal with. His lies are so loud, you need not prick up your ears to catch them. His very generosity leads him into excesses. He is not an accurate scientific liar. My advice to Indian visitors dealing with shop-boys in London is to use despatch as well as decision. Don't higgle; don't ask for discount, pleading "I come from India," &c. That will make matters worse for you. Such higgling will often provoke giggling among the girls behind, besides making the boys stare at you rudely.

My impressions of London shop-girls in this respect are more favourable. Whether at the shop, the open stall or booth, or in the restaurant, they have, as a rule, dealt fairly with the stranger, sometimes generously. Poor little things!—hungering for a kind look, a kind word, which they seldom get. How they hover about you, clearing the table, holding up the things you want, explaining the difference between them, sometimes venturing upon a bit of advice! Poor, weary, ill-paid drudges! What a mistake you are! What a freak of fortune! I almost wish at times the law allowed infanticide at the birth of girls like you.

It is not unusual to see English boys and girls amusing themselves in a manner that might take one's breath away. Climbing trees and walls, rolling down the slopes of hills, skating, jumping across bars and through hoops—these are some of the common amusements for children of tender years. Boxing and wrestling belong to the same order of amusement, in which the wild beast peeps occasionally out of the British nature. When English boys or men fight in earnest, they seem for the moment, like Nelson, to know not what fear is; they cannot think of consequences. Children show the same pluck at a very early age, the same impulse and resource. One day I saw at Brixton Station a trotter of hardly three, rushing after an express train which would not stop for him and his sister. The girl had to pursue and to hold him back by main force. But I suppose the little fellow felt he was quite within his rights, and perhaps wanted to butt at the engine in order to arrest its progress. It is neither possible nor desirable for children in India to act like this *enfant terrible*, but I wish the same impulse might sometimes seize our children of a larger growth when pursuing a career of usefulness to themselves and their country.

What has been said above applies generally to town life. In the country it is sometimes very different. I have a little bumpkin in the house, whose courage seldom goes beyond blubbering whenever the street arabs take him in hand. There is hardly anything to choose between this Hodge in Lunun town and our Bhagla at Mumbai Bunder.

In the course of an omnibus ride through Edgware Road, one evening, I see a row of carriages before me, moving slowly along. It is a miscellaneous crowd of cabs, hansoms, waggons, wheelbarrows and private carriages, large and small, many of them drawn by a pair. The coachmen crack their whips and swear at some one in front, but they make no better progress for all that. I ask the driver what this means, and he explains that the traffic has been blocked by a costermonger "standin' on his roits." He directs my glance beyond the carriages, and there I see a miserable looking boy driving a wee little donkey, looking more woe-begone than himself, to which has been attached a sort of basket, little larger than what is used by a regimental mess in India. He happens to be in the middle of the crowd, and he sticks to his rights, regardless of the vehement protests flung after him by the minions of wealth and fashion. The sight becomes exciting as a crowd gathers to cheer the costermonger's boy. At last, one of the coachmen, losing his temper, yells out—"Look 'ere, Radishes, 'ow long are ye goin' to crawl alon' of this blessed road?" The costermonger's boy, who is smoking his pipe serenely, gets up, and putting the finger to the tip of his nose, slaps it with the other hand—which means, I suppose, "I don't care this rap for you all." The crowd of boys and girls cry *hurrah!* Stately coachman collapses.

*
* *

Never having been to a theatre or a dancing saloon in England, I cannot say how much of the bad odour associated with these haunts of public amusement is due to prejudice. But, the best of them excepted, theatres in every large town are likely to do more harm than good. Author, manager and actor have often to consult a low taste, a mawkish sentiment; sometimes to create these.

The posturing of men and women for hire, the getting up of what is unreal in nature, and merely artificial in art, cannot but affect the common run of play-goers injuriously. As an index to the reputation they enjoy, one has to see that not a few of the theatres and dancing-halls in London stand in the back slums, not far from taverns, public-houses and similar resorts of doubtful utility. The smaller of such establishments have a tendency to gravitate towards the theatres. A moist tongue is fit companion to a moist eye; and the two give their owner a soft moist brain which acts as readily on his lachrymal as on his risible faculties.

Girls of tender years are generally impressed for the ballet, perchance seduced by flattery, intoxicated by applause, and thus in some cases rendered insensible to the claims of modesty. I have observed a nascent protest against this particular species of public amusement, and am inclined to think it will work for good.

Amongst indirect results of an excessive love of the stage, no less serious than the foregoing, are late hours, in all kinds of weather, stimulants, late rising, bad health and worse temper, neglect of children, diseases like consumption, and so on.

But it would be absurd to suggest this as a complete picture in itself. There is the other side to it; at least there are a good many redeeming features.

The theatre is a national institution. Neither sermon nor law can do much to suppress this form of popular excitement. The best way is to provide counter-excitements, healthy, natural amusements. The English cannot do without their plays. If they can't have plays of the right sort, they will put up with the wrong sort.

* *
*

An inordinate desire to make the largest fortune within the shortest space of time appears to culminate here in a rage for circulars and advertisements. Englishmen spend millions of pounds on these, in order to push their business all over the world. I should not be surprised if they spent more on manufacturing these veracious circulars and advertisements than on manufacturing their equally trustworthy wares. It pays them—that is all they care for. Good men of business, these advertisers of the West !

Every trade, every industry, every art in London floods the streets with its circulars, advertisements, and handbills. It litters walls, windows, pavements, making the thoroughfares hideous with large, loud, staring type. Railway stations are covered over with trade notices, so much so, that it is with difficulty a stranger can find out the name of the station he is to get out at. He finds everything else there but the name-board he wants. Tram-cars, 'buses, stalls, waggons, wheel-barrows, even match-boxes, are clothed with flashy advertisements. Nay, these are, as a rule, smuggled into the package you bring home from the market—fruit, biscuit, fish, eggs, pastry— all reeking, as it were, with the smell of specious advertisements.

Look at this placard, representing a bull—a splendid animal—about to be, or in the act of being, killed,—with the large words explaining—"Over 60,000 slaughtered annually for Bouillon Fleet," a stuff to make soup with. Whether it makes anything like soup, it is for the purchaser to find out. What I am baffled to understand is that men and women should stand admiring the sight.

You may see scores of men, sometimes hundreds of boys, in a procession, tricked out in all colours and costumes, parading the steeets every day, with advertisements stuck on to their hats, the front and back of their coats, and so on. How piteous is the sight of these peripatetic human advertisements! What is it but shame for a man to expose himself thus ? But the men seem to be less to blame than their employers and the public generally. Is it not cruel to put the image of God to such uses? No sight repels one so much as this, and that of the black minstrels, English lads dressed like negroes, their faces covered with soot and grease, all but the lips—which makes them look like lepers. It sickens me to see one of the latter dancing and jabbering before a crowd. Why, the collier is a prince and a hero by the side of this ragamuffin of a knave. To think that his antics should pass for fun !

Another kind of advertisement may be seen some-times in the figures of women posted here, there, and everywhere. The prints represent the women, standing or sitting in various postures, all but naked. Indeed, the very slight covering used in order to elude a stupid law makes the figure more hideous in its suggestiveness than if it were quite nude. All this is done in broad daylight, not only to invite the lewd to the dancing or swimming bout, but also the unwary to a purchase of worthless articles. Oh, London, London, what is to be the end of thy ethics of business ?

This reminds one of what euphemists are pleased to call " living pictures." What are these but adver-tisements for the benefit of the stage manager or his company ? It is well for society that recent protests against such exhibitions of flesh and blood have proved effective. It shows that sportive London is not quite without conscience. And what about the display of nude art? Can nothing be done to avert this holocaust on the altar of high art? There is no need, and certainly no defence, for some of the pictures one sees exhibited in odd corners of London. If artists and lovers of art cannot live without these, let the artless masses, at least, be saved a sight that corrupts their taste as well as morals. Think of artists, that is poets, having to set the eye of flesh on fleshly images before they can reproduce them on canvass or in stone. What creative power, and how pure! Think of the law allowing this basest form of slavery in the name of freedom of contract. What free contract can be possible between the wealthy and well-patronised artist and his starving model? Crude painting or sculpture of this kind is as much a perversion of art as is rash vivisection of science. Is there no guild of artists in London? Where is its Church, where is its State, where is its vaunted Public Opinion?

Here is a lady's advertisement:—" A beautiful silver set, bought for £ 30 only a fortnight ago. Owner going away. Anxious to *give* it to a *lady* for eight guineas." Women rush after the offer. Can't they see that the original seller himself would be glad to have it back for £ 20?

There goes a draper's circular, offering to send you a parcel of " beautifully assorted dresses for mother and baby. Could not have it under £ 5; we will send it to you for one guinea cash, prepaid. This is our clearance sale."

Perhaps the most tempting circular I have seen is this, received in July, 1891, in tip-top business form, duly dated and signed :—

"Sir,—Having a very large capital at my disposal, I am prepared to make *immediate cash* advances to any amount on note of hand simply. All communications treated in the very strictest confidence."

What a windfall ! Why, I could marry off all my widows in India with the "large capital" for "immediate cash" on "a note of hand simply." I would not insist upon "the very strictest" or any other kind of "confidence." I consult Dr. B—— about it, and find the bait is no better than it should be. These philanthropic financiers may never advance you anything in cash or kind. But they may make some friendly advances to you after you have been entrapped by their overtures. They may ask for consultation, stamp, registration, and other fees, putting off the real "advance" day after day. They may make you pay for the lawyer's draft, and may then wriggle out at the last moment. Give "on note of hand"? If ever they do give, they give on nothing short of security in gold, silver, house, or furniture, at exorbitant rates, and with a tendency to foreclose. Many a widow and boarding house keeker has been thus driven upon the streets, after the harrowing experience referred to. No, no, give me my much-abused Marwari money lender, though he and I have never yet shaken hands.

I am told, however, of a good deal of *bonâ fide* business done in London this way, which circulars and advertisements as a rule only caricature.

It is not a little humiliating to reflect that the newspaper press should allow itself, though indirectly, to aid and abet this spread of falsehood and indecency through advertisements. I can say so consistently, having refused to accept trade notices and advertisements about patent medicines, patent only in their glitter of shame. But, on the whole, it is creditable to the press that the more respectable portion thereof do not admit notices that are flagrantly misleading; and that, as a rule, they do not honour them with editorial attention.

What a power the Newspaper Press of England is! Perhaps the greatest power of our times—greater than church, greater than state, if it will only know how to use itself. As it is, the Press declares wars, and concludes peace. It makes and mars ministries. It exercises an almost super-regal power over royalty. But it is powerful for evil as much as for good. For good or for evil, however, it is a power to be reckoned with. I do not see why they still call it the Fourth Estate. Let us hope, at least, it will deserve in time a higher title. God guide the counsels of the British Press! I owe so much to it, that it is easy to forget any shortcomings it may have. Its instincts are generally sound, though swayed by policy. I think the British Press helps more in stimulating than in educating public opinion. And some of its very faults, in politics and religion, seem to add to its power of stimulating the opinion of the country. Long live the Press of England!

The same shall I say of the Press in India, Anglo-Indian and Native. Long may it live!—fighting, and blundering, and sometimes plundering; but often showing its teeth to tyranny. With all its short-comings, what a stride the vernacular press has taken during my brief experience of fifteen years! What ideas of public journalism we used to have in the early eighties! I remember having read an announcement, in all the honours of editorial type, somewhat to this effect:—"Our *this* (wife) having taken ill, our daughter Javer had to bring us a can of hot water. Unfortunately, she upset the can and scorched herself badly. We had to attend to this and other troubles, and could not come out in time last week. The reader will, please, excuse." Who could think of publishing such an apology in the year of grace 1891? Not the smallest print, done in the obscurest corner of the mofussil.

The Press in India is getting on very well on the whole; and the cry to gag it seems to be amazingly idiotic. I say this without hesitation, though few have smarted, as I have, under the stings of the mosquitos of the Native Press. Of course, there are bad papers in India, as there are in England, backed by worse men from behind the scenes. If the public have a quarrel with these, they will know how to settle it. Government, or their officials, have really little to fear from them. But if they violate the canons of public criticism too much, or otherwise abuse their liberty, it is open to Government to withdraw their subscription, to strike out their names from their annual report, and to stop the supply of official information to them. Beyond this I do not see what the State can do with advantage.

The aggrieved official may prosecute a libeller, as any private individual can. The revival of a Gagging Act is out of the question. Lord Ripon wrote it off as a bad legacy, never again to be bequeathed to his successors.

Among other things, Lord Dufferin once complained to me at Simla of the attitude of a section of the Native Press towards his Government. He spoke as an aggrieved parent would speak of spoilt children. I explained that, coming after an extremely popular Viceroy, he must expect to be victimized to a certain amount of misgiving; that newspaper opinion did not always represent public opinion. I also advised a friendly chat with proprietors of the more respectable journals, whenever possible, besides putting them in possession, as far as might be, of the aims and objects of Government. There was some talk at that time of starting a Government organ,—in order to set things right with the public. I felt this might prove to be a remedy worse than the disease. The carpers would go on carping all the same, and discrediting the utterances of an accredited organ all the more effectively. Besides, Government have their weekly *Gazette* for purposes of information.

Whilst venturing to advise successive Governments to this effect I have never missed an opportunity of bringing home to the Native Press a sense of the sacredness of their office. They enjoy a most enviable position. They must use it well if they wish to benefit their country. It is as much to the British love of freedom as to their own merits that they owe this position. They must remember that the press in India enjoys greater liberty than the press on the Continent of Europe generally. Look at Russia, for instance. "The progress of Russia" is all very well to conjure with. But directly you come in contact with it, you may find that the magician's wand turns to a knout. Dost know what a knout is, my brother? I had rather poor India perished under the sword than lived under the knout. So dip not thy pen in gall, my knight of the goose-quill.

The ordinary newspaper in London seems to be run much more upon business principles than I expected. True to its name, it goes in greedily for news—telegrams, special reports, and things—employing a large staff for the purpose, and issuing several editions daily, with one sensation or other for each edition. If the poor hacks cannot find news, why, I suppose they must make it. In short, the cheap newspaper seems to live on *publicity run mad*. Whatever the advantages of this plan, its drawbacks are certainly more serious. What is the good of reports of divorce suits, with their unsavoury details, of other scandals and crimes, of suicides and murders, every circumstance of which is clothed in ghastly realism and appears under bold black headings? Whatever good there may be in the thing is more than neutralized by the widespread mischief it causes amongst the people. It must lead inevitably to a depraved public taste and imitation in evil-doing. How often do we see servant-girls and shop-boys poring over Police Court reports? This is the dark side of po-

pular journalism in London. Respectable journals
do not encourage the system of newsmongering, and
their leaders are master-pieces in their way, though
often disfigured by party spirit. For vitality and re-
sourcefulness the native Indian Press cannot be
mentioned in the same breath with the Press in
England.

As in making, so also in selling the newspaper,
the English have an immense advantage over us in
India. They sell by tens and hundreds of thousands, to our paltry hundreds. Thousands of men
and women and children are engaged daily, not only
for distribution from door to door, but in selling the
copies at railway stalls, in the 'bus, the tram-cars,
etc. You sometimes find boys and girls of hardly
six, rushing off with fresh editions, and spreading
their placards in odd corners of the thoroughfares,
shout the contents and drive a roaring trade for the
hour. They jump up the 'bus going full speed, and
after hawking the paper for a few minutes, jump
down in order to catch another 'bus. Each has to
sell some fifty copies before he can make fourpence
to carry him through the night. Poor little orphan
of the press! I cannot get him out of my mind for
weeks.

As for despatch, I have only to mention a boy
running up to my carriage at Newcastle between 2
and 3 A.M., with the familiar cry of "Mornin' papear"
long before it is morning. This is taking time by
the forelock.

⁎

Her enterprise is the making of England, and her

P 2

organization the proof thereof. Look at some of her Exhibitions. The best are said to have been those managed by public citizens, and partially subsidized by the State.

Beginning with the great Exhibition, opened by the Prince Consort in 1851, of which they have a living memento in the Crystal Palace, the Londoners count about a dozen of these national shows of which they are justly proud. The Fishery, Health, Inventions, and the Colonial and Indian Exhibitions, owe much of their success to the Prince of Wales. Following in the steps of his renowned father, who will be best remembered, perhaps, as the patron of these immensely popular movements, H. R. H. worked on the committees harder than many other members. As a result, these Exhibitions were most successful. Then came the Danish, the Italian, the French, the Irish Exhibitions, meeting with more or less success; followed by the Military, the Naval and the German Exhibitions. Most of these latter groups seem to have been managed by private companies, with an eye to business. They could hardly prove such an unqualified success as the former. But still, they have been witnessed by millions, with no less profit to the promoters than instruction and amusement to the public.

I am myself a poor sight-seer, very shy of crowds, and with but little leisure on hand. For years I have given up sight-seeing on purpose, as also study and culture. Human progress is my only study now; human nature my only interest. Besides, I have weakened my eyesight, not so much by consuming the midnight oil as by straining the eyes in search of beauty in nature and art. How long have I watched the moon courting the sea; the stars frisking and gambolling in the silver sky; the wind playing, with pity or passion, to the hill, the river, the streamlet, abashed by his boisterous wooing. To climb mountain sides, in order to catch the sun peeping out of his cerulean chamber, or to witness his unwilling entry into it, to the music of birds, and the dancing of beasts around—to lose myself in solitary rambles, keeping the eye on the rack for hours—this was the delight of my earlier days. But I overdid it, and have had to bear the consequences. My eyesight was given to me not merely for my own selfish enjoyment. What is one's knowledge of art, science, literature, if acquired for himself at the expense of the most precious gift of life? I see my mistake, perhaps too late for myself, but not for others.

Don't I use glasses? Of course I do, as a necessary evil. The wearing of them is no pleasure, nor do I use them in pursuit of pleasure. My glasses are reserved for business. I can't bear to use them when looking at a pretty face or picture: they show blemishes in beauty. I want my ideals to be perfect; prefer to believe them so. What has one left to admire if even his ideals begin to show flaws? Besides, the extravagance and venality of art drive one more and more to puritanism as he grows.

Thus it is, that I am seldom drawn to art galleries and shows. But I make a point of visiting the Naval and the German Exhibitions. The latter interests me more, though in saying so I run the risk of displeasing some of my readers. It has more variety, more general interest. The German band is a novelty to me, so are the German faces, and lastly, the German exhibits. The Naval appears to be on a smaller scale. The Panorama of the Battle of Trafalgar disappoints me. But that apart, it is a thoroughly representative show, of which the English may well be proud. And they are, you may be sure. Don't they go to it in crowds?—men and women and children, from prince to peasant, from Dowager Duchess to dancing girl; grandma with H'anna's youngest baby in her arms, grandpa with his little ducky in the perambulator; old and young, rich and poor, healthy and invalid; all gazing, chattering, laughing, drinking, munching cake or fruit before your eyes! Yes, sir, making love to each other, and looking saucily at you if you happen to be a marjoy! Come in, ladies and gentlemen, there is ample accommodation for you all, more than enough attraction. What with the exhibits, parades, drills, music, and working of machines; what with the food and drink available, not one of you need remain uninterested, nor go away disappointed. There is life for you all, lively enough to prove the death of your distracted critic. And above all, there are the inevitable advertisements, telling all the lies that liar ever told without coming into the clutches of a lie-encouraging law.

One of the most striking instances of European organization, that I witnessed in London during my third visit, was "Constantinople"—that is, a reproduction in the Metropolis, of the capital of Turkey.

Properly speaking, it was a panorama of Eastern and Western Civilizations at their best. Having heard much about this grand exhibition, I induce Dr. B. one morning to take me over to it. He yields so far as to accompany me to the door, but then turns away, dragging me back with him. He has been offended by something, unknown to me. "This is no place for us," he decides; and away we drive again homewards. It is a weary long drive. The same week I happen to meet a Parsi friend who, on hearing of my misadventure, insists upon taking me to "Constantinople." He has seen it, and is simply in raptures over it. I ask Dr. B. to let me have a look at the forbidden show, which he does, not without much ado, and not till our Parsi friend tells him he is depriving me of one of the most memorable sights London could show that year. Well, so we are off next morning. Whilst my friend is buying the tickets I take a look round, and see several clergymen, and two nuns, emerging from the theatre. Surely, it cannot be so bad a place, after this. I take heart of grace, and enter, bent upon making the best of it. The very first sight repays all the trouble, expense and struggles with conscience. What a sight it is! The whole of the gorgeous East, instinct with life, spread out before the spectator. It is a marvel and a mystery of art, which even the most sanguine imagination could hardly have been prepared for. Apart from the scenery—the warmth and variety of the East sobering down to the solid monotony of the West, and this dull uniformity of the West again catching

the glow and versatility of the East—the diversity
of tongues and of costumes, of manners and customs, is bewildering. It is like one fairy scene
succeeding another, and striking the spectator with
the magic of its power and its beauty. Pageants and
processions chase one another, representing almost
all nationalities of Asia and Europe, their music,
their costumes; their everyday life, in short, at home
and in the market place, from prayers down to
drinking bouts. How perfect is the representation
of men and women, both as regards the age and
the country; as also the part each has to play!
And the horses, the camels and other animals—
how well trained these are! There is not one flaw
that I could detect in the get up of the whole. As
the Persian procession comes on, and forms itself
into a Durbar, my heart jumps for joy. It is a real
Iranian Durbar, as sung by Firdousi. Then come
Cairo, Alexandria, Constantinople, from the public
street to the private zenana with its inmates charm-
ingly reproduced—and the Thousand Pillars. Oh
wondrous organization! Will India ever show it?
I am afraid it is not in her genius. The only thing
that jars upon my nerves, here and there, is that the
profane comes too soon after the sacred. As we leave
our seats reluctantly, I thank my friend for the
treat. Not for the world—or its opinion—would I
miss such a sight.

The same friend inveigles me into the Aquarium
one afternoon, with the assurance that it is "all
right." I join him without Dr. B.'s permission, in
fact, without his knowledge; and am well punished

for it. Not that I see anything that is positively bad. There is a good deal of daring performance by men and women—jumping, swinging, swimming; some clever sleight of hand, mimicry, ventriloquism. But somehow, the sights wound whatever little artistic sense I possess, apart from moral sensibility. The Aquarium is a place I would not visit a second time. Thus I make up my mind as I clear out and go straight to the Doctor for confession. He does not throw up his arms, but asks mildly how my neuralgic pains are. This question is a crusher, coming on the top of my self-abasement.

Among the sights that interest me most in London are Westminster Abbey, the Houses of Parliament, St. Paul's Cathedral, the Crystal Palace, Hampton Court, the South Kensington Museum of Natural History, the Art Gallery, the British Museum, Madame Tussaud's Exhibition, and the Zoological Gardens. The Abbey, as well as the Cathedral, rather falls short of my expectation. But both are striking enough, and their associations invest them with a grandeur of their own. The interior is adorned with fine statues, worth study, and worthy of a pilgrimage from the East. As works of art, however, they hardly come up to similar collections on the Continent. The absence of the painter's skill, again, is keenly felt here, as one is reminded of the conspicuous part that branch of art plays in the decoration of places of worship elsewhere. Nor is it cheering to see the fair sex jealously shut out of these sacred national walhallas. There is not a single bust in the Abbey or the Cathedral, that I could see, devoted to the memory of a woman. This omission cannot be accidental. If it is designed, it may be taken as another instance of the disfavour with which Mother Church has viewed the liberation of her daughters from religious thraldom. Is it not too late now to deny that there have been women in England, worthy of a place side by side with some of their illustrious countrymen whom they (the women) have aided materially in winning a niche in the Temple of Fame?

My visit to the House of Commons is very brief. Two friendly Members take me in to the Strangers' Gallery and point out some of our common acquaintances addressing the House. I cannot see their faces, and hear the voice of but two of them, discussing a rather technical point. Shortly after, my friends bring over several other Members, and two Ministerial guns, who give me a hearty salute. We have some desultory talk, and part with mutual regret, promising to meet again. I feel somehow oppressed by the hum of voices, and leave the gallery with a sense of relief. In other parts of the House I have more than once had consultations with friends.

My visit to the Lords is equally brief, and even less formal. It happens to be the afternoon of the Manipur Debate, though I go there to meet a friend whom there is small chance of catching elsewhere before long. Lord Ripon opens the debate, calm and self-possessed as ever, but with the same dauntless courage that marked his Viceregal career. No Englishman, who ever came to India, has clung to her interests with such tenacity. Lord Ripon makes some very good points in the course of his speech this afternoon, and is evidently seeking to strengthen the bands of the Government of India. This the other side cannot see; or, is it that they see through more than I can? Lord Cross gives a reassuring answer, and combats one or two of the mover's arguments. Lord Kimberley tries to pour oil over troubled waters, or rather waters that are about to be troubled. Perhaps he reads something in the Duke of Argyll's face, that bodes no good to the Opposition. The Duke speaks with his wonted fire. His is the speech of the evening, so far as it impresses my Lords, though I feel it is the speaker's personality more than the pertinence of his remarks that so impresses the audience. Lord Northbrook follows the Duke with equal warmth. Here my friend comes up from one of the Opposition benches, and we walk out after a few minutes' whispered conversation.

How like our Diwan-i-Khas and Diwan-i-Am of old are these Houses of Parliament! And yet how much more unlike, both in themselves as national institutions, and in their modes of transacting business! After seeing what little I have seen of British parliamentary life I have no reason to be ashamed of the manner or the spirit of similar work done in India—for instance, in the days of Akbar. No less real than imposing were those Durbars, presided over by the Grand Moghul, and attended by Hindu as well as Mohammedan counsellors, representing different interests and opinions. Akbar welcomed even Zoroastrians and Christians to help to build up

the unity of his Empire and add to the happiness
of his subjects. When will enlightened Christian
England admit Indians to the Councils of the Empire, or to the Command of the Army?

Another time I am asked by friends in the House
of Commons to attend the discussion of the Indian
Budget. Some of them are good enough to telegraph to me in time. So one afternoon I start with
the indispensable Dr. B., to witness the most important Indian Debate of the year. On entering
the Gallery I find Sir William Wedderburn labouring through a string of figures, a sort of defiant
martyrdom lighting his face—as if he meant to say,
"do what you like, I'll have it out this time." And
what is the strength of the House? So far as we
could count at the moment, there are 13 on the
Liberal side, including the Ministers, and 8 on the
Opposition benches. Where are our Indian Parliamentary Party?—150 of them, stalwart and true.
This thinness of attendance, and the indifference
of the few that are present, chill me. Who can tell
but that Sir W. Wedderburn is oppressed by the
same feeling which, however, he is too brave to
betray? On and on he goes, in the hope, the vain
hope, alas, of convincing this final court of appeal,
determined not to be convinced. He is followed
by Mr. Samuel Smith who, by an unlucky chance-
shot, gives himself away to the masterful Secretary
of State for India. Mr. Fowler is nothing if not a
tactician. Being also a capable financier, he handles
his subject well, although he makes some amusing slips in dealing with details. In the course of

an eminently lucid, but here and there plausible, exposition of our finance, he traverses the statements of several of the previous speakers, including Mr. D. Naoroji whom we came in too late to hear. The voice is, no doubt, Mr. Fowler's—and it is a clear ringing voice of conviction so far as he is concerned—but the facts and figures, and more so the inferences that hang so loose on them, belong evidently to the India Office. What a rattling pace he goes on at !—brushing aside objection after objection, in that light-hearted fashion, dear to the heart of the official expert. Away he runs with his optimistic oration, till flesh and blood can bear it no longer. Here Sir W. Wedderburn puts in a humble caveat, whereupon the Maharaja of Westminster turns upon him fiercely. There Mr. Samuel Smith ventures, in the mildest of his mild manner, to correct a mistake. He is rewarded with a shrug of the ministerial shoulder amid cheers from the Opposition. Never in my life have I realized India in this position of utter helplessness. My poor country, such is thy fate; and such it will remain till thou knowest how to help thyself. But who is this clerical-looking critic, standing slowly up as Mr. Fowler sits down triumphant ? He begins in a deliberate, half-trampling, half-apologetic tone. Who can it be ? Dr. B. whispers it is Mr. Chaplin. I am all eyes and ears. Mr. Chaplin quotes our Secretary of State himself, and then condemns him out of his own mouth. He hoists the Liberals on the horns of a dilemma. In his sledge-hammer style he charges the party with false pro-

fessions of friendship towards India, and in one or
two instances proves the charge to the hilt. Mr.
Fowler now turns wistfully to the ministerial bench
which he finds deserted. His critic here worries
him with questions to which the erstwhile rampant
representative of officialdom makes very humble answers—he does not know, he cannot tell offhand, he
will look into the matter, and so on. Now stop this
game of worrying, Mr. Chaplin; it is not fairplay.
Instead of worrying their new master, you ought to
worry the old rats of the India Office. Bait them
all the year round, if you really feel for India.

With the exception of this part, the Indian Debate has been a sore disappoinment to me, intensified by the look of blank despair in Mr. Dadabhai's
face. Oh if he could only speak his mind! But
the rules are against him, as are the fates. By this
time our friends in the House have become fewer
than need to be counted on the fingers of one hand.

Compare this lack of interest with the attention
paid by the Ministers, small and great, to Irish
Members questioning them on details of administration. Very rapid is this Irish sharp-shooting, and
the official responses are as prompt as they are
definite—"yes, Sir; no, Sir; we shall inquire and
let you know, Sir." Every Minister seems to feel
that evasion or discourtesy may mean as much as
his place is worth. No wonder, then, he tries to
humour even the crank or the bore intent on asking questions. There is only one Minister in the
House, who disdains to do this. The answers given
by the Chancellor of the Exchequer to such critics are

at times crushing in their laconic brevity. After this questioning-and-answering is over, Sir W. Harcourt comes up with a motion to the effect that Government business should have precedence over all other, for the rest of the session. And scenting opposition from some quarters, Sir William puts on extra stiffness. Here, on Mr. Balfour coming to his rescue, a Scotch Member makes some ill-natured remarks, at which the Chancellor of the Exchequer snorts like a warhorse, and exclaims—"If I do not serve the House faithfully, they may dismiss me." This elicits cries of No, No, from some Members, with other assurances of respect and confidence— just what the old Parliamentary hand wanted, I suppose. Here a Division is ordered; and taking the wave of temporary popularity at its height, the Ministers, aided by the bulk of the Opposition, get their motion carried. The House then go into Committee, as it is called; and the demure-looking, oddly dressed figure, sitting under a' sort of canopy, quietly sidles out.

All through the proceedings, dull as well as lively, I have kept looking at this figure, with growing interest. At first I take it for a statue. But see, the figure moves its hand. It stretches what looks like a leg, safely ensconced under its seat. Meseems it now opens its eyes. Now the figure is looking really alive and awake. Why, it is stifling a yawn, and stuffing its nose, being too polite to blow it in the face of the august assembly. Dear me, how very like a human being! There, it has just cracked a joke that sets the whole House laughing. I look at it intently from my perch, and now feel as if I could claim it as a cousin. And yet, I know not what to make of this droll figure and the ornamental piece of furniture it occupies. I turn to my guide, who explains it is the Right Honourable the Speaker of the House of Commons, sitting in his chair of state. What an ironical race the English are! This quiet, quaint, elderly gentleman the *Speaker*, who has hardly spoken five sentences in the course of as many hours? For a real live Speaker you must go to Ireland, to Bombay, or, better still, to Bengal.

To judge from such proceedings in the House, and their echoes in the party organs, the keynote of English politics seems to be—Nothing Succeeds Like Success. The parties exist mainly to worry each other —the one out of office striving to oust the other, only to do very much the same sort of work they denounced their rivals for. At times one feels as if the honour of the Empire or the wellbeing of the people was a mere incident of this eternal party strife, rather than its one pre-arranged object, as students of constitutional history are tempted to believe. This is, of course, a superficial view: much that is truly patriotic may be found under the surface of current politics. Anyhow, He who shapes the destinies of a nation knows how and when to adjust, and where need be, to redress, the balance. So fight on, gentlemen politicians, flourishing your party cries about Free Trade and Fair Trade, both of which have a tendency to drift perilously near to Protection when outside interests are involved; your cry of one-man-one-vote, where a dozen votes may be commanded by any one man with enough of money or influence at his back; your cry of three-acres-and-a-cow, where thousands upon thousands are never likely to have half-an-acre each, with or without the cow; with all your bids and your promises that, you know, will come to nothing. In this huge struggle for success, which typifies the political life of England, what chance is there for her far-off Dependency? God help India! Neither Conservatives, Liberals nor Radicals will help her, seeing how much they have to help themselves every day of the year.

Haunted by these grim thoughts of our future, I leave the House of Commons, stiff in the back, frozen in the feet and the stomach, and sweltering in hot perspiration on the forehead. The cold wind outside aggravates my troubles. The pilgrim-reformer is in for his usual fever which developes this time into neuralgia. Oh my tooth! Poor scapegoat—victim of misdirected patriotism. And yet, patience, my pilgrim-patriot, patience. But this horrid toothache! Any ache but toothache, O Lord! Headache, if Thou so willest, which I have been spared. Heartache, of which I have had enough to break a hundred hearts. Any ache or pain but toothache, please. I am not a professor, nor an orator. Nor yet am I partial to toothsome dishes. Why, then, this tearing, shooting pain? But just are thy ways, though inscrutable; and if I have deserved bitterer martyrdom than hitherto endured in my passage through this vale of tears, methinks it were a mercy to send me right off to the stake. In that, there would be some glory, at any rate, for a vainglorious nature.

Q

The tortures from an angry tooth may not be so elevating to the spirit as are the agonies of the stake; but are they not more excruciating to the flesh?—harder by far for a sinner to bear? Lo how the victim of toothache writhes as the beast inserts its fangs into his ears, his eyes, his brains. It saps the foundation of his Fortitude, makes his meek Contentment itself rise up in wrath to smite the infidel dentist. And—there's the rub—one has to endure all these miseries of martyrdom without being entitled to any of its merits.

The Crystal Palace is my special favourite. It is near enough to Dr. B——'s; and as I do not care for theatres, music halls, and so on, I make the most of this palace of crystal and endless curiosities.

The Natural History Museum interests me much more than the British Museum of Antiquities. The plants, flowers, birds, beasts, and other trophies, products of flora and fauna, that I see in the former, are so life-like. They are wonderfully well-stuffed, and surrounded by their natural accompaniments. This, to me, is the perfection of art. It is only from very near that you find life wanting in these interesting objects—and then *only that* wanting to mark it off from Divine workmanship.

I am not sufficiently learned to fall in love with the Museum of Antiquities. The broken pieces of stone, iron and brass; the pots and pans, belts and buttons and other dead bones of history, pointed out to me, throw their charms away on a hopeless ignoramus. Dr. B—— expatiates eloquently on their genuineness and their value as connecting links between past and present. I can only shake my head moodily. If the blessed things are real, I leave them for real lovers of antiquities. In another room I try to snatch an interview with Queen Cleopatra's Mummy, without success. The sight of her companion in the silence and helplessness of death haunts me for days. I would rather visit a charnel-house that is real, more recent. The beads and bones used by living savages come nearer my rude comprehension than all these fossils of ancient fashion and relics of royalty.

Far better than these I like some of the inmates of Madame Tussaud's Exhibition. What a wonderful show it is! I begin with the Indian, Anglo-Indian and Afghan celebrities on the ground floor. Some of them are wrongly numbered, thus giving rise to ludicrous mistakes. But they are life-like, one and all. The figure that strikes me as most curious among the vast variety exhibited on the top floor is the one with its head nodding every minute. If I forget not, it is old Mr. Cobbett, with a snuff-taking face that winks knowingly at you as soon as you smile recognition. The Sleeping Beauty is another remarkable piece of art—a lady asleep, with the breast gently undulating in imitation of nature. We do not care to visit Madame's Chamber of Horrors, to be introduced to many of the criminals and cut-throats known to history. We have just had our throats cut by the waiter at the restaurant, who charged us half-a-crown for two plates of mud-water which he passed off as mulligatawny soup. There were horrors enough in that costly repast.

The Zoological Gardens in Regent's Part are even more interesting to me. Here one feels as if moving about amongst his kith and kin, all of them real and alive—very much alive, indeed, judging from the overtures made to me by a greedy old beast of a baboon. I have a friendly chat with some of these "poor relations," and listen to the song of the birds— a chorus in a sort of universal bird-language. I admire the limbs of the antelopes and the giraffes, shudder at sight of the pigs and the rhinos, and humbly salute His Majesty of the African desert, as he sits, like a grand old Nawab, wiping his moustache after dinner. It is a sight more striking than pleasant to see the lions, tigers, leopards, wolves, foxes, seals, &c., tearing away at junks of beef, or gobbling down fish, mice and other live food thrown to them by the keepers. What is even less pleasant to me is the applause of a crowd of men and women as they witness these goings on.

One day in July I set apart for a pilgrimage to the Parsi Burial-ground at Woking. A party of five, all Parsis, one of them a lady student, make for that solitary retreat in the afternoon. We have some trouble in reaching it, though Dr. B. and two of the other friends seem to have visited it before. It is a beautiful spot in which we count eighteen graves, large and small, some handsomely made, others, plain to a fault. No fear of vultures here, however. The sight fills us with solemn thoughts; for a time none attempts to speak. Poor, weather-beaten wanderers from the East; what hopes, what longings lie buried with you in this foreign land!

What a wrench your departure from home must have been to the dear ones left behind! What anguish this final parting at a distance, without the consolation even of a brief meeting! But rest in peace and hope, dear exiles. There is reunion even for such as you. With some such thoughts agitating our breasts, and with moist eyes, most of us, we place the flowers brought over from Covent Garden on all the graves, each breathing a prayer in his or her own way. Having attended to this sadly-agreeable duty, we wander about awhile, visiting the spots assigned to other nationalities for the rites of sepulture.

The parks of London are my favourite resorts of an afternoon; later they become crowded, and undesirable after eventide. What an aid they are to health! What a relief to mind and body! What a delight to the eye! Hyde Park, St. James's, Kew, Richmond, Greenwich, and many another paradise, private as well as public; each of them forms an oasis in this dreary dismal fogland, brightening the landscape and purifying the air; at times ridding it of the germs of epidemics. And the people, rich and poor, seem to know how to use these centres of health, judging from the immense turn-outs every afternoon, by river and rail. Bands of music inside, shows, games, picnics, add to the attractiveness of the parks, which, in this way, keep many a poor family from the grog-shop, especially if the weather happens to be fine. There go a knot of lovers, arm-in-arm, in search of quiet corners. Here you see an elderly Darby and Joan couple, spread out on the bench, leaning against each other, and drinking in their wedded bliss by the hour. In front of these you see a grandmother 'taking the h'air'. She holds up her skirt, which is in rags, right over the knees, disclosing a pair of stockings perforated almost like a sieve. She is drenched in the rain, and covered with mud. And yet how proudly grandma passes the pair of ancient lovers—her nose up in the air! A princess in her own right could not carry herself more daintily. Yonder you see a group of ragged children, frisking and jumping, rolling down slopes, and running about the grounds, who will come up to you before five, the leader asking, "Please, sir, ken yer tell me the toime?" If you ask why, he will answer " Cose we are goin' 'ome." They must be home before long. Poor little children! They would rather spend the night here, if it rested with them. We in India know less of this park life than of the club life which is just growing into favour with us. Not only do we want the parks of London; we also lack the Londoner's appreciation of them.

Though rich in parks and gardens, London seems to be miserably poor in its markets. I have seen not one worth mentioning; not one to match our Crawford market. Covent Garden is badly built, and worse kept. I have visited it half a dozen times in search of fruit and vegetables, with Dr. B———. Billings gate is about the same. The only time I called there I found it deserted by the fish-wives. Some of the markets on the Continent compare very favourably with those in London, but even the former hardly seem to rival our own little gem.

Both at Covent Garden and at the shops I have

seen fruit and vegetables rotting for want of timely
disposal. Beautiful pine-apples, peaches, pears ; fine
mangoes, pomegranates, water-melons, figs, sugar-
melons, coming over from the Continent or the West
Indies, may be seen at the same stalls for weeks; yet
the seller won't sell them under his price. I have
paid as much as a shilling for one peach ; at other
times buying a basketful for eighteen-pence. You could
hardly expect to buy a decent pine-apple under six
shillings till the canker has eaten well into its core.
And then the man will rather cut it up into slices
than sell it as it is. Few shopkeepers know brin-
jals and other vegetables coming over from France.
They ask the customers " what them furrin things
are," and how they are to be cooked. In short,
the better sorts of vegetable and fruit are just
struggling into favour with Englishmen. If a company of foreigners, including Indians, were to nurse
the business, they might make handsome profits,
besides educating the dull and conservative British
appetite.

* * *

"I like them roses," says a daughter of the people
to her companion in the south-east of London, as
a stranger wends his way home from Westminster, with a bunch presented to him by the wife of
a friendly M. P. in the House. The words are addressed by one maiden to another, but are intended
for the present owner of the flowers. The stranger
is amused by this sly manœuvre. To keep up the
joke, he turns instantly back, and holding up the
flowers, replies " I like them lips." Does the maiden

shriek and faint right off in the arms of her companion? Nothing of the sort. She simply steps forward, and holds up her face, with just a suspicion of a pout, while her friend looks demurely on. There is no retreat for the stranger now; no backing out of the bargain. He hands her the roses. The maiden takes them, blushing ruddier than the flowers, and waits for a moment to pay the sweet debt which the stranger is loth to exact. She seems to pout more at this omission to keep to the terms of the contract than at the original proposal. But whatever she may be thinking of the ungallant foreigner, he feels it would be mean to exact ransom from a captive so natural, so honourable. It might, perhaps, take away the smell of his roses, the merit of his kindly act. Goodbye, sapling of the sturdy oak, daughter of the working man of London; God keep thee in thy frank ingenuous innocence!

It is curious how we Orientals differ from Europeans in the matter of kissing. We hold it too sacred to be overdone, or to be done in the public. We kiss the eye-brow or the cheek, gently and sparingly. Sometimes the lips, but sparingly, sparingly, like grace before meat; and never before a witness, save in the case of children. There may be exceptions when we drink a kiss. But we never devour it.

Kissing seems to run riot among Europeans. They kiss with excuse or without it—let them alone for making excuses. They kiss baby for mamma, mamma for baby; wife for husband, husband for wife. They kiss at meeting and at parting, at the door, in the drawing room, in the street. They kiss in broad day light, in the shade, in the dark—I hope without making mistakes as to identity. Wife and husband kiss each other at the railway station, so do male friends in France. In India, the most devoted and the most uxorious of husbands would think no more of kissing his wife at the station than of knocking down the station-master and dancing on his prostrate form.

Look at these old ladies carrying it on. They are not content with kissing each other, nor with the one kissing the other's progeny. One of them must needs hold up her cat to be kissed by the departing friend. And the latter does it with a whack that makes poor Tom draw in his moustache and present a rueful countenance.

Of course, it is not the cat, but her mistress that has been so affectionately saluted. Poor woman; perhaps the cat is her only family. See, again, how like a rhinoceros that fat old gentleman is biting the skin off his lean young companion's cheek!

What an amount of kissing! Is the climate of Europe at the bottom of this peculiarity, too? Be that as it may, I am inclined to think that if the strength spent upon kissing were to be reserved for a few years, it might furnish materials for another big war. England herself might work an electric railway with the current of energy she could command by foreswearing her osculatory extravagance. However, if the doctors think that kissing helps to keep the mouth and the teeth clean, I am sure I do not mind.

One of the saddest sights I have seen in London is that of the organ-grinder. It may be a man or a woman. This latter is generally a foreigner, looking like an Italian, with a couple of birds in a cage deposited on the top of her instrument (of torture). There she stands, one arm akimbo, with the other plying the handle, changing the tune now and again, for a chance copper that comes in her way. She seldom asks, seldom grumbles.

There is another class of organ-grinders, probably English, who do the streets, so many every day. They use larger instruments, and seem to get on better. Off and on you are treated to vocal music in the street, by men who have nothing else to do. They parade the street, hand in hand, singing or telling a tale of woe. Once I heard an elderly tramp sing 'Ome, Shweet 'Ome, in tones so sweet as to drive one away from home. These itinerant music-makers have always to be on the alert. They dread the policeman, and walk away as fast as they can at sight of him. I suppose the Police Code cites them as 'public nuisance.'

Yet another organ grinding party—a man and a monkey, with a small organ between them, worked alternately by the man and the monkey. These two look so alike at a distance that you can hardly tell, but for the accident of dress, which is which. The monkey is the attraction of the show; then comes the instrument; last, and of least account to the street boys and the servant girls, is the man.

Perhaps the sweetest street music I heard in England was at Brighton, one evening. A blind woman apparently Irish, stood in the midst of a large crowd. She had a very comely face, with thin delicate outlines, the loss of eyesight making it more pathetic. Her voice was soft and musical, at times tremulous with emotion. She sang *The Better Land* with exquisite feeling; and as she came to the words—"Is it there, sweet Mother, that radiant shore?"—she seemed to move forward in an ecstasy of eager anticipation. The acting of this question was very well matched by the action accompanying the answer—"Not there, not there, my child." There was moisture in many an eye, besides the singer's, that evening.

A passing mention may be made here of another kind of street music—that played, by a venerable-looking tramp, on glasses. Some of the glasses, or tumblers, are empty; others hold a little water in them, perhaps in order to adjust the tones or to make them uniform. Here stands our aged musician in a corner, passing his fingers airily over the edge of the glasses, and eliciting some of the sweetest strains I have heard in undertone. This time he is playing a hymn, the words of which I cannot catch. His best hit is said to be "Home, sweet Home." He reminds me very much of Maula Bux with his *Jaltarang* on cups and saucers.

Another sad but rather unattractive sight one encounters in the streets is that of the knight vagrant of paint and brush. He is a sort of amateur painter in colours, who draws capital figures on the pavement, and then stands near his handiwork, hat in hand, mutely inviting the passer-by to patronize his evanescent art. He seems to be a pessimist, every inch of him, enamoured of his dull aimless existence.

More interesting than this is the sight of blind people sitting at corners, neatly dressed, singing quietly, as if to themselves, or reading aloud from the Bible by the feel.

One of the queerest sights is presented by ladies parading the streets with pet dogs held by chains, on whom they seem to lavish all their affection. Here goes one of these dressed-up dolls, carrying a pet in arms more fondly than she is ever likely to carry her own offspring. The sight is rendered more incongruous by her husband or brother walking listlessly beside her, without offering to relieve, or even to escort her through a crowd. I am inclined to sympathize *with the husband or brother.*

One evening, while in the Crystal Palace, I am tempted to look at the ballet-dancing in progress there. I find it different from what I was led to expect. What I actually see here is a troop of little girls tricked out in fancy dresses, like the Peris of our Eastern plays, going through an animated dance to the tunes of equally lively music, or a cleverly contrived pantomime, very much after the Oriental fashion. There is nothing positively unseemly about it so far. A wealth of lights and shades is thrown round the scene occasionally, the effect of which is very striking. The dance itself is not so artistic as the best to be seen in India—for instance, that shown by the Tanjore girls. Years ago, when a boy, I used to see at Surat a Panjaubi girl go through the sword dance with marvellous grace and agility. I never witnessed a dance since, till this evening. Of course, one does not feel comfortable at the sight of the poor little children having to work thus for their own living, or perhaps for idle or drunken parents. I hope their future is not to be worse.

*
* *

Oh the street arabs of London! Dirty, unkempt little urchins, out at elbow, often out at knee too, if I may use the phrase; lean and hungry as a rule, yet full of life, and always amusing. We have an encounter with some of them near Westbourne Park the day after our arrival in London. Crocodile and I are walking about, my companion in white Indian long-cloth, and myself in dark. The white catches the fancy of one of the little monkeys, who yells " Yaw, Johnny, jist out o' the laundry?" The other boys laugh and take up the cry. Crocodile asks what it all means. I explain that the boy wants to know if his washer-woman has just turned him out on the streets after washing and wringing his frame. He turns away in disgust, and I cannot help joining the laugh against him, little knowing how very near is my own turn.

Next morning I go out to the Bank with my land-lady's daughter as guide. Poor Annie pilots me through the rocks and shoals of street-arabism. I am dressed in a loose flannel suit, such as we often use in India on a rainy day. They do not seem to use flannel here, save for cricket or lawn-tennis. So, near Paddington Station, I am assailed with the sneering question—"Yaw, gov'nor, foine day for creeckit?" (It was drizzling.) I turn to Annie for explanation, as Crocodile turned to me yesterday. I make up my mind to discard flannel. But that is not enough for my tormentor. After disappearing for a minute he returns to the scene with two or three other imps of mischief, and cries out—"Jim, look at 'is 'at; look at 'is 'at, Jim; hoo, look at 'is 'at, George." Annie apologizes, and explains that Indian pugrees are new to these boys,—"though I am sure we like them." She may be right. But I am determined to be revenged on the London rough. Scarcely have we come to a turning when two or three ladies walk up to me, and one of them asks if I'll let them look at my hat. These ladies are not street arabs. Annie suggests they may be photographers or artistes. Very likely. But I would rather not give them a sitting.

And now for the revenge. Smarting under a sense of my wrongs from the street-arabs, I jump up a 'bus one evening, that is about to start from Victoria Station, when, whom do I find in charge but my old friend of Edgware Road? Jehu is as jolly and rubicand as ever; but something ails his hand which he has kept wrapped up. I ask what it is, whereupon he silently unwraps the limb and holds up the thumb which has swollen to the size of a well developed beet-root, and is about the same shape. I look at it with the air of a surgeon-general, and prescribe a poultice, adding it is nothing serious. As he nods gratefully, I ask—"Have you consulted a veterinary?" "Oom?", queries my patient uneasily. "A Surgeon Veterinary," I repeat sententiously. The conductor, who is with us, here explains—"them doctors as treats 'osses and loikes." " Thank ye kindly, says coachman, turning to me with a sneer, and digging my right side with his elbow.

Another day, stepping out of a Palace train, I ask the porter on duty if I am at Ludgate Hill Station. "Yes, Sir, Laget I'll," he replies.

"Is it Ludgate Hill from which one goes to the City?"

"Yes, Sir-r-r."

"May I ask why they call it Ludgate Hill?"

"Dunno as I knows," looking suspiciously at the stranger.

"What I want to ascertain is the etymological significance."

"Never 'eard of 'Etty nor Molly down 'ere," replies the disgusted carrier of packages. As he joins a chum, he cries aloud in my hearing, "rum uns, them furriners," and probably repeats to him the up-shot our learned interview.

How many "rum uns" is India sending out to England, for study, business or for pleasure? The vagaries of the student class we have elsewhere glanced at, except that there are some Indian students over here, who live upon 'nothing a year.' They are supposed to live on their wits; more correctly, they live upon the credulity of their witless victims. And they justify their ways sometimes by explaining, "if the English rob and plunder us every day in India, why should we not do the same by them when we get the chance ?" To these may be added the Indian eye-doctor and ear-doctor, surgeons itinerant, who loaf about London and the provinces, undertaking to cure the blind and the deaf in the cheapest and most expeditious manner, as if by magic. How gullible their English patients must be ! Last of all, there are the pleasure-seekers, or those who visit England partly for pleasure or health, and partly for business. Here goes a Parsi gentleman at large, in evening suit capped by his conical paper turban, followed by ladies of his family, dressed in the height of the season, with the saris thrown airily round, drawing half of Oxford Street behind them. They seem to enjoy the attention.

More picturesque than this party are Rao Sahib Moro Punt and the Rao Sahiba, dressed impartially, half in the English, half in the Indian style, in which the buff-coloured sari, the scarlet shawl, and the cartwheel of a puggri play a prominent part. From the hotel, where they have put up, to the private drawing room or the public hall, the shop, the theatre, the hospital or the park, do Mr. and Mrs. Moro Punt repair, a pair of " Indian princes," taking all they meet into confidence, asking queer questions, and drinking in the doubtful admiration which the London mob knows how and on whom to bestow.

Then there is the Indian Raja—the real one—with an Englishman for bear-leader ; dressed in silk and embroidered stuff, and yet half naked in his person ; with a fair command of the English language, and yet three-quarters of a savage in speech ; dining at the head of the common table, but using his paws even for the fish and butter he swallows; paying court to the chamber maid, and offering his seat to the girl who has come to receive orders for the day.

***

Some of the street cries of London are very like the cries of our Indian hawkers. The words, of course, are quite different, but the sound is almost the same in both. The first cry one hears on getting up is the cry of "papeaw"; that is, *paper* or newspaper, with a variety of names rattled off by the criers. Towards the evening this is heard at its best in the City—spa-shul (special), Fryfuasden (frightful accident), N'ather klopsity bank (another collapse of a City Bank), &c. Of this we have not much in India. The next cry is "mihi", or "mehew", or "mi-ho," that is *milk-ho*, uttered in a shrill voice. The sellers are all men—which is a pity—but the voice is so much like what we hear from our milk-maids in the mofussil, that if I were to hear the London "Miho" in India, I could hardly tell it at a distance from the lactic "dudho" of Gujarat. Is the similarity in the sounds, the words being utterly different, an accident or a part of nature? Or, has England borrowed the sounds from the East?

There are many other street cries that I have listened to with interest—the costermongers hawking vegetables, fruit, flowers, etc. Here is the flower wench at the station, with her "Penny a bunch—them beautiful flowers—all for a penny, sir, on'y a penny, please." Flower girls in London would be

R

very pretty but for underfeeding and exposure. Some of them have the prettiest noses I have seen, though I do not think they come up to our *málans* of Surat. Then there is the strawberry boy, with his " t'puns a pun stro-bree, foine laj stro-bree." Or the fish boy, with his cry of " Elive-shrimps oh, thrupuns a pint ho." (Alive shrimps, threepence a pint), or " fresh laj mackrels ho, six for a shillin-ho."

There is one street cry that baffled me—a fellow with a sort of Sindhi hat, singing out, *Cachimalai* (very much like our street cry *Tajimalai, i.e.* fresh cream). I follow the hawker about, anxious to know what article it is whose virtues he is singing so glibly. Unable to make head or tail of it, I appeal to Dr. B——, who unravels the mystic triplet— " Cachimalai, nasty fly, make baby cry." The man is selling fly-paper to catch flies on. His *cachimalai*, translated into Queen's English, is *catch them alive*.

Perhaps the queerest street cries I have heard are those set up by an old-clothes gatherer, and a man hawking " fresh oysters," many days old. " Oin boin ould cilose," (I buy old clothes); " Me boin-boin, me boin ould lumber." And " freshoisters, shweet-oishters, foinoishters " (fresh, sweet, fine, oysters). Poor old Irisher! He is dead, and no one has yet risen at Nunhead to treat us to " freshoisters," at sight of which the stomach is apt to revolt.

One more street cry—of the bustling little shoe-black—" Shoe-blake, sir, shoine, sir, shoine?"

* *
*

Looking at a crowd of London roughs, one feels

that the brute instinct of the Briton has not left him quite. The love of fight for the sake of blood still clings to the people. You will often see a big boy thrashing a small one; and a crowd looking on and cheering the small one, till he is "smashed up." Then the crowd remonstrates with the bully. Perhaps the small one likes his baptism of blood. Perhaps his father and friends wish him to rough it out for himself.

In out-of-the-way places you may witness cock-fights and dog-fights at certain hours. Look at the faces of the dog and its owner carefully. You may be excused for imagining traces of a common parentage between them. One knows not which is the more repulsive of the two. From a moral point, of course, that of the owner of the dog. What a specimen of humanity! I doubt if the world holds another such. His language is about as human as are his looks. The women belonging to this class are not positively ugly, unless they make themselves so with drink. But I have seen faces amongst them, such as could hardly be matched outside the Zoo.

"B——y cheek that," growls a cadger, as he feels scratched in the arm by two of Carter Paterson's horses on a spree. "B——y cheek, loosing them 'osses," he repeats, as he sees the driver emerging from a gin-shop. The driver apologizes in a way, by asking, "What is I to do with them b——y hanimals?". Cadger and driver soon make up over a pipe; and as the latter drives off his restive horses, the huckster remarks "Oll right, chum, b——y 'ot day," meaning he was angered by the heat of the day

R 2

rather than by the scratch from the horses, and that he did not care now.

Of all the expletives I have heard in London streets this "b——y" seems to be the commonest—b——y cheek, b——y hard, b——y fat, b——y fool, b——y flower (blood and flower in one breath). Now, I may as well explain to my Indian reader that "b——y cheek" means nothing more dreadful than bad or great impudence. It has nothing to do either with *blood* or *cheek* as explained in learned lexicons. But what I cannot possibly make out for myself is—where does the British rough get this hideous expletive from, and why does he use it so often? Has he got it from the soldier whose business is with blood? or, has he got it from the butcher? or, does he owe it to his own instincts? Our terms of abuse or reproach in India are bad enough, many of them being aimed at the female relatives of the party abused or reproached. That shows the Orient-al's respect for the sex. Here, in England, the ag-grieved seems to thirst for blood. You smell blood in his protest, in his familiar conversation; there is blood even in his jokes when John Bull is in a jocular mood. Who can say how much of the blood-thirstiness and blood-guiltiness of the people is due to this love of blood, or how much of the latter is due to his innate supply of bad blood? Several of my English readers have been at pains to explain that b——y is only a vulgarized abbreviation of By Our Lady. There can be no question as to this, nor as to the obligation I am under for the kindly correction. But do those who use the expletive in

the streets of London to-day use it in the Shake-
spearian sense? They smell too much of blood to
mean anything so harmless.

***

And now farewell to London! Dirty little pool
of life, that has grown and expanded into an ocean
—the biggest, the muddiest, and yet the healthiest
of this iron age.

Great in varieties, great in contrarieties; unequal-
led in the power of contrasts and in the wealth of
extremes; I sit entranced, watching thy divergent
forces. The noise and bustle—the everlasting clang of
feet, the whistling of engines and smoking of chim-
neys—are music to my ear. But it is music which,
like my native tom-tom, I should prefer hearing at
a safe distance.

CHAPTER VII.

THE CONTINENT RECONNOITRED.

Paris—Cologne—Munich—Ober-Ammergau—Florence—Rome—
St. Peter's—The Vatican—Naples—Venice—The Passion
Play at Ober-Ammergau—Trieste, Two Days of Suspense—
Trieste to Bombay—A Channel Crossing—Some other Con-
tinental Cities.

THIS morning, the 15th of September, 1890, I leave
London for Paris with Dr. B——, who kindly undertakes to see me off at Trieste, after a run across
those parts of the Continent which we missed on
our way up. Dr. B—— knows London as probably
few born Londoners do. He can name all the streets,
lanes and bye-lanes, can ferret out the darkest hole
therein, running into corners like a rat, to save time.
He carries a map of all the railway, tram and 'bus
stations, of all the steamer lines, on the palm of
his hand. It is seldom that he needs to look at
the map or question a constable. And then, oftener than not, he has to correct his informant. He
is familiar with almost the whole of England, Scotland and Ireland, and knows a good deal of the
Continent, too, having lived in some parts for study,
and visited others in search of health. He has also
been to Australia and the United States. His company is indispensable to me. It costs but little.
Really, we two together spend less than when I
am travelling by myself.

I say good-bye to all the stations from Nunhead to Dover, never again feeling likely to return that way.

The Channel is rather boisterous, but we keep walking the deck all the while, after a simple fare. Going into French territory, we find it looks somewhat like my own Gujarat. The soil is very rich —a contrast to some parts of England. For the first time I see bullocks in the fields at St. Just. We reach Paris in the evening. Leaving our things at the Hotel Moderne, we go off for a walk and a look at the streets. Rows of people are sitting at their meals outside the restaurants, and some of them inside. Many of them are sitting in groups, like so many separate families. It is a very fine picture, all laughing, talking, sipping wine or coffee. But the picture looks scarcely homelike to me. They are a quiet, cleanly lot, showing no traces of drukenness—another contrast in favour of France. But the people in the streets have a look of dependence and discontent, and are by no means so robust and pushing as the English. Here is a feather in England's cap. The Parisians seem to work leisurely, as in an Indian city, and are equally languid in the street. You miss in them the hurry and bustle of the London crowd.

As in drink, so in dress and food, the Parisians have much finer instincts. They seem to prefer bread, milk, grapes, or other fruit or vegetable, to the bacon, ham, cheese, and beer, which Londoners of the same class are wont to eat.

We have no time for sight-seeing, and no inclination. Of the few sights we stumble upon by accident, I can recall only the Galleries and the tomb of Napoleon. This latter is a splendid work of art, representing the emperor in his full glory— with so many of the bravest of the time at his feet. But where is he now ? The life of Napoleon reads like a Persian story out of the Shahnameh, with the simple well-worn moral—pride goeth before destruction. Poor old Nap ! I had a sort of admiration for him even when he lay withering in his water-bound prison. What a meteor-like career ! He was badly needed to quicken the blood of Europe, stagnating in venal and voluptuous repose. He gave her a complete rousing, shook her into healthy activity. He gave her a new life, but buried himself under the ashes of the old. In spite of his miserable ambition, Napoleon Bonaparte was a far greater man than insular prejudice will ever acknowledge.

But there are phases of ambition, to which even the souls of Napoleon and Alexander could not soar —their genius seems to have quailed before the goal. And yet they are more or less within every man's reach—*To be good; to do good*. The former ideal is far the best, though least attainable save through grace from above and without. The latter is largely dependent upon the former. What are crowns and coronets to man, kingdoms and principalities, compared with the power of being good, of doing good ? That is an ambition worth living for.

We expect no friends in Paris, as the season has just ended. Only one friend I miss, one dear as a brother. But that cannot be helped, seeing we have caught *La Belle Paris* asleep. She is in a lovely trance. Some day we must see her aglow with life, in the drawing-room or on the promenade.

The friend whom I missed in '90—no other than the gifted *savant*, James Darmesteter—I am privileged to see during my third trip. We meet in Paris, at no small inconvenience, he running down for a few hours all the way from his country house, I making a brief diversion from my journey down South. It is destined to be our last meeting on earth. The lunch over which we sit is a mere pretence—we are so absorbed in conversation. When and where shall I again see the face of that divine alchemist of literature, the glance from which no subtlety of art or nature could remain long hid, the hand at whose magic touch the gates of Truth flew open? Oh that face, illuminated with knowledge, the simple child-like voice, the delicate hand of a born gentleman! In his fragile little body my Darmesteter carried a grand soul. Those who dare to call him an atheist ought to have studied the man as well as his work. For me, James Darmesteter will ever live a believer, as he was a seer; and, as is alleged of Afghan saints and heroes, he will grow in his grave. What truer testimony could be had of his greatness than that he has left no one behind to take his place?

After a day and a half in Paris we push forward to Cologne. Great are the straits to which John Bull is reduced while travelling, not knowing how to talk with the " furriner " who asks for an examination of his luggage in a crowded train at 1 A.M.

It is very vexatious. All of us have to take our things out. John is sulkily polite to "Monsoor," but swears viciously behind his back. The inspector is over-strict with him, peeping into his letters and papers, emptying his hat-box, &c. He lets us off easily, seeing we are strangers. "Hang it! how lucky some people are," growls John. This frontier inspection is really a nuisance. Why perpetuate a relic of barbarism? The inspector pops in at unholy hours, takes you and your luggage out, and coops up both for a time in a bleak cold room. Italy and Germany seem to delight in thus persecuting passengers. John Bull assures me, it is mainly to extort blackmail. On the other hand, I see that Mrs. J. B. has something like a mania for smuggling. She will do it, if only to overreach that heathen. But, apart from this Christian consideration, I think she does the thing often for the love of it. It is a weakness with her sex. She has an eye for curios and souvenirs, which she will convey into the corners of her multifold drapery. What is travelling worth, without the privilege of these petty little larcenies?

As we proceed, we find a simpler life everywhere, drawing nearer to India. The people are simple— men and women carrying loads, barefooted. At Cologne we have the hottest and the noisiest tram ride. I doubt if Bombay could be hotter; and yet the people seem to work more heartily than in Bombay. On the Bavarian side we pass through a fine country, looking remarkably like India in the habits of the people and their way of ploughing.

Next day we leave for Munich, and glad we are to get there. It is a very interesting old town, with large broad streets, clean and sweet, spacious roads, paved side walks as wide as our roads. The river adds largely to its industrial activity. In short, Munich wears a decidedly prosperous look. We enjoy ourselves for a day at the picture galleries, which are worthy of its traditions. The Austrian track looks very fertile, studded with valleys and lakes. I see crows here for the first time. The snow-capped hills delight me very much. Going on to Ala, I am reminded of the Ghauts. The scene strikes one by its rugged magnificence.

This noon we leave for Ober-Ammergau by a branch railway. The country stretching beyond is lovely. It spreads itself out like a carpet, dotted over with rivers, hills, dales; a picture of rural beauty, very enchanting indeed. After two hours' drive we have to get into a horse carriage with two German ladies. They are very kind to the pilgrims coming all the way from India. We proceed slowly—an immense calvacade or caravan. Messrs. Cook & Co. have the management of it. They have to work hard, but seem to be unequal to this sudden influx. We are put up at Herr Speigle's, on arrival. He is a woodcarver, and looks like a Jew. But he is a jolly old Jew, if a Jew he be, though rather innocent. His wife attends to business for him and for herself. Where would the poor man and his large family be without that masterful wife? Her daughters are equally business-like; the sons seem to be loafers. Lena is told off to look after our room. She is apparently a bright hearty worker, but is so tired just now that we catch her crying. We spare her all needless trouble. That puts her on her mettle, and a few purchases of the local art-ware through her give the girl a new interest in the signors. Lena speaks decent English, and can run up her account quicker than she can return you the balance of your sovereign. She pouts very prettily when chaffed for her sharp practice. She is as arch as she is pretty; but from the way in which she thrusts a certain cab-driver upon us whenever we want a drive, we see that a certain rivulet of human affection has drifted towards a big iceberg.

Lena has a younger sister, looking older and stouter. She is positive in manner, and very tooth-achy. She gives us excellent fare. Her bill is very stiff, but we do not grudge it at all. She takes the gold from the table, and quickly puts down the balance in silver and copper. I push back the balance towards her with a smile. She takes it up demurely, with a slow, deliberate, well-masticated, "Tank you, ser." She offers me a nice, warm, sisterly hand to shake; Lena offers her cheek.

The Germans are hard smokers, and heavy eaters and drinkers of beer; but they are not drunkards, so far as we can see. We do not meet with a single instance of wrangling in the streets of Ober-Ammergau, with all the crowds swarming over the village. The streets are all clean, the crowds peace-ful—people walking leisurely in small knots, each their own way. The villagers look happy. The women seem to be very hospitable. But the smoke and smell of towns is already penetrating this rural paradise of Europe.

One morning we drive up to King Ludwig's Palace, doing part of the way on foot. Going up at a stretch, we are rather fagged. But the scenery more than repays us. It is grand in its soft harmonious beauty. For the moment it makes me forget Simla and Mahableshwar. Nature luxuriating in rivers and mountains; art lavishing herself on waterfalls, variegated lights and shades, lovely grottos and arcades—the whole makes a beautiful picture of rural grandeur.

Coming back to Munich from Ober-Ammergau, we then enter Italy *via* Ala. Italy seem to be rich but flat, with the hand of Autumn already laid heavy on her. At once we run up to Florence, City of Flowers and Flower of Cities. For the first time in Europe we see on our way a regular *vanjar** of bullocks, goats, sheep, with the familiar sound of their bells, and of the song from the shepherd, very like our Kathiawar *paraja.*

The street cries here are peculiarly like ours— more so than elsewhere. The people are slightly tinged brown. Little meat seen at the shops. Plenty of vegetable, fruit, grain. In this respect Italy is perhaps the best country in Europe, because nearest to the East.

Florence is a splendid town, with large, handsome houses. The streets are rather narrow for such a town. I get here the best tram ride I have ever had—at a break-neck pace—given by gallant horses and a gallant driver. The tram runs close to the

* A large flock going to a distance.

houses, within less than a foot here and there. The poor folk sit out of doors in the evening, on chairs, stools, etc. ; men and women apart, in a group, gossiping, singing, eating, just like our Indian villagers. Inside the villager's house we see a bedstead with one or two old chairs, sometimes a table, for furniture. The house is often made up of a shop in front, and a back room for the family.

The Picture Gallery at Florence seems to be, perhaps, the best I have seen. Paris and Munich make a good show in statuary, but not so good as Florence; whilst for paintings Florence surpasses both of them in quality and quantity. The study of heads alone is a splendid treat, besides the designs, sketches, coins and so on. But as I return home to the hotel I muse—What is all this to the people, the hewers of wood and drawers of water? And what is it now to the founders? Oh vanity of vanities !

From Florence we hurry off to Rome. This hurried travelling mars a good deal of its interest. Rapid change of air, water, food ; suspended functions and sundered associations—all tell upon one's health. But we cannot help it. Life is too short even for pilgrimages.

Rome presents a capital outlook as we enter. The Grand Hotel stands in a noisy quarter; but it is very convenient, with train, tram, 'bus, donkey cart, cab—all at hand. Standing at the window we see happy, busy crowds below. They are very interesting, but slow. Somehow, the Italians strike you as a fallen race ; certainly, as fallen behind in the race of life. We secure an enthusiastic Roman as our guide, a citizen member of the Municipality. He is an excellent fellow, throws his heart into his work, and has almost every detail of the history of his race at heart, which he explains with a face all aglow

The service at St. Peter's is very like what we see in Parsi and Hindu temples. The interior weighs you down with its gloomy splendour, itself overlaid with a thick air of mystery. We see sinners seeking forgiveness on their knees, sobbing out their hearts in an agony of repentance. How often they do the same every week! And yet they feel the need of doing it over again.

The priests pray for the sinners, give them absolution in a high pitch of voice, with uplifted hands, very much like our priests. The censers, flowers, the offerings in coin and cloth, all remind me of the devout East. What is Rome but the East? What are her traditions but Eastern?

St. Peter's is the most magnificent pile I have yet seen. Our Tajmahal is a toy before it. I cannot attempt a description of it in this place; but from what little I have seen, it is certainly unsurpassed in its magnificence of wealth and art devoted to religion. The interior looks grand and imposing, with its columns, domes, and paintings by old masters. These, with their precious collections and ornamentations, have each of them a history which the guide explains to us, lifting us off our legs, as he himself leaps in excitement.

We dart through the Vatican, and are struck dumb

by some of its masterpieces. The gardens, the hospitals, the colleges, the Pope's palace, with his Swiss guards, all bespeak a little kingdom in itself. It is a miniature—I dare not call it a caricature —of past glory. It is a remnant of, perhaps, the greatest sovereignty wielded by man on God's earth; greatest, because wielded in God's name.

The Fountains of Rome are a feature in themselves—charming and significant conceits—here combining all the winds, there all the largest rivers of the world. These and other works of art we manage to glance at.

The city of Rome is a world in itself. Some of the deserted parts show the most notable sights of antiquity, scattered all over their extent. In every street, almost, there is something curious or interesting to show to the student of human progress—trophies of victory achieved by a nation now lying at the feet of a modern world, with even its modern grandeur gone. We are shown the new church of St. Paul building, the old Forum, the Colosseum, houses of famous men, ancient temples, altars, pulpits, &c., that we have read of in Roman history. We have been on our legs almost the whole day, and return to the hotel faint and weary, but with a sense of inexpressible satisfaction, not unmixed with sorrow.

Rome, City of Priests—honest, devoted, uninquiring, ubiquitous, repulsively rotund—what a future thou hast to look forward to! Rome, City of Ruins —scenes of glory alike with shame and iniquity that pass the imagination of poets! We listen to the

guide breathless, as breathlessly he expatiates on thy
chequered past. What a past to look back upon!

From Rome we branch off to Naples. It stands on
a splendid site, not unlike Bombay. Here it is very
hot during the day, and very close at night, though
our hotel faces the bay due north. The Neapolitans
seem to be a mixed community of various shades
and sizes. The poorer people speak a sort of Asiatic
patois, a dialect, half Turkish, half Urdu; as the
Italians sometimes seem to me to speak Bengali.
We rush about sight-seeing during the day, and
after a night of rest, badly disturbed by an insect
stinging my right hand, we depart early.

Back to Venice in a couple of days. We do the
galleries here at leisure. Some of the larger pictures
seem as if carved out of the walls. The effect from
a distance is very striking. But there seems to be
a little too much of scriptural monotony in almost
all the galleries of Europe. One thing that strikes
me most painfully is Christ exhibited so much in
His sufferings. Of course, this is His principal character. But I venture to think that even this is apt
to be overdone in its cruel onesidedness.

Throughout Southern Europe—Florence, Rome,
Naples, Venice—we find the people remarkably sober.
They are an orderly lot, but look as if weighed down
under some hidden curse—a depressed and dependent
race. They seem to lack the crisp elasticity of the
French, the robust self-assertion of the English or
the German. It is in Southern Europe, also, that
one comes across the more obtrusive forms of street
mendicancy. But one may not be often so badly off

S

here, as in Germany or Austria, in making himself understood, though he finds it, perhaps, as difficult to get at the hotels what he needs. At Venice, for instance, the waiter runs through his bill of fare for our behoof—roast beef, beef steak, ham and eggs. We ask him, however, for mutton cutlets, well dressed and well done, as in India. The man takes his order cheerfully enough, but returns with huge pieces of meat, as clumsy as Scotch chops at a third-rate restaurant. We protest, and explain that we want the meat to be minced fine and to be dressed in the usual butter. "Ah, ah, ah," says the waiter at the end of our explanation, " now I superstand." His " superstanding," however, is of a very inferior order, for he returns with the mutton simply hacked into bald little boluses, less tempting than before.

* *
*

This year of grace, 1890, is to witness the Passion Play at Ober-Ammergau. For believers it is to be, perhaps, the most notable event of the decade in Christendom ; invested with more than its usual interest, as it is likely to be the last of the revelations in rural innocence of the divine humanity of Christ. I am anxious to witness the Play, if by so doing I could better realize certain phases in the life and teachings of the Perfect Man whose suffering grace fascinates an Asiatic more than his triumphant victory.

In the name Ober-Ammergau I catch a familiar sound, as if of one of my own Indian dialects—*Upar-amar-gaum.* The village (gaum) on (upar), amar (the river Amar). All the three words are literally

Indian, very sweet to my ear, especially the last, meaning *immortal*. So I break off engagements in Scotland and Ireland, cut down my programme for the Continent, and make hurriedly for the little hamlet nestling in the heart of what feels like a little paradise on earth.

The origin of this Passion Play has a deep human interest. Ober-Ammergau, a village in the highlands of Bavaria, was visited by a plague in 1633. The simple villagers, finding the ravages of the pestilence too terrible, vowed that they would, in the event of its ceasing to cause them further suffering, reproduce in their own persons the Passion, that is, the suffering of their Saviour, every ten years. The vow has been religiously observed from sire to son, from mother to daughter, for nearly two centuries and a half. Such vows are not unknown in the East; in fact, they are made more frequently, and perhaps kept more devoutly there than in the West. What is singular is, that the sacred drama we are going to witness here is performed before an admiring audience of faith as well as culture, by simple village folk under the guidance of their priest and elders. The man who composed it, in German, must have done so under some higher inspiration than he was aware of. And almost the same might fairly be said of many of the poor wood-carvers of Ober-Ammergau, who have rendered their respective parts with a success that could hardly be claimed by the most cultured of their co-religionists in Europe. Faith and love have worked wonders ere now; the Passion Play at Ober-Ammergau is certainly one of the most wonderful of their achievements in the history of religion.

We are not quite unfamiliar with the Passion Play in India, though it is the Mahommedans only, and those the followers of Ali, that engage themselves in it. The Mahommedan Passion Play, moreover, depicts the trials of faith more than its triumphs. In some respects it is really more effective than the representation at Ober-Ammergau. The spectators are kept in almost a perpetual tumult of tears, as the sufferings of the faithful are described. The exhibition of grief is as fierce as the Arab nature could make it. But we also see in the Mahommedan Play a certain softening and harmonizing of the fiercer elements of the reaction from idolatry, which is the essence of the Prophet's creed. This chastening influence of humanism is most marked where we see the leaders of the faithful—the Shahids, that is, martyrs—suffer without complaining. Terrible is this silent suffering of the children of Ali—most terrible in that they deny themselves most where the suffering is most unmerited. It is, as I have said, a trial of faith. May not this feature of the Imambara performance be a modern Christian graft on the Jewish tradition of old, as taken by the Mahommedan poet?—a fulfilment of prophecy, making the mission of the Prophet two-sided in its character of protest and of patient resignation? The softening of the rigour of Arabic vehemence falls in curiously with the original Persian nature. The Passion Play of Islam obtains only amongst the Shiahs of Persia and India.

Hindus are not without their Passion Plays, enacted perhaps more than once a year, but bearing only a remote resemblance to those in favour with their Semitic brethren.

We must now hasten to the stage, erected somewhat on the outskirts of Ober-Ammergau. Everything about the stage bespeaks a natural, one may say, a pristine simplicity. No tawdry trick of art defiles this sacred structure, though improvised for the occasion. It breathes the spirit, as it were, of scriptural history, and reminds one vividly of the men who have contributed most to the making of that history. The narrative throughout is suited to common intelligence, and therein it shows off the talent of the author at its best. The prologue is ushered in to the tunes of sweet music, given by a chorus composed of eight men and ten women, dressed with a simplicity perfectly in keeping with the character of the times, each face wearing a quiet dignity, wrapped in its sacred surroundings. The Choragas, who leads this band, briefly explains the nature of the *tableau* representing the fall of Adam and Eve, and their expulsion from Eden. It is a most effective sight.

Talking of *tableaux* generally, I may add that I never before saw scenes so absolutely real. The groups of men, women, and children, even these last, sit or stand motionless, and, at a distance of some fifteen yards look like paintings and statues rather than living characters—all of them sitting or standing in appropriate attitudes. They must have been most carefully trained. Their behaviour throughout shows how conscious they are of the dignity of the parts they have to sustain, and how anxious to acquit themselves to the best, as if the success of the whole depended upon the success of each one of the actors, singers, managers, and accessories. Faith alone could sustain these most artless of artists in their arduous task. In fact, the acting that follows could not justly be called *acting*. It is actual impersonation, every actor being inspired by and absorbed in the original. We Asiatics can understand this, perhaps, better than Europeans. Every one of the singers is gifted with a clear sweet voice, which is never broken by so much as a false note, and which sometimes exhibits a rare compass. One or two of them show a wonderful faculty for gesture-making, more significant to me, of course, than the words of their music. Singers and actors alike seem to be the flowers of the valley, that the priests could pick out for this sacred performance. A few of the chorus appear to be dummies, who have only to stand or move with the rest. The majority have to take up a separate part, more or less important. One only of the singers breaks down for a minute, singing by himself. The get-up of the whole Play is Hebraic—dress, stage, scenes, and so on; the language alone being Bavarian. The part given to the Choragas is very fatiguing. Christus has doubt-less an infinitely more delicate and trying part, Judas a more formidable part to render. How they walk about the stage, from highest to lowest! What dignity and grace in words and movements alike! None but an eye-witness could realize the effect.

Marvellous is the acting of some of these untutored rustics. To me it is a miracle in itself. The *tableaux* manage to keep up their realistic character; but the music begins to pall by occasional monotony, as we enter into the thick of this sustained representation of sacred history.

Christ's entry into Jerusalem appears to me to be perfect, both in the principles and details of art, according to the best canons of criticism. It is so entirely like what one should wish it to be. The whole picture is real, besides being a faithful picture of the life and circumstances it represents. The face wears a heavenly dignity and calm self-consciousness, untinged by pride. The pretty little animal he rides, too small though it is for the rider's height, seems to share his conscious dignity.

As I see the ass move gently forward, I can have a better look at the face of the rider. If that face shows anything more than self-consciousness, it shows indifference to the praise and worship that burst from one side, and to the looks of contempt and hatred from the other—a meek resignation, an intelligent appreciation of what is coming. The greatest merit of his acting is, that amidst all the temptations to show himself off, Christus forgets himself throughout, seems to be elevated out of his self. Even when he drives away the pack of buyers and sellers who desecrate his Father's house, he does it, not so much in anger as in a sort of energized grief. The chorus of Hosanna that follows his entry is a treat in itself.

The members of the high Council, who now meet,

seem to be more energetic than wise or eloquent.
The Council looks very much like a Persian Durbar
of old, deliberating as to how to encounter an invad-
ing host. The barking, howling voice in which some
of these men discuss the question before them, and
their fierce gesticulations, testify to the insolence of
the unregenerate priest. Even here the actors show
the artlessness of their art, though they are rather
tedious, and some appear to be anxious to catch the
eye of the audience.

Christ's departure for Bethany is introduced by a
chorus, led by a fair soloist. She sings with exquisite
feeling. On her face you find a soul suffused with
the melody. The Bride's lament is equally touching, as is the music that swells up from within.

The anointing of the Saviour's feet by Mary Magdalene is a capital piece of acting. Mary's voice has
a strange weird sweetness in it. It thrills me. Both
in looks and words she stands next only to the
Virgin Mother. The parting at Bethany nearly over-
powers me, that parting between mother and son.
I find my eyes glistening—after what a length of
time! Tears seldom come to the relief of some suf-
ferers. I am one of these unprivileged mortals. This
afternoon, however, I have need of the handkerchief. The situation is contagious. Few eyes can be
dry amongst the thousands that surround me. The
mother, as she develops her part, becomes more and
more motherly, till, with a broken heart, which you
almost see reflected in her face, she helps to per-
form the last sad rites of her holy office on her
babe. Is he not still a child?—this son of the im-

maculate, suffering for the sins of others that have gone and that are to come.

Here comes in Judas. His part is only next in importance to that of Christus, and at some points seems to require even more power. It needs art and craft alike, to portray the terrific passions, and the struggle for mastery, that rage in his breast. Judas is not without some innate good—the worst of us has something in him to be saved by. But the evil overwhelms him—his avarice. He shows a wild energy of purpose towards the end of his career. There is some superb acting in his acceptance of the money, the price of the betrayal, and in his flinging it at his own pious betrayers, the destroyers of his soul. As he nears his self-invited doom, Judas looks like a hunted tiger, hunted more from within than without, more by himself than by others. Conscience! Who can escape thee? Do people really escape the qualms of conscience? Oh that there were no such word as *betrayer !* The sight of it makes one tremble all over. And yet, methinks, there is no betrayer so loud, so relentless, as the "shrill small voice within," if you once decline to have him for your good genius.

As to acting, I have seen Hamlet done by a very capable artist. But the portraiture was not half so vivid in power and passion. The actor was a gentleman of talent, who had made a lifelong study of his part. In the present case, Judas is represented by a common villager! His best acting is, of course, the very last, showing how a sinner is tempted, hunted, frenzied into despair. Even for such a

sinner as Judas, however, I find the Church is not
without hope. The curtain drops just a moment
before the last rash act of his life overtakes him.
It is a wise and humane arrangement. I wish they
reserved it also for the principal character in the
drama.

The washing of the disciples' feet by their Master,
Peter's humble but earnest protest, Christ's gentle,
dignified reply, are all very effectively rendered.

The agony in the Garden is, to my mind, the
best representation, better than the final tragedy.
How the disciples doze away in spite of warnings!
It is a masterly study of human nature.

Peter denying Christ is equally natural. The
crowing of the cock is feeble; it rather spoils the
effect of the whole.

The sight of Christ in the hands of the cruel
soldiers, and his more cruel countrymen; their gibes
and jeers, their coarse laughter and vulgar taunts,
only add to the pathos of his sublime self-sacrifice.
His patient bearing has something of the divine in
it, though to the human eye it may, perhaps, appear
the reverse. The music seems to hallow the situation with its sad impressiveness. Different emotions
affect different natures among the audience.

Peter's repentance is a powerful piece of acting.
It is his best. The old man seems to be torn by
remorse. But there is nothing vulgar in his exhibition of grief and shame. John, his Master's favourite, is quieter, though no less effective.

The acting of Pilate and Herod is very good, indeed. Again I wonder how these village wood-

carvers could possibly sustain such parts. Are they all villagers? There can be no mistake about it.

The Saviour is now introduced, to the sound of sad music, and, alas! to the sound of scourging and hooting. Christ bears himself truly like a Prince of Peace. The scourging and hooting well bring out what is brutal in the soldiery and in their heartless abettors, the Jewish mob. On the other hand, what is divine in Christ is strikingly brought out by his human suffering. He is greater in his suffering than in his triumph. The priests, egging on the mob, show us a terribly true representation of priesthood typified. Pilate, the Roman Governor, presents a very fine contrast to this infuriated and demoralized mob of murderers. Pilate washing his hands of the sin implied in the impending murder that the priests have insisted upon, preferring to have Christ for their victim, rather than Barabbas, as suggested by the Governor, is very natural. Here Christ may appear to some to be indifferent to the fate gathering round him. No fatalist he! He knows that the greater the agony in store for him, the greater the self-control and self-communion necessary.

Most painfully vivid is the picture of the Saviour bearing his cross to Calvary. It is a reality, rather than a picture, of physical and mental prostration, through which the spirit has to carry out her assigned task. How he stumbles, yet stumbling, goes on, agonized at every step in which he glorifies the Father—a woman's pious hands wiping the drops of blood on his forehead! More cruel to witness, even than this cruelest of trials, is the first look of recognition between the divine sufferer and the mother, sharpened by her gasp of agonized despair. It is an appalling sight. My heart is frozen, withered—I cannot weep. The representation is wonderfully real, including the voluntary relief afforded by Simon in this hour of extremest need. Human language is not sufficiently developed to describe this penultimate act of the divine tragedy.

The Crucifixion is too much for my nerves. I turn away from it for a moment, but to be drawn to it again; the scene is so fascinating. One of the most notable incidents of this tragedy, surpassing in human interest much that has yet been conceived by poet or prophet, is the last message from the Cross—"Woman, behold thy Son; Son, behold thy Mother." Here the ties of human kinship are sundered. Does he mean himself or John, as he entrusts the latter to his earthly mother, who is now to be a mother to the favourite disciple, the child of his spirit? The thunder and lightning that follow harmonize well with the darkness of the deed done. The exemption from the usual breaking of limbs, and the piercing of the side instead, to see that all is over, and thus to satisfy his malignant persecutors; the removal of the body, so tenderly, so reverently; the hushed weeping and whispered conversation among mourners, appear to awe the audience into an agony of suspense and silence. The acting is perfect throughout. The laying of the body on Mary's knees; the anointing and dressing; the carrying it to its temporary resting-place

—all these details are real in their naturalness, and natural in their harrowing reality.

The scene of the Resurrection breathes joy, hope and triumph—the triumph of good over evil, of spirit over flesh. They do not seem to linger on the details of the Ascension or Resurrection, though some of the minutiæ of the latter are very well managed—such as the falling open of the grave, the walking out of Christus, the panic among the soldiers on watch. Mary Magdalene and others ought to have been represented here, as also Mary's mistaking Christ for the gardener. On the other hand, I wish we were spared some of the details of the Crucifixion.

To sum up, the Passion Play at Ober-Ammergau is a marvellous triumph of faith in art. The writer of the play seems to have purged the Gospel narrative of some of its later accretions, and though scrupulously faithful in the details that bring out the life and the truth thereof, he seems rather to have avoided the incomprehensible. Herein, I think, he shines at his best, as an artist. I regret Christus having to be shown so much and so often in the one sad aspect of helpless suffering, mortification, agony and despair—*Eloi, Eloi, lama sabachthani?* That, no doubt, is the essence of the grand self-sacrifice ; but it familiarizes the uninitiated mind too much with a totally one-sided view. The same remark I have been compelled to make regarding many of the pictures in the Art Galleries of Europe. The drama has also undergone considerable improvement, I am told, in which the more careful students have observed a tendency to gratify the purely artistic taste. Such as I see, however, the performance is calculated to appeal directly to whatever is true in our nature. The principal characters leave nothing to be desired in this direction. The charge of venality, or of personal ambition, does not seem to have been made out. Far from being worldly, some of the men lose more than they gain by observing the traditional vow. It doubtless costs them an almost superhuman effort. That they are not actuated by love of pelf or of fame, may be further seen from this, that our simple village artists have declined repeated offers of what might be to them a princely fortune for a performance outside of Ober-Ammergau. They have been so much disturbed by these temptations, and by the gradual tendency to vulgarize their sacred institution, that the elders are thinking of breaking it up rather than incur further risk to their faith and character. They have kept the vow as long as they could, they argue; the times are against a longer observance of it. I think they argue wisely. Nobly and long have they illustrated the Lord's sacrifice. It may be nobler now to sacrifice their own feelings, in order to keep the example of that sacrifice pure and undefiled. I am desirous of a nearer look at, and a talk with, Christus. But it will hardly do to disturb him at such a time. Besides, I am afraid of being disillusionized. The humble wood-engraver is not expected to be at home what he has been on the stage under the inspiration of the hour. From all reports, however, he is believed to be thoroughly genuine. The same may be said, more or less, of the others. But it is a rude shock to me to be told that one of them, who bore a prominent part yesterday, and showed on the stage as if her whole nature had been penetrated by the presence of grace, was found giggling at home shortly after. I gather this, on our way back, from a Florentine noble who seems to have taken lodgings in her family.

As to whether it is well to keep up the Passion Play, one is really puzzled in coming to a definite opinion. There is much in it, offering the highest edification, of which one should be sorry to deprive the believer. It is a most powerful representation of life and nature, with an absorbing human interest. Even as a work of art it claims very high praise. On the other hand, however, the interest manifested by a majority of the audience appears to be too much of the sense, sensuous. They are drawn to the spot more by curiosity, love of art, considerations of health and pleasure, than by actual sympathy. Now, the eye and the ear are valuable ministrants to our physical and, indirectly, to our spiritual enjoyment. But the heart of things divine is best seen by the eye of faith, its throbbings best heard by the ear of the spirit within. The issues here involved are far too momentous to be trifled with by the hands or head of man, however reverent. It is noteworthy that in the Passion Play of Islam the principal character is never brought upon the stage. Do not Christians claim for Christ a greater affinity to the invisible Father of Grace?

It may be asked why the pious villagers of Ober-

Ammergau may not be left undisturbed in the enjoyment of their privilege. The demand is apparently reasonable. At any rate, we have no right
to withhold it. This concession is the easier to make,
seeing that it is not a new departure from the æs-
thetics of faith, and that the performance comes off
only once in ten years. But I do not see that the
objection in principle is thereby removed. To take
a practical view of the matter, if the outside world
is to be shut off from the representation, perhaps
one of the most powerful incentives to success might
be lost to the rustic performers. The withdrawal of
all outside contributions might prove fatal. Will the
peasants of Ober-Ammergau care to undertake another performance, before themselves, in the absence
of all extraneous aid, including the rich contributions
to which they have so long been accustomed ? On
the whole, therefore, one is constrained to advise,
not without a pang of disappointment, that the now
historic drama of life should be considered a matter
of history, to be profaned no longer by the eye of
flesh.

Such, at any rate, is the opinion of a non-Christian
who has no wish to be un-Christian.

* *
*

Trieste looks like Bombay on a small scale. The
people are more lively than contented. Women of
the working class dress very like our Mahommedan
women of Gujarat. Being a seaport town, Trieste
wears a rather dissipated look ; but we do not find
a single drunkard in the streets. As regards sani-
tation, it is distinctly inferior to Bombay.

Here, in Trieste, we pass a couple of days in acute suspense. I find no letters waiting for me, either from India or England. This is very disappointing. Dr. B——keeps running between the Post Office and the office of the Austro-Hungarian Lloyd. He also wires to his housekeeper in London, to ask how many letters she has forwarded. From the housekeeper we get an evasive reply, winding up with the words—"Mamma died yesterday." Poor Dr. B—— breaks down while reading these words. He takes "mamma" to mean *his* mother in India, while I feel certain it is the housekeeper's mother in England. The thing is so plain that it vexes me to see my friend shaking his head. He is disconsolate. I enter fully into the context of the reply, discussing it word by word in the light of his message to London. The housekeeper could not possibly say "mamma" for his mother? But it avails nothing. Then I take up another cue. I pretend that my letters are as dear to me as his mother is to him. That startles him out of his melancholy. Like a truly unselfish friend, he offers to resume inquiries, mourning his mother silently all the while. I prevail upon him, also, to wire to his housekeeper once more, asking *whose* mother it is that has died. It takes nearly a day to get the reply, as the housekeeper has been out of town to attend her mother's funeral. Here is suspense piled upon suspense. But the reply comes at last. "*My* mother." We are very sorry, indeed, and wire our sympathy to the bereaved.

Dr. B——again resumes search for my letters;

T

but we are doomed to another night of torture. It is my friend's turn now to soothe me, as I keep chafing under my ill-luck. The head of the Lloyd Office is extremely kind, making hourly search for the letters, and offering to do anything Dr. B—— would suggest to get at them. But we are all at our wits' end. At last, on the 3rd of October, we go on board the steamer which is to sail almost immediately; and there, as I step up the deck, I am saluted with a large packet unasked. The mystery is now solved—these letters seem to have been kindly taken off on board by one of the office clerks, as they came in. His ignorance of English is his only excuse. Had he been able to follow our instructions, he would have spared us his very cruel kindness.

From Trieste to Bombay is a very smooth passage. It goes without saying that this return voyage is even less eventful than was our trip to Europe six months ago. The *Imperatrix* is as splendid a vessel as her mate, conscious of her proud title and of her position in the fleet. The captain is not less energetic than his colleague in charge of the *Imperator*, but lacks the martial bearing of the latter. The officers and crew are about the same, willing hands and hearts, but more or less tongue-tied. By this time, however, I have become an adept in the language of signs, and manage to make myself understood by dumb show. The *Imperatrix* keeps a good table, but seems to give less variety, and is decidedly inferior in the supply of fruit. This is because the fruit season is over for Europe. The captain cannot help his helplessness, as he naïvely puts it in his own English. Another trouble, which he is even more helpless to cope with, is the heat experienced in the Red Sea. I never felt it so hot in my life before, although I have visited some of the hottest districts of India. The cabin feels like an oven at work, and the voyagers have to be out mostly, during night as well as day. Everything on board is hot, from the food in your plate down to the water in your bath. Your deck chair is as uncomfortable as your bed in the cabin. Your meal becomes tiresome; and though you like to be in your bath, you have to change the water every few minutes. I happen, one afternoon, to have fallen asleep in my bath, overpowered by the heat. But for knocks and kicks at the door by an impatient German, it is hard to say what might have been the result of this protracted immersion. Ladies and gentlemen are seen at all hours of the night, running about from corner to corner, bed-clothes in hand. One often finds the bodily functions almost suspended, and the balance of mind sadly disturbed. The children cry incessantly, knowing not why. Oh the misery, the agony of those three October days! On the fourth we are in sight of the dear old Indian Ocean, inhaling his balmy breeze, feeling more refreshed in body as we draw nearer the shores of India, and more picked up in spirit as we get a clearer view of Home, Sweet Home.

In 1891 we take the Brussels route on our return to Trieste. Three times have I had an easy passage across the Channel—a privilege to be envied

T 2

by heroes and statesmen. But the witch of the
Atlantic revenges herself on me the fourth time I
have to cross her path. It is a bleak morning towards the end of October. A strong gale is sweep-
ing over the Channel, which lashes the sides of the
mail steamer and makes her dance fantastically.
As she weighs anchor the dance becomes more fantastic. The sky begins to be overcast, and in less
than five minutes we have to beat a hasty retreat,
and are driven below by pelting rain on the top
of piercing wind. Here I try to fortify the inner
man, inducing Dr. B——to do likewise. My friend
munches a sandwich with the air of a martyr.
He has a presentiment of what is to follow. The
prophet of evil! In less than a minute the poison
seems to be working in him. He asks me to run
away. "Let me alone," he pleads ; "I'll try to
sleep." I take an umbrella in one hand, a stick
in the other, and try to hobble upstairs. Walking
is hopeless. A frantic effort to steady myself sets
me sprawling. I bang my head beautifully against
the railings. Thus baffled, I have once more to
descend to the regions of gloom below, sheepishly
eyeing the bowls and the towels, and the prostrate
forms of some of our fellows in misery, who look
as if lingering between life and death. As I approach my friend he starts up electrified, and stag-
gers forward, very unwell. "Shame ! shame," I
laugh, catching him by the shoulder. "Don't," he
groans in reply, with another *haw*, and another, and
yet another. The cry is taken up by a lady next
to us, and by her son, followed by an old gentle-

man whom I mistake for Mr. Spurgeon. But hist! What have we got here? The contagion is spreading this way. A sense of giddiness is creeping over me. I feel as if a feather were being smuggled down my throat, soaked in some noisesome mixture. I crawl towards my chair, leaving the doctor to his fate. I close my eyes and pretend to sing—which sounds like moaning. I try to recall old jokes, but it is useless. I thump my chest, and rub and slap my face vigorously. All to no purpose. I have to get up, in despair, and reel forward to meet my fate. For a while I forget everything. I get back to my seat, clenching my teeth and closing my eyes, only to find Dr. B——in a similar plight. I feel guilty at my selfishness, in leaving him alone. But I have no will-power left. I doubt whether I could move if the engine on my right were to burst this moment. There I sit, limp and loose, in mute, moist sympathy with my fellow-sufferers. It is a passive sympathy, not active, as usual with me; and I despise myself for it. But what is one to do in such a strait? One may face a lion, go through flood and fire, in order to help a friend. He may brave fever and cholera. But to attend to a sea-sick friend, when one is himself in trouble, is beyond human friendship. I think it would be easier to die for a friend than to serve him in sea-sickness when you are in for it yourself.

Shortly afterwards we catch the welcome sound of the gong. Two carriers walk off with our baggage, the doctor and I tottering behind. I feel keenly the discomforts of the situation. It is my second experience of sea-sickness, the first having been acquired off Gogo Bunder some eighteen years ago, from association with a dirty Bania family in a dirtier little coasting vessel. But there is one consolation. The doctor has fared much worse. Poor fellow! Does he not look like one of the survivors in Noah's ark?

Landing at Calais, we take train immediately for Brussels. The doctor is anything but complimentary to the British authorities—who won't build a tunnel under their "dirty little ditch." It is, really, sad to see what an amount of suffering the English put up with and impose upon others, by resisting a tunnel so doggedly. Surely, they could guard the passage well enough against invasion. I am told it is not a question of cost. Why, then, pile up such agonies upon themselves, not to speak of others, nor of other than personal discomfort?

The capital of Belgium has a peculiar interest for the tourist—part French, part German, part English, and part, as it appears, American. It has an air of freedom, of cleanliness and comfort, which one often misses elsewhere. The upper town is detached from the lower. Here for the first time I see dogs yoked to little carts, and worked pretty much as horses and bullocks are worked in other countries. This practice we observe in parts of Germany also. The dogs are as large as our *genius* of Gujarat, and seem to be well cared for. They have light weights to drag, and look rather proud of the work. We have not seen a single dog whipped for scamping work, though there seems to be no limit to their barking, especially when at rest. Brussels has a large market, where buyers and sellers are almost all women, except meat-sellers. This looks natural. I see some cheese here, exactly like our Surat *panir* (cheese), same colour, shape and make—little basket and all. In the afternoon we run over to the Picture Gallery, which strikes one more as a menagerie—such a confusion of profusion it presents to the view. Every one of the continental schools is, I believe, represented here. Some of the statuary is very effective, and so are not a few of the paintings. But far more effective, to my mind, is the Wierst collection in an isolated part of the town, close to an iron foundry. Wierst must have been an artist of stupendous powers, bold and original to a degree, but also extravagant and irregular. He may be described, off hand, as Byron, Burns, Goethe and Rabelais, all rolled into one—sharing as much of the strength as the weakness of each. Unhappily for the artist, the man seems to have been a little too conscious of his genius. That self-consciousness was his curse in life; it has also clung to his memory and kept it out of its legitimate recognition. That accursed self-consciousness has burnt itself into the most splendid of his handiworks. For all that, however, Wierst has no need to hang down his head in the presence of the greatest masters.

Another sight of Brussels is the Palais du Justice, perhaps the best constructed court-house in Europe, commodious, with ample light and ventilation, and very fine acoustic properties. It is a contrast to our gloomy labyrinth at Bombay, not unfit for lawmongers and blood-suckers to live in.

Part of next day we spend at Antwerp, the most ancient of seaport towns in Europe, which at one time traded with the whole of the then known world. During a long period it seems to have fallen into decay, but is reviving again. We walk right along the harbour, with its splendid docks. The whole line of buildings opposite is dedicated to Bacchus, and wears a very dissipated, if not disreputable, look. Here the hard-worked sailors have to empty their pockets on arrival, and to fill their stomachs with fire-water. Antwerp boasts of a venerable cathedral, which contains two of Rubens' masterpieces. These are in themselves worth a pilgrimage, though, for my part, I would place the poet's creations any day before the painter's. The filigree work on the dome of the cathedral is another attraction worth mentioning. From the cathedral our guide, a schoolboy picked up in the street, takes us to a church, inside which we find a very clever representation, in stucco or clay, of the scene on Calvary.

We make a brief halt at Frankfort next day, and are struck with the size and solidity of some of its buildings. In the evening we take a turn round the shops, and see a bevy of women gazing at them, though not perhaps so aimlessly as they do in London. The German lady seems to be modest, simple, industrious, but rather slow in apprehension and in movement. She looks somewhat like her Parsee sister; comfortable in girth, with a face on either side of which you may put a new-born baby to sleep. One misses here, as elsewhere on the continent of Europe, the fresh looks, the light, free movements of the Englishwoman. Germany has a great future before her; and with the Colossus of modern statecraft removed from the scenes of his activity, she may well look forward to some peace and progress at home. The people in general seem to care very little about politics, nor do they think much of the influence of women on public life. Clever women seem thrown away on Germany. The German has yet to learn that though military prowess may make an Empire, it is mainly the influence of women of the right sort that will keep the Empire pure and strong. In this respect, as in some others, Germany is almost the opposite of France.

On our way to Vienna from Frankfort, overnight, I see a steady fall of snow keep up till the morning. The hills around are silver-lined, and look beautifully grand. But we feel frozen inside the carriage, in spite of a service of hot air. Think of the poor conductor having to walk along the foot boards in this bitter cold, while the train is rushing at breakneck speed into the dark hilly tract before us. He can hardly open out his hand as he enters the carriage to punch our tickets, and is breathing hard, as if about to choke. Could not the tickets be punched or examined before the train leaves the larger stations? It is on our way to Vienna, also, that we have to pay a heavy transit duty on a few table requisites purchased at Frankfort. This is the first time we have been thus fined in Europe for patronizing its art. Before reaching our hotel, we have again to pay a franc, I suppose as toll-tax or

wheel-tax. At this rate Vienna will take a long time
to be won to the fold of free trade.

After a little rest we rush out, in a close carriage,
to do the town, being at the mercy of an incessant
snowdrift. Vienna has some truly palatial buildings. Even private houses are large and well built.
What are your London and Glasgow and Edinburgh beside some of the continental towns? One
must not speak in the same breath of the mean
and the magnificent. I think the American geo-
grapher was not far out in describing England as
" a small island in the Atlantic "—only he forgot
to add, " which sways the destinies of nearly a
fourth of the human race."

It ceases to snow as we leave Vienna for Trieste;
but here we have to face a chill, biting wind. We
are fairly driven before a blast as we near our
carriage. Even the horses find it an effort to breast
the gathering storm. With this high wind blowing,
we see women of the poorer class return from
market, shivering in almost every limb, with lips
compressed and cheeks blistered red all over. It is
a piteous sight. I thank God we, have no wind,
such as the *mistral*, in India, nor the delicate skin
that suffers so acutely under its influence. I almost
think the Trieste lasses eye us enviously as we go
past in our thick brown cuticle.

The train from Vienna is belated during my third
trip down; and we have to go from this station to
another, to catch the mail for Trieste. To miss this
train overnight is to miss the steamer starting next
day for Bombay. I am in a fever of anxiety. A

German fellow-passenger sees this, and is so very kind as to get a carriage to drive me to the other station, himself accompanying. It is a drive for dear life, the coachman yelling and cracking his whip without pause. But we arrive too late by a minute. The train is in motion. I am bathed in despair, but not yet quite despondent. The ticket has to be bought, the luggage to the examined. A mute appeal to the station-master, however, with the scattering about of all available silver in my hand—and I make a blind rush towards the train. The guard and another official haul me up over the wheel of a ladies compartment, in which my coat is very near getting entangled. There is uproar and outcry all over the platform. But I am safe up at last, thanks partly to the help extended by a motherly occupant of the compartment. The German friend throws the ticket and the luggage in after me; and I throw at him, in return for his unaccountable kindness, a glance of unworded gratitude with a bundle of braided silk handkerchiefs I have carried in my breast pocket. Here we are quits for the nonce, friend; at any rate, till you chance to come Indiawards.

On our way from Trieste to Bombay this year we are having a very lively time of it on board. This is due mainly to the presence of several English passengers. These people know how to make themselves at home on the wildest and the bleakest of islets, how to extract some sort of home comfort from it. Why not, then, from the good ship *Imperator*, which is a mansion in itself, with drinking, smoking, and dining saloons of its own, and a music-hall to boot?

In the intervals of creature comfort the voyagers go in for amusements of various kinds—sports, dances, concerts, fancy balls, and so on. Very few of them could have come on board provided with the requisites of a fancy ball; yet they manage somehow to improvise one—this gentleman personating a Parsi priest, that a Chinese mandarin, the other a Bombay policeman. What they lack in art they make up by good humour. This fancy dress ball is an immense success, so far at least as clapping of hands, and cheering and laughing, could make it. The same may be said of the concert, in which I here at a distance one good voice singing, and see one pair of deft hands playing. The dancing is more successful, to judge from how the partners puff and pant and go at it again and again. The sports are no less amusing, except when ladies and gentlemen try to drive turkeys, geese, and hens in a straight line before them. This part of the sport is torture to me. What must it be to the victims? But our sportsmen and sportswomen persevere with their gruesome game, urging the victims with a cord or a pointed stick. The poor little bipeds do not, as a rule, go straight. How are they to know what they are wanted to do? They fail to see the fun of it, and persist in running back to the coops. The more they are worried, the more frantic they grow, till they are ready to bite their tormentors, to peck at them viciously, and then lie exhausted on deck. If, by chance, one of them manages to run straight, in hopes of escaping, it is greeted with shrieks of delight from the ladies, and shouts of applause from their gallant knights—which only fluster the unhappy things. The sight is altogether depressing, and I offer to pay five times the original subscription, to be spared a further experience of sports which, without being intended as cruel, are certainly managed with unseemly cruelty.

A few days after starting it is whispered that the *Imperator* is timed to reach Bombay earlier than usual. This is owing no doubt, to the presence on board of the Bombay agent, Mr. Janni, with his demure looks but eminently business-like habits, as also of the Calcutta agent of the Company. The *Imperator* is determined to do his very best this trip.

Among the other notable voyagers I must not omit to mention two cats, a grey and a black one. The former appears to be strangely drawn to those who speak English, and sits patiently before them whilst conversing. Now and again it wags its head knowingly, as the speaker waxes eloquent, and then takes a few turns across the deck, with all the dignity of an ambassador. If I believed in magic, I would take that cat to be an emissary of the Austrian Government, watching the movements of the subjects of Her Britannic Majesty abroad. Its dark companion seems to have more wit than wisdom. It helps itself to any piece of cake or biscuit lying about, with that lofty disdain of the law of *meum et tuum* which characterizes the dealings of the feline tribe. The cats are much in request with some of the passengers, more so with the crew who caress and feed them every morning. It is a sight to see these soft-hearted fellows sharing their bread crumbs with them, and talking to them, as if they were one family sitting at a common table. The carpenter is very fond of the grey one, whom he takes up in his arms daily for a fatherly kiss. The cat receives his salute with a look of unutterable disgust, as it runs off to wipe its moustache against the door rug. I wonder why cats are averse to kissing, to which dogs take so kindly. Perhaps they see nothing in it. Perhaps they suspect foul play in the average kiss.

About 3-30 P.M., on the 4th of November, 1891, we see a magnificent rainbow, half way between the Adriatic and the Mediterranean. It adorns the firmament above in the form of a semi-circle, depicting a trinity of most delicate tints—there is the light scarlet, emblematic of the British Empire, the pale yellow of the Rajput, and the deep green of the Moslem. The rainbow looks about a foot and a half in girth at this distance of, perhaps, a million miles. That would give its real girth about—how many thousand miles, with how many million miles for its length all over? What a fascinating phenomenon, reflecting itself on the waters below, and producing an exact duplicate side by side in the skies!

On the 7th of November we pass a steamer going the other way. I ask the carpenter to say what ship it is. " Pino, Ser," he replies. By this time I have become familiar enough with Austro-Hungarian English to understand that it is a P. & O. steamer. A splendid vessel, one of those palatial water-ploughs that cut their way majestically by, scarcely touching the fringe of the waters. The *Imperator* and the P. & O. steamers pass each other in stately dignity, unfurling the flags, and waving hankerchiefs. This ceremony of salutation over, the flags are lowered, and we soon begin to lose sight of the giant which, only a few minutes before, loomed so large before our eyes.

No such giant do we espy again till the evening of the 18th, when the *Imperator* slackens its speed all of a sudden, and putting itself in charge of the pilot, hobbles laboriously along, like a wounded elephant. It comes to a dead pause every few minutes. During one of these intervals we obtain a good look of our harbour, dotted over with steamers and country craft of all shapes and sizes, and sparkling with the reflected beauty of its background. What would Bombay be without its harbour? But this is hardly the time for speculation. The *Imperator* makes no sign of moving; so, with a friend, I jump into a dingy by the side, and make way for the Bunder, thence off to Hornby Row in a victoria, beating the official forecast by nearly twenty-four hours. What a surprise on the enemy's camp! Here we are, spoiling their game for to-morrow, stealing a march on rank and file, startling from their sleep the mercenaries that have come from far and near, to be at the Bunder on receipt of the earliest report. For a minute there is confusion and clamour all over the camp. The invader is charged with foul play. "People don't come back prowling like this, from such a distance, to mar the pleasure of a regular reception." Come, come, all's fair in love and war. May I always be blessed with such delicious home-coming!

THE END

PRINTED AT THE APOLLO PRINTING WORKS, FORT, BOMBAY.

www.ingramcontent.com/pod-product-compliance
Lightning Source LLC
Chambersburg PA
CBHW080550090426
42735CB00016B/3199